ENTERPRISE
AND THE
IRISH ECONOMY

EDITED BY
Andrew E. Burke

Oak Tree Press
Dublin
in association with
Graduate School of Business
University College Dublin

Oak Tree Press
Merrion Building
Lower Merrion Street
Dublin 2, Ireland

A catalogue record of this book is
available from the British Library

ISBN 1-86076-004-X

Printed in Ireland by Colour Books Ltd.

A toast to the demise of that Irish social animal —
The Begrudger.

CONTENTS

II
FIRM CREATION AND DYNAMICS

10. Legal Factors Affecting Enterprise: Ownership and the S-Firm

11. Education, Training and the Growth of the Owner-Managed Firm: Recent Evidence in the Irish Context

III
RENT-SEEKING AND IRISH ENTERPRISE

Contributors

Dr Sean Barrett, Senior Lecturer, Department of Economics, Trinity College, Dublin.

Dr Andy Bielenberg, Lecturer, Department of History, University College, Cork.

Dr Andrew E. Burke, Research Fellow, Department of Economics and Centre for Research into Industry, Enterprise, Finance and the Firm (CRIEFF), University of Saint Andrews.

Dr P.J. Drudy, Senior Lecturer, Department of Economics, Trinity College, Dublin.

Mr Eric Hanvey, Research Officer, The Northern Ireland Economic Research Centre (NIERC).

Dr Mark Hart, Senior Lecturer, School of Public Policy, Economics and Law, University of Ulster, Jordanstown.

Dr David M. Hitchens, Reader in Economics, Department of Economics, The Queen's University of Belfast.

Professor Kieran Kennedy, Director of the Economic and Social Research Institute (ESRI).

Professor William Kingston, Department of Business Studies, Trinity College, Dublin.

Professor Dermot McAleese, Whately Chair, Department of Economics, Trinity College, Dublin.

Professor Patrick McNutt, School of Public Policy, Economics and Law, University Of Ulster, Jordanstown.

Professor Patrick O'Farrell, Department of Economics, Heriott-Watt University, Edinburgh.

Dr James Walsh, Lecturer, Department of Management and Marketing, University College, Cork.

LIST OF FIGURES

LIST OF TABLES

FOREWORD

The Irish economy needs more enterprise. Specifically, it needs more entrepreneurs who will seek out market niches and employ people to exploit them. This is rightly seen as the only way of generating sustainable employment at home.

It is often said that the Irish can be very enterprising. Sometimes the enterprise is not economically-motivated, as in the case of the missionaries. Also, much Irish entrepreneurial talent of the economic kind has been deployed to the benefit of countries overseas. Think of the huge numbers of Irish emigrants who made good. Sometimes, the enterprise is located at home, is energetic and motivated by financial self-interest — in short is typical of the classical textbook entrepreneur — but is unproductively applied. Think of the boom in the compensation culture, the abundant supply of "rent-seekers" in the professions, the relentless search for grants, the pressure for better pay and working conditions unrelated to productivity. As this book makes clear, Ireland is not short of enterprise in a general sense. It is short of the right type of enterprise. It needs much less of the *zero-sum* enterprise of lawyers, doctors, trade unions and other pressure groups squeezing more out of the taxpayer, and much more *positive-sum* enterprise directed at market demand, making money for entrepreneurs and their employees, contributing to state revenues and general welfare instead of draining them.

How to generate more productive enterprise is a key issue. Since entrepreneurial supply responds to financial incentives, a good place to start would be to make it financially attractive. This has obvious implications for Irish income tax rates, capital taxes and tax/welfare interactions. We must also create a supportive and encouraging environment. This means education — entrepreneurs get nowhere without skilled and motivated staff — up-to-date and effective physical infrastructure and positive attitudes to business. It is easy to forget the depth of anti-business feelings in our society only two or three decades ago. Happily attitudes have changed for the better. There is now extraordinary interest and enthusiasm for business among young people and a level of commitment to work which is unprecedented. Unfortunately, Ireland's tax and entitlements systems has been much slower to adapt. Irish business itself has been slow to appreciate the wealth of talent at its doorstep.

A book on the topic of enterprise in Ireland is to be warmly welcomed. The editor, Dr Andrew Burke, is a distinguished scholar in the field of enterprise economics, and he has displayed an entrepreneurial streak in his pioneering research into the music and entertainment industry. Like the best entrepreneurs, he is engaged in a positive sum exercise. This valuable book will enhance the reputation of its contributors and add to our understanding of a comparatively unexplored and vitally important subject for the Irish economy.

Dermot McAleese
Whately Professor
Trinity College, Dublin
September 1995

PREFACE

The recent international proliferation of entrepreneurial analysis within economics, business studies and historical research has now manifested itself in the form of a plethora of courses on entrepreneurship in Irish third level institutions. Simultaneously economic policy in Ireland has placed increasing emphasis on the pivotal role played by entrepreneurship in the determination of the vibrancy of the Irish economy. However, despite these developments the researcher, policy maker and student of Irish entrepreneurship have not, up until now, had access to a book which provides a general overview of entrepreneurship in Ireland.

This volume seeks to serve three purposes. Firstly, to provide a reference point for third level courses on entrepreneurship; particularly those with a significant economic content. The book provides a general introduction and overview to entrepreneurship in Ireland and is therefore suitable as a foundation text to various specific courses on the subject. Secondly, the book is aimed at encouraging further research on enterprise; particularly in an Irish context. Finally, it is aspired that the content of the book will help stimulate policy debate and activity in a manner conducive to the fostering of productive enterprise.

An extensive and diverse group of people have contributed towards the completion of this book. It is not possible to thank all of these individuals within the confines of this preface but a few deserve special mention. Thanks are owed to Oisin Murphy-Lawless, Neil Elliott and Ian Minch who provided fresh eyes and editorial assistance in the proofing of the final drafts. Paul Murphy and Economic and Business Analysis provided similar assistance in the checking of the printing proofs. David Givens and Oak Tree Press proved to be innovative, encouraging and highly efficient publishers who deserve praise for the foresight to back this volume of research. The members of the Department of Economics at Trinity College, Dublin provided much advice and assistance and Cathy Lennon, Francis O'Toole and Marius Bruilhart are owed a special thank you. Regrettably, the volume has helped to increase the Departmental telephone bill to a significant extent! Andy Bielenberg and the CESR at University College, Cork are owed thanks for assisting at the incubation period of the project. Finally, all the contributors of the volume deserve credit for their efficiency in meeting publishing deadlines and their flexibility in accepting many pedantic editorial recommendations.

Andrew E. Burke
September 1995

I

HISTORICAL BACKGROUND

1

THE RE-EMERGENCE OF ENTREPRENEURIAL ANALYSES

Andrew E. Burke

> ... neoclassical value theory did not develop a theory of enterprise. ...The new paradigm took ends as given, explained allocation of scarce resources to meet these given ends, and focused attention on equilibrium results rather than adjustment processes. It therefore left no room for entrepreneurial action; the entrepreneur became a mere automaton, a passive onlooker ... (Herbert and Link (1982, p. 52).

Within the purely neoclassical school economics students are told, or rather bullied into the belief, that firms always maximise profits. With this sweeping assumption neoclassical economists isolate themselves from the main challenge of the business world and indeed, the analyses of their academic colleagues in business schools. The neoclassical school has very little to say about enterprise and in the words of Parker and Stead (1991), it is apparent that:

> If markets move smoothly and predictably from one equilibrium to another and if in employing factors of production firms are assumed to know *in advance* their marginal products, so that optimal input combinations are employed, entrepreneurship appears to be devoid of any rationale. Moreover, technical progress and innovation appear to fall "like manna from heaven" in neoclassical market models (p. 74).

In the neoclassical framework, the composition of industrial evolution and historical paths virtually do not matter. The emphasis is on a theory explaining net change rather than the gross adjustments involved in the generation of such changes. Therefore, for example, if a 5 per cent fall in real wages generates a 1 per cent increase in employment, it is of no interest to the neoclassical economist whether this 1 per cent change was made up of a 20 per cent increase in employment generated in services, accompanied by a 19 per cent loss of jobs from the manufacturing sector, or whether the 1 per cent growth was generated by a small expansion in one industrial sector. Similarly, the actual composition of the aggregate 5 per cent fall in real wages would be of little interest to these economists.

Through this analytical approach, neoclassical methodology seems to exhibit the hallmarks of "schizophrenic rigour", where analysts systematically veer from a delusion of business world realities to extreme caution and attention to detail with a handful of axiomatic assumptions. The result is akin to a predictive model of rail transport, basing its analysis on railway track without reference to locomotives. The theory can accurately predict railway journeys "as long as the locomotives make all possible trips". However, one can assert that governments have not been willing to take neoclassical economists at their word and in a departure from the expected causation, economic policy has preceded research policy recommendations within the realm of encouraging the exploitation of profit opportunities (for Irish examples, see the chapters by Drudy and Kennedy). Indeed, the economics of entrepreneurship has only begun to permeate mainstream economic analysis over the last fifteen to twenty years. However, it has not led to a superannuation of neoclassical economics but has augmented and, for the most part, adapted the neoclassical approach to include areas of analysis such as the dynamics of industrial organisation, a flow approach to labour economics, endogenous growth and regional economics. With an emphasis on dynamics as opposed to statics, this development has begun to lead to a convergence of research interests between economics, managerial science, political science and history.

In Ireland's case the pattern is similar. Since independence, government policy has taken an active role (under many guises) in encouraging enterprise. In tandem with this development, over the last decade a plethora of courses on entrepreneurship in third level institutions have been introduced across the aforesaid disciplines. However, apart from some notable examples, research in this area is still in its infancy. The aim of this volume is to build on these developments. The volume contains a collection of chapters from some of the best Irish academics who have conducted research in the area. The contributors originate from three disciplines, namely economics, business studies and history.

The volume seeks to serve three purposes. Firstly, to provide a reference point for third level courses on entrepreneurship; particularly those with a significant economic content. The book provides a general introduction and overview to entrepreneurship in Ireland and is therefore suitable as a foundation text to various specific courses on the subject. Secondly, the book is aimed at encouraging further research on enterprise, particularly in an Irish context. It is ironic that the formidable rise in the importance of enterprise among the Irish business community and government dwarfs the activity of academics within the same area. Thirdly, and relevant to the latter, it is hoped that the content of the book will help stimulate policy debate and activity in a manner conducive to the fostering of productive enterprise. This is as much relevant to the laws and regulatory environment under which firms operate, as it is to the incentives they are offered.

The book is structured in the following manner. The remainder of this chapter provides the reader with a brief history of the evolution of economic thought on entrepreneurship and how this has led to the current upsurge in research on enterprise. This provides a general overview of the current framework of analysis for entrepreneurial research and is followed by a section summarising the contents of the chapters of the volume. The chapter closes with some concluding remarks concerning policy and future directions for research.

The book is divided into three sections. Section one provides a historical background to Irish enterprise in the late nineteenth and twentieth centuries. It assesses the dynamism of enterprise over the period, the nature of enterprise policy and provides a new data set. The second section of the volume is entitled "Firm Creation and Dynamics". A theoretical model of the supply of enterprise is provided as well as empirical analyses of Irish enterprise through research on new company registrations data, VAT registrations data and surveys of existing firms. The section also provides an analysis of Irish enterprise in an international dimension with comparative analyses of both Northern Ireland and the Republic, the Republic and Scotland and also the impact of economic integration on Irish enterprise. The section closes with two chapters assessing the effect of education and company law on entrepreneurship. Section 3 deals with the very pertinent issue of the role of rent-seeking in determining the productiveness of Irish enterprise.

DEFINING ENTERPRISE

It is important at the outset to be clear about the meaning of the term "enterprise" in its application to the Irish economy. In far too many instances of economic research, unnecessary ambiguity and debate have been generated by a lack of rigour in defining enterprise. This point has been made eloquently by Casson (1982):

> Most studies of the entrepreneur make no attempt at definition. They rely instead on a stereotype, that of the swashbuckling business adventurer. Anybody who conforms loosely to this stereotype is dubbed an entrepreneur (p. 1).

We assume that enterprise occurs when there is a coincidence of a profit opportunity, and an economic agent willing and able to exploit this opportunity.[1] This, in effect, is a supply and demand approach to enterprise (see Casson (1982) and Schultz (1975) for an outline of the framework and Black et al (1992), Foreman-Peck (1985) and Kihlstrom and Laffont (1979) for examples of the analysis in practice). The approach has become widely accepted and utilised because it accommodates the various schools of entrepreneurial thought within a general framework. Each school identifies entrepreneurship with a key characteristic (for example, risk-taking) and the supply and demand approach treats these characteristics as resources that are allocated through their respective markets. In each case, an individual's endowment of entrepreneurial characteristics determines the level of income that he or she may expect to derive from enterprise. Thus, each individual makes a career choice by comparing entrepreneurial income to income from non-entrepreneurial employment. Through aggregation, a form of a supply schedule for enterprise may be derived. The interaction of this supply of entrepreneurs and avail-

---

[1] The income from enterprise, therefore, is a reward for the co-ordination of resources necessary to exploit a profit opportunity. In this manner, the income from enterprise can materialise directly to a sole proprietor of an enterprise and/or indirectly in the form of wages to an employed entrepreneur.

able profit opportunities (i.e. the demand for enterprise) determines the level of enterprise.

The Knightian school of entrepreneurship is based on the seminal work of Frank Knight (1921), where an entrepreneur is defined as someone who undertakes economic activities involving uncertainty, i.e. facing an unknown probability distribution and hence involving uninsurable or impure risk. Kihlstrom and Laffont (1979) use Knightian risk-taking as the key feature of a general equilibrium, supply and demand model of entrepreneurship. In this model individuals choose between wage work and setting up a new firm; the wage rate clears the market. If, for example, enterprise was low, this would be exhibited in unemployment which would drive the wage rate down, increasing enterprise and generating a full employment equilibrium.

In the case of Schumpeter's (1939) approach to entrepreneurship, *Classical* risk is assumed to play no role as entrepreneurs can find investors to back their projects. ". . . risk bearing is no part of the entrepreneurial function. It is the capitalist who bears the risk" (p. 104). For Schumpeter the key characteristic of entrepreneurship is the ability to conceive and implement "new combinations". This approach has been adopted by Evans and Jovanovic (1989), where risk neutrality is assumed, and an individual's endowment of entrepreneurial ability determines her income from enterprise. Since banks require collateral for bank lending, Evans and Jovanovic assume that self-employed entrepreneurs cannot avoid Knightian risk-taking. Blanchflower and Oswald (1991) describe a similar model based on entrepreneurial ability but argue more coherently that the need for collateral for bank loans is due to asymmetric information between the lender (usually the banks) and the borrower (entrepreneur). Under asymmetric information, collateral is necessary to avoid problems of moral hazard and adverse selection among entrepreneurs. This style of model (of entrepreneurial supply) is commonly coupled with a theory of profit opportunities in order to explain a model of enterprise within a supply and demand framework. Two recent examples are Black et al (1992) where a controversial link between house prices and firm start-up is mooted, and Johnson and Parker (1994), where intertemporal effects between firm start-ups and firm deaths are examined.

Since Schumpeter's view of entrepreneurship is more commonly associated with creating disequilibrium, it may seem counter-intuitive to embody this theory within an "equilibrium" framework. This would of course be true if the entrepreneur's sole activity was disequilibrating. However, profits from enterprise can also be made by equilibrating activities. This point of view was recognised by Schumpeter's fellow Austrian school economist Israel Kirzner (1979), who saw rewards for enterprise existing as long as disequilibrium persisted. He argued that as entrepreneurs exploited opportunities, the market moved towards equilibrium. Both Casson (1982) and Schultz (1980) have necessarily included the equilibrating roles of entrepreneurs within a supply and demand framework. Casson chose to construct a general synthesis of definitions and identified an entrepreneur as ". . . someone who specialises in taking judgmental decisions about the co-ordination of scarce resources" (p. 23) In this definition, both the equilibrating and disequilibriating entrepreneurs are captured by Casson's generality. Schultz (1980) draws a distinction between innovation and imitation of innovation. Within Schultz's schema, an innovating entrepreneur throws the market into disequilibrium, while an imitating entrepreneur helps the diffusion of an innovation reach maturity, thereby moving the market towards equilibrium.

The key feature of the supply and demand approach is that the discussion moves away from a search for an elusive entrepreneur (or what Kilby (1971) described as "the heffalump"), and towards an examination of enterprise as a resource. Each individual is assumed to be endowed with a level of enterprise acumen (i.e. innovative ability in the case of Schumpeter and Kirzner, or willingness to take risks in the case of Knight), and this resource is allocated as individuals choose careers. In this setting an individual who is an entrepreneur under one vector of incomes may seek non-entrepreneurial employment under a different vector. In this manner, the supply and demand approach moves the emphasis of analysis away from the individual and towards the allocation of entrepreneurial acumen across areas of the economy. Thus, risk-taking could be an important attribute for enterprise in one industry, while a unique skill could be crucial in another. Therefore, the supply and demand framework does not have to search for the "heffalump", as it assumes at the outset that entrepreneurship is a set of heterogeneous attributes which change in emphasis between industries and over time. With this perspective, it is not surprising that attempts at a general characteristic approach to enterprise have always generated debate.

Baumol (1990) makes an important augmentation to the supply and demand framework. He argues that entrepreneurship is not always productive and in some cases is actually destructive. Baumol claims that certain forms of entrepreneurial activity do not enhance total wealth in the economy and may even reduce it. This activity, commonly referred to as "rent-seeking", has important welfare implications for a supply and demand approach to enterprise. In this framework, entrepreneurs aim to maximise their income and do so by exploiting profit opportunities. Some of these opportunities entail the generation of new wealth, namely new output generated by an entrepreneur, in addition to multiplier effects to other firms. However, some profit opportunities arise from a redistribution of wealth where entrepreneurs are actually unproductive. If such a redistribution of wealth reduces entrepreneurial activity in another sector then it may have the effect of being destructive.

Baumol's contribution implies that the supply and demand framework must be augmented if it is to fully explain economic performance. In effect, the demand for enterprise must be divided into productive and unproductive enterprise. In this manner, a modest level of productive enterprise may not merely be due to a lack of qualified entrepreneurs, or a lack of opportunities, but to an imbalance between "pure entrepreneurial" and "rent-seeking" opportunities. Within the supply and demand framework, this would be reflected by unproductive entrepreneurial opportunities "crowding out" a proportion of their productive counterparts.

Foreman-Peck (1985) further qualified the use of the supply and demand analytical approach. He argued that in a market for entrepreneurs, where incumbent firms seek to hire enterprising individuals, entrepreneurs who are rejected by these firms are likely to start up their own firm. Presumably, firms reject individuals with relatively low entrepreneurial ability so that new firms created by these individuals are likely to represent low quality enterprise. In the words of Foreman-Peck, they represent the "chaff" of incumbent firms rather than the "seedcorn" of future industry. Thus, any measure of the supply of enterprise would have to distinguish between "seedcorn" and "chaff" in terms of assessing an *effective* supply of enterprise.

We can summarise the literature with reference to Figure 1.1. The figure is divided into three levels labelled 1, 2 and 3 respectively. Level 1 represents the supply of entrepreneurs in both the self-employed and employed sectors. As we move to level 2 we separate entrepreneurs into two "quality" groups i.e. seedcorn and chaff. We would imagine that most of the chaff would be concentrated within the self-employed sector although it is conceivable that a static incumbent employer may also push dynamic entrepreneurs into this sector. Baumol's distinction between productive and unproductive enterprise further subdivides the supply of enterprise as we move from level 2 to 3. Here we are left with four groupings of entrepreneurs: high quality entrepreneurs in productive enterprise, high quality entrepreneurs in unproductive enterprise and low quality entrepreneurs in productive and unproductive enterprise respectively. Since enterprise policy ought to be directed towards maximising the first of these groupings, three objectives arise which affect the supply of enterprise at each of the three levels in Figure 1.1. Firstly, productive opportunities should be encouraged and destructive opportunities ameliorated. Thus, for example, a policy aimed at reducing rent-seeking opportunities would reduce the flows along the right hand streams between levels 2 and 3.

In the second instance, and as far as is realistically possible, policy should be aimed at increasing the seedcorn/chaff ratio to ensure that any given supply of enterprise is most effectively employed. No doubt, it is easier to propose than implement such a policy, and it is likely to involve elements of enterprise training, and guidance on the ease and viability of market entry. The third facet is the most long-standing approach and involves encouraging an increase in the supply of enterprise, either indigenously or through imported foreign enterprise. However, what is clear from the chart is that the impact of policies can only be gauged by tracing the effect from level 1 to level 3. An attempt to ignore this process may not only neutralise the impact of the policy (for example, encouraging the supply of enterprise when the main constraint is the demand of enterprise) but may even reduce the supply of effective enterprise (a possibility in a case such as the provision of capital grants which may divert productive enterprise to unproductive activities).

FIGURE 1.1: THE DEPLOYMENT OF ENTREPRENEURS

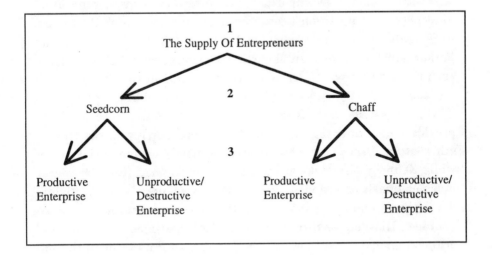

OVERVIEW

The book is divided into three sections, comprising of an economic history of entrepreneurship in Ireland, analyses of firm start-up and the development of Irish firms, and finally, a section dealing with the distribution of profit opportunities between rent-seeking and productive enterprise.

The first section serves the dual purpose of providing a historical perspective on Irish entrepreneurship and also initiating some research issues for future analyses. It begins with a chapter by Andy Bielenberg who conducts a re-appraisal of the performance of Irish enterprise in the nineteenth century. Through a survey of new and existing data relating to entrepreneurship and investment, Bielenberg argues that Irish economic activity seems to have been fairly robust over the period 1850-1900 and particularly so in the 1890s. Bielenberg's analysis raises a number of important research questions for this period and for the evolution of Irish entrepreneurship in general. Firstly, it must re-open the debate concerning the performance of the economy during the nineteenth century. Secondly, it would be of interest to know the determinants of the patterns of investment and enterprise which are illustrated in the data. Such an analysis might shed important light on the driving forces behind the dynamics of economic performance in this period. Thirdly, and related to the two previous issues, is the role played by Ireland's economic integration with Britain. How important was Britain in terms of generating multiplier or competition effects for Irish entrepreneurs? Contemporary analyses such as Carree and Thurik (1994) or Johnson and Parker (1994) provide a suitable research trajectory to follow. To serve such research purposes the new data contained in Chapter 2 (which was collected by Bielenberg and Burke) is published in Chapter 3.

Chapters 4 and 5, by Kieran Kennedy and P.J. Drudy respectively, provide a historical account of Irish entrepreneurship in the twentieth century. Drudy's chapter focuses primarily on industrial policy, while Kennedy also looks at industrial performance. Kennedy places much emphasis on the view that Ireland's weakness is due to its late development and being susceptible, therefore, to a "late mover disadvantage". His chapter points out that to a large extent the Irish government endeavoured to overcome these constraints through the importation of foreign enterprises. He also describes and discounts a selection of mainly sociological propositions relating to factors that may have inhibited the supply of Irish entrepreneurs. Each of these explanations are only relevant to particular epochs of Irish history in the twentieth century and according to Kennedy could not, therefore, account for the pedestrian performance of the Irish economy across the whole period. However, it must be contended that the cumulative effect of the impact of these factors could go some way towards constraining the supply of Irish enterprise more consistently across this period. Kennedy does, however, postulate that the supply of Irish entrepreneurs may be misallocated into unproductive areas due to the distribution of profit opportunities in the economy. This point concurs with the thesis of Baumol (1990). Kennedy maintains that to further understand the Irish economy properly, analysis needs to be extended into the realm of the economics of the firm. In this regard, if the Economic and Social Research Institute (ESRI) follows the vision of its Director, then the future for research on Irish entrepreneurship looks bright.

The chapter by P.J. Drudy focuses on the role of industrial policy in stimulating entrepreneurship. He argues that the market environment is paramount to the extent that it determines the long-run formulation of industrial policy. In agreement with Kennedy, Drudy argues that a small domestic market acts as a major constraint on the development of indigenous enterprise. Therefore, despite an initial desire for protectionist policies, market forces acted to push government policy, initially in an "outward-looking" export approach and ultimately towards free trade and support for Irish enterprise to facilitate market penetration. While maintaining that policy seems to be moving in the right direction, Drudy is critical of its current form. In particular, he rightly finds it ironic that industrial policy is formulated to favour manufacturing while most jobs have been created in the services sector. Further, he finds that the emphasis on encouraging enterprise in predominantly agricultural and peripheral areas of Ireland may be displaced to some extent, given that most unemployment is concentrated in urban areas. These points highlight the importance of an analysis of the composition and evolution of industry structure. In conclusion, Drudy raises the issue of the cost effectiveness of industrial policy — an area of research interest in the years of fiscal difficulties in the early 1980's which has "slipped off" the agenda in recent years of primary exchequer surpluses.

Section 2 begins with two chapters of my own which deal with the supply of enterprise in Ireland. Chapter 6 provides a theoretical framework for analyses of the supply of entrepreneurs. It highlights the means through which a range of economic factors can affect the supply of enterprise. Therefore, the analysis indicates that a variation in the determinants of the supply of entrepreneurship (that is, the degree of rigour in which profit/business opportunities are exploited) is also likely to vary across time. Thus, it highlights that an analysis of economic performance which only examines the demand for enterprise (as in the purely neoclassical framework) is unlikely to provide a comprehensive account of such activity. The chapter also emphasises the importance of relative incomes (particularly in the context of defining seedcorn and chaff) and cautions the over reliance on aggregate wage measures as a means of accounting for changes in economic performance. The analysis also critiques the impact of capital grants on enterprise and uncovers some paradoxical effects resulting from this policy approach.

Chapter 7 conducts an empirical analysis of the determinants of new firm formation in Ireland. Although assessing the influence of factors such as migration, collateral and capital grants, the chapter is mainly interested in the importance of economic integration to enterprise development in a peripheral economy. To this end it estimates the impact of product and labour market spillovers from Britain on new firm formation in Ireland. While as expected, British product market spillovers are found to positively affect Irish enterprise, labour market spillovers are found to have a negative and more important influence on Irish enterprise. Since British wages grow faster during British upswings, this result indicates that Irish new firm formation is negatively related to British aggregate economic performance. This illustrates the importance of sectoral analyses of the composition and evolution of industry structure, as well as demanding further research in this area since at an aggregate level Irish economic performance is usually viewed as being positively related to that of Britain. Thus, it may be the case that the rising importance of small firms in Irish economic growth plays a significant role in explaining the recent divergence of Irish and British GNP growth rates.

The emphasis shifts from firm start-up to firm performance as we move onto O'Farrell and Hitchens' comparative analysis of business service companies in the Republic of Ireland and Scotland. They find that the functioning of business services companies is fairly consistent between the two regions. In both areas companies derived most of their sales from local demand. However these firms did not serve much of the blue-chip high price/quality sector of the market which seems to have been catered for by large London based firms. O'Farrell and Hitchens note that these sales pattern present a dilemma for business service companies in Scotland and Ireland. These firms tend to be "generalist" in order to succeed in the local market but if they desire to break into the larger London market they need to specialise (serving niche markets) in order to compete with established firms. The chapter also represents an interesting methodological approach as it expands economic analysis along the lines recommended by Kennedy in Chapter 4, namely researching the "black box" of the firm. Through this means, economic and business school research is brought closer together as economists conduct something akin to a

SWOT (strengths, weakness, opportunities and threats) analysis of firms.

The comparative approach to enterprise analysis is continued in Chapter 9 where Hart and Hanvey compare the creation and performance of firms in Northern Ireland and the Republic of Ireland. The analysis also looks at the crucial issue of job creation. They find that new small firms are the main source of job creation in Northern Ireland, while in the Republic employment creation is mainly accounted for by the growth of existing foreign firms and new foreign and indigenous firm foundation. Their dynamic approach to job creation raises as many issues in terms of the causes of the differing patterns of job formation in the Northern Ireland and the Republic, as it does in terms of the most relevant form of economic policy to enhance employment generation and durability in both parts of Ireland. In general, Hart and Hanveys' analysis highlights the importance of industry and firm dynamics in evaluating economic performance and particularly the impact of economic shocks on the latter. This has begun to become a focus of research within industrial organisation and labour economics.

In Chapter 10 Patrick McNutt draws attention to the fact that a rapidly evolving enterprise economy is increasingly comprised of firms that do not match up to the principal (shareholder) agent (management) structure assumed in the traditional theory of the firm. He argues that in recent years entrepreneurship is best characterised by firms offering flexible working hours, minimal fringe benefits, retraining opportunities, subsidised child care while encouraging tele-working, outsourcing and sub-contracting, namely an enterprise culture interspersed with contract workers, contingent workers, and "portfolio workers". He postulates that these developments represent an alternate culture within which it is predicted that the supply of enterprise seems destined to outstrip demand. He refers to such firms as *s-firms* and the workers as *stakeholders* in the firm — they are part of the firm, managing themselves, monitoring quality and productivity. McNutt's analysis not only suggests that there is a need for a re-appraisal of the black box of the firm, but that the new structure of firms should be accompanied with new company law to address the needs of s-firms.

The issue of education and enterprise has long been an area of debate. One view believes that potential entrepreneurs may be trained/educated with skills relevant for successful business venturing, while another perspective regards education to act as a hindrance to entrepreneurship; as it teaches the individual to conform to existing standards and beliefs which are the anathema to the innovative abilities required for entrepreneurship. At an empirical level a further difficulty is encountered as it is awkward to obtain and separate data on individuals' education which coherently divides into skills relevant and irrelevant for entrepreneurial activity. In Chapter 11 James Walsh sets out to address some of these issues in relation to the performance of small firms. He finds that there has been a significant level of education and training in the small business sector. In addition, he finds that employment growth was positively related to the amount of training undertaken by managers. However, he finds that attempts to break this influence down into more specific forms of manpower characteristics (for example, learning styles) does not derive statistically significant results. In this regard his chapter raises important research issues and interestingly illustrates a convergence in the analytical approaches of managerial science and economics to the extent that the latter are now beginning to employ characteristic based analyses, for example Evans and Leighton (1989) and Blanchflower and Meyer (1994).

In Section 3, the final two chapters of the book deal with the issue of rent-seeking. Both authors take the pessimistic view that profit opportunities in Ireland are skewed in favour of activities which Baumol (1990) described as unproductive and destructive entrepreneurship. Together the two chapters provide a comprehensive coverage of rent-seeking in Ireland. In Chapter 12 William Kingston provides a conceptual framework for assessing Irish rent-seeking. Kingston states that a society has a fairly discrete choice between law and private property rights which promotes productive entrepreneurship, or collectivism which promotes rent-seeking. He stresses that in its most extreme form, the latter was apparent in the former Soviet Bloc but is also highly prevalent in "mixed" economies. He argues that Ireland has always vied towards collectivism and that a combination of political, judicial and economic change is necessary in order to

overcome Ireland's inherent tendency to generate rent-seeking opportunities.

Kingston's analysis is complemented by Sean Barrett's applied
economic taxonomy of the range of rent-seeking opportunities in Ireland. Barrett casts a cold eye on the various forms of government intervention and private sector market imperfections which have led to
the creation of these rent-seeking opportunities. He argues in favour
of a rent elimination policy where market deregulation and the roll-
ing back of government intervention are central features. There can
be no doubt that Barrett's analysis will "rattle a few cages", so to
speak, and hopefully will stimulate a productive debate.

It is by no means an understatement to say that the above chapter
summaries are extremely terse and by no means exhaust the range of
insightful points raised by the authors. In this regard, it is virtually
impossible to discuss all the potential policy, analytical and research
issues that stem from these analyses, especially in a global context
and within the confines of this volume. However, it is possible to or-
ganise the research implications into three general points. Of course,
this taxonomy is subjective to the extent that it reflects the research
issues which this author feels are important.

1. **The supply of entrepreneurs matters:** For any given level of
   profit opportunities available in the market, the extent to which
   they are exploited depends on the number of individu-
   als/firms/institutions seeking to exploit these and the ability of the
   same to achieve these ends. Therefore, factors such as attitudes to
   risk, availability of capital, education, information and (relative)
   wages are likely to play a role in determining the robustness of
   profit exploitation within a market. In such an analysis economists
   should not have a monopoly and it is likely and indeed prudent,
   that a significant amount of multi- and inter-disciplinary research
   should be conducted.

2. **Relative incomes matter:** Relative incomes are significant for
   two reasons. Firstly, they affect the supply of entrepreneurs directly and secondly, they determine the distribution of this supply
   between Baumol's taxonomy of productive, unproductive and destructive entrepreneurship. The ability of an economy to compete
   and innovate, therefore, can only be partially accounted for by ag-

gregate measures such as wages, GNP etc. To this extent, this volume of research indicates that a rigorous understanding of the Irish economy demands a much greater amount of analyses than most researchers have bargained for.

3. **Dynamics and evolution matter:** The composition of industrial growth and its technical characteristics are dynamic and evolutionary objects. *A priori*, one cannot assume that such a transient economic structure is likely to react in a consistent manner to economic shocks in different time periods (this was also the central thesis of the Austrian school of economics). This volume of research supports current developments within the economics profession where analyses of the firm, employment and industry dynamics are being conducted. The volume contains some initial analyses along these lines in the areas of firm start-up (chapters by Burke, Hart and Hanvey) growth and development (O'Farrell and Hitchens, Hart and Hanvey, McNutt, and Walsh) and the importance of small firms in output and employment (Hart and Hanvey, and Walsh). However, further research is required in terms of the causes of the rise in the importance of small firms, such as falling minimum efficient scale, a rise in the heterogeneity of consumer tastes and a rise in switching costs associated with a need for flexibility in a more turbulent economic environment. An analysis of such factors is useful not only to formulate policy to assist small enterprise, but more importantly to investigate whether the recent rise in the importance of small firms is a long-term development or an aberration from the previous trend of the rise in the size of firms over time. To this end the work of Brock and Evans (1989) and Acs and Audretsch (1989) provide a blueprint for research. Also along the lines of Johnson and Parker (1994) and Carree and Thurik (1994) an analysis of the intertemporal interaction between firm births and firm deaths, firm births and firm births, and firm deaths and firm deaths is required — especially in the light of the high rate of business failure in Ireland. In particular, it is important to assess across each industrial sector the importance of competition and multiplier effects spilling over from firm starts and deaths. Related to this style of analysis, is the issue of turbulence (that is, the sum of firm births and deaths) where it is of interest to know whether markets operate differently

in periods of rapid change as compared to more stable environments. These analyses at the firm level each have their counterpart in the study of employment where issues such as job creation, job destruction, employment turbulence (the sum of jobs created and destroyed), job flexibility and employment mobility all demand the attention of a dynamic approach to Irish economic performance.

This volume will have been a success if it both alerts students and policy-makers to the important caveats that apply to the successful functioning of economic policy and markets, and at the same time if it stimulates debate and research which increases our understanding of the enterprise process and hence, therefore, of the functioning of the Irish economy itself.

REFERENCES

Acs, Z.J. and Audretsch, D.B. (1989): "Editors Introduction", *Small Business Economics*, 1: 1-5.

Baumol, W.J. (1990): "Entrepreneurship: Productive, Unproductive and Destructive", *Journal of Political Economy*, 98(5): 893-921.

Black, J., de Meza, D. and Jefferys, D. (1992): "House Prices, the Supply Collateral and the Enterprise Economy", mimeo, Exeter University, and forthcoming in *The Economic Journal*.

Blanchflower, D.G. and Oswald, A.J. (1991): "What Makes an Entrepreneur?", Manuscript, Dartmouth College, N.B.E.R. and Centre for Economic Performance, LSE.

Blanchflower, D.G. and Meyer, B.D. (1994): "A Longitudinal Analysis of the Young Self Employed in Australia and the United States", *Small Business Economics*, 6(1): 1-21.

Brock, W.A. and Evans, D.S. (1989): "Small Business Economics", *Small Business Economics*, 1: 7-20.

Casson, M. (1982): *The Entrepreneur: An Economic Theory*, Oxford: Martin Robertson and Company.

Carree and Thurik, R. (1994): "The Dynamics of Entry, Exit and Profitability: An Error Correction Approach for the Retail Industry", *Small Business Economics*, 6(2): 107-117.

Evans, D.S. and Jovanovic, B. (1989): "An Estimated Model of Entrepreneurial Choice under Liquidity Constraints", *Journal of Political Economy*, 97, August: 808-827.

Evans, D.S. and Leighton, L.S. (1989): "Some Empirical Aspects of Entrepreneurship", *American Economic Review*, 79(3), June: 519-535.

Foreman-Peck, J.S. (1985): "Seedcorn or Chaff? New Firm Performance of the Interwar Economy", *Economic History Review*, 38(3): 402-422.

Herbert, R. and Link, A. (1982): *"The Entrepreneur"*, New York: Praeger.

Johnson, P. and Parker, S. (1994): "The Interrelationships Between Births and Deaths", *Small Business Economics*, 6(4): 283-291.

Kihlstrom, R.E., and Laffont, J.J. (1979): "A General Equilibrium Theory of Firm Formation Based on Risk Aversion", *Journal of Political Economy*, 87(4): 719-748.

Kilby, P. (1971): "Hunting the Heffalump" in Kilby, P. (ed.) *Entrepreneurship and Economic Development*, New York: The Free Press.

Kirzner, I.M. (1979): *Perception, Opportunity, and Profit: Studies in the Theory of Entrepreneurship*, Chicago and London: The University of Chicago Press.

Knight, F.H. (1921): *Risk, Uncertainty, and Profit*, Chicago and London: University of Chicago Press, 1971. Originally published in 1921 by Houghton Mifflin Company, Boston.

Parker, D. and Stead, R. (1991): *Profit and Enterprise: The Political Economy of Profit*, London: Harvester Wheatsheaf.

Schultz, T.W. (1975): "The Value of the Ability to Deal with Disequilibria", *Journal of Economic Literature*, 13: 827-846.

Schumpeter, J.A. (1939): *Business Cycles: A Theoretical, Historical and Statistical Analysis of the Capitalist Process*, 2 Volumes, New York: McGraw Hill.

2

ENTERPRISE AND INVESTMENT IN IRELAND: 1850-1900

Andy Bielenberg

INTRODUCTION

Despite the proliferation of international literature on investment and enterprise on the nineteenth century, as yet little work has been undertaken which concentrates specifically on these issues in an Irish context.[1] A number of authors have touched indirectly on the matter. The objective of this chapter is to draw together some of their conclusions, which will be used in conjunction with some new statistical data, in order to gain a broad overview of investment and enterprise between 1850 and 1900.[2] The evidence presented here suggests that the traditional gloomy assessment of investment and enterprise during this period needs some re-appraisal.

The only work which deals directly with the issue is Caskey's unpublished investigation of northern industrial entrepreneurs during the second half of the nineteenth century, which concludes that their performance was not as impressive as popular perception suggests (Caskey, 1983). As Ulster was the region which experienced the highest degree of industrialisation, this implies that an even more pessimistic conclusion should be drawn for the southern industrial sector. In the same vein, but in a sociological context, Desmond and Keating (1993) have made an assault on the poor performance of southern Irish entrepreneurs. They attribute this to a cultural environment which was unconducive to enterprise. From a historical perspective their evidence is thin, but a similar argument was frequently used

---

[1] For an overview see O'Grada (1994), pp. 324-30 and footnotes, pp 511-13.

[2] Statistical data is to be found in Chapter 3 of this volume.

within British historiography prior to the 1970s, where entrepreneurs of the late Victorian era were widely condemned as the major cause of Britain's relative decline as an industrial power.

In recent decades, however, a range of new research has to some extent exonerated British entrepreneurs and a more complex and varied picture has emerged across different industries and different firms (Payne, 1988). In an Irish context, recent investigation on different aspects of Ireland's economic history has also taken a more sympathetic view to Irish entrepreneurs of this period (O'Grada, 1994; Kennedy, 1978; Ollerenshaw, 1988).

It has generally been accepted in the historiography that there was no great shortage of capital in the Irish economy. Lee (1969) was an early proponent of this position. This view was also held by a number of informed contemporaries; an agent of the English Globe Insurance Company noted in 1835 that it was not capital, but confidence that Irish investors lacked (Lee, 1969). In 1863, Hancock (an Irish economist) noted growing investment in railways, large holdings of government stock and increased deposits in Irish banks, all indicating that there was a fair supply of surplus capital (Kennedy, 1978). Given the availability of capital, what then were the factors which were inhibiting development in Ireland? O'Grada (1994) and Thomas (1987) suggest that the size and nature of the economy only provided limited investment opportunities. They argue that where obvious opportunities existed they were exploited by both native and foreign entrepreneurs.

How dynamic was the economy during this period? Cullen (1972) and more recently Williamson (1994) have taken a more optimistic outlook than most. Williamson points out that purchasing power in Ireland increased dramatically during the period as the Irish economy experienced a high level of convergence with that of Great Britain. Between 1848 and 1914 income per head in Ireland rose from about two-fifths of that of Great Britain to about three-fifths. Irish real wages rose even more (from 59 per cent of those in GB to 88 per cent over the same years). Williamson isolates two major factors which contributed to this between the mid-nineteenth century and World War One (which was probably the most dramatic period of real wage convergence before or since). Firstly mass migration out of Ireland raised wages as the labour supply diminished. Secondly, the significant growth in trade facilitated by falling transport costs helped to accelerate convergence with Great Britain (Williamson, 1994, pp. 12-22).

By the 1920s, Ireland had achieved a level of per capita income which was between a half and three-fifths of that in Great Britain which at this point was the wealthiest country in Europe (Kennedy, in this volume). If Ireland's performance was relatively good in a European context (despite the fact that part of the story is to be explained by unprecedented levels of emigration), this growth would also have been reflected in a general increase in investment in the economy. The following sections will therefore examine investment patterns in different sectors of the economy.

SERVICES

Railways

The railways absorbed more fixed capital investment than any other part of the economy during the second half of the nineteenth century (see Figure 2.1). They revolutionised Ireland's transport and communications network, which was critical in an economy so heavily dependant on trade for expansion.

By 1914, about 50,000 shareholders (who were mostly Irish) held about £45,000,000 of Irish railway stock which yielded an average dividend of 4 per cent. This compared favourably with British and European railways, despite its relatively low traffic density as construction costs were much cheaper. The 4 per cent average return on railway stock compared favourably with government stock which yielded in the region of 2.5 to 3 per cent (Lee, 1973, p. 110).

Lee has detected a certain degree of risk aversion among native entrepreneurs in the early years of Irish railway construction, when English investors bore a disproportionate share of the initial risks in Irish railways. Only 35 per cent of the capital in the Great Southern and Western Railway (Ireland's largest rail company) was in Irish hands in the mid 1840s. After the company had paid its first dividend in 1850 and raised this to 4.5 per cent in 1852 native capital was more forthcoming accounting for 73 per cent of the total capital invested by 1860 (Lee, 1968, pp. 48-9, 62-3). However, in the long term Irish investors provided most of the substantial capital demands of the railways and reaped most of the dividends. Once railway shares had demonstrated their metal, Irish shareholders were more forthcoming and a major transfer took place from other Irish asset holdings, like government stock. About 700 miles of track had been built by the end of the 1850s rising to 2,000 by the end of the following decade. By this time the most important and profitable parts of the network had been built and the stocks of major rail companies had become one of the most solid and dependable Irish stocks available. During the 1880s and 1890s a number of light railways were built with public assistance at a cost of about £6 million though these never brought the expected profits (Thomas, p. 112).

FIGURE 2.1: CAPITAL IN RAILWAYS

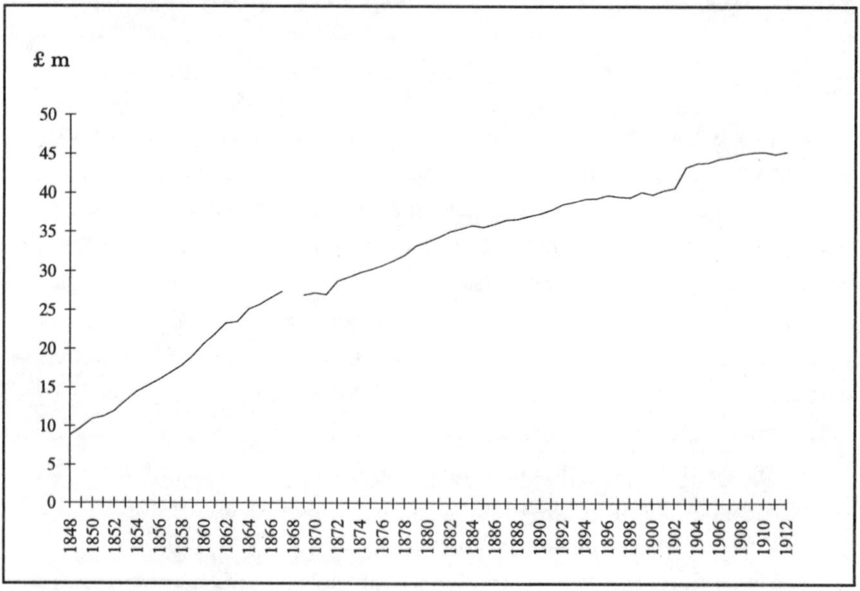

Source: Mitchell, 1988.

The railways made an enormous improvement to the country's transport infrastructure, reducing costs, raising speed and bringing the Irish economy closer to its main trading partner, Britain. In this respect the rail network was the single most important infrastructural investment in the economy and the increase in trade which it facilitated most certainly improved investment opportunities in the economy at large.

The Catholic Church

At the turn of the century Horace Plunkett earmarked Catholicism as a major cause of Ireland's poor economic performance. More recently, Larkin (1967) has argued that the Catholic Church reduced the supply of capital in the Irish economy by redirecting a large part of the country's wealth into unproductive enterprises like church building, thereby retarding potential economic development in other areas (notably during the second half of the nineteenth century). Kennedy (1978) in a spirited defense of the faith has argued that the church was not guilty in this respect, as a lack of capital was not a factor which inhibited development. He argues that a lack of profitable investment opportunities and risk aversion are more likely explanations and the church if anything may have marginally assisted economic growth by raising demand for goods and services.

By the 1890s, the Catholic Church had surplus capital above and beyond its requirements for working capital and building purposes due to legacies, bequests and other gifts. These funds were invested safely in government securities, railway debentures and first mortgages on land (Larkin, 1967, p. 869). The church in this respect merely reflected patterns of investment evident in the wider society.

The Banks

Irish banking in the period in question has been frequently criticised for its conservative lending policies and a perceived unwillingness to assist a host of potential entrepreneurs who lacked nothing but credit. The growth in deposits in Irish banks from about £8 million in 1850 to over £71 million in 1914 dramatically increased the potential capital available for investment purposes. The question is did the banks prevent this major resource from being utilised? A recent reassessment by Ollerenshaw (1988) has argued that the traditional negative view is not very accurate. Ollerenshaw concludes that:

> in the later nineteenth and early twentieth centuries total advances continued to rise on trend, although at a slower rate than deposits; that discount business declined compared to overdraft business; and that investment loomed much larger in bank asset portfolios in 1914 than they had in the 1860s. Investment of funds outside Ireland had long been a necessity for Irish banks, since securities could not be bought and sold in quantity on the small

Dublin Stock Exchange. For this reason purchases and sales were made via the London Stock Exchange (Ollerenshaw, 1988, p. 223).

The growth in banking facilitated an expansion of investment during the period; in particular the banks provided working capital on a short term basis. This was important in an economy where much of the demand for credit was seasonal. Ollerenshaw's work indicates that by and large the banks provided capital to most investors who had a viable business proposition with reasonable security.

Joint Stock Companies in the Service Sector

It is possible to gain some idea of investment patterns in the service sector as a whole from the register of Irish joint stock companies which were published annually. This register (see Figure 2.2) provides some indication of the periods of high and low investment in services during the second half of the nineteenth century, although they need to be interpreted cautiously (see Bielenberg and Burke, Chapter 3).

Investment in joint stock companies in the service sector was initially sluggish, with the notable exception of the gas sector which accounted for 39 new companies between 1856-62. The first good year for service investment was in 1864; from here it climbed rapidly to a peak in 1868 with gas continuing to be prominent, although insurance, banking, and hotels also featured. Investment fell off somewhat until 1871 when a number of steamship companies were registered. Investment in services remained steady in the 1870s with a number of companies registering in the area of transport, warehousing, distribution and retailing reflecting the general expansion of trade and commerce. With the increase in mobility resulting from the railways, investment in hotels continued. Peak service sector investment during the decade was in 1877-78. The next upturn in 1883 was the highest for the period in question. This was a consequence of new legislation which provided the interest on railway capital with a baronial guarantee; in addition, public assistance was given to light railways and tramways, all of which resulted in a number of new transport floatations between 1883 and 1896. The increase in investment in joint stock service companies through the late 1880s and most of the 1890s seems to be closely related to the international trade boom during this period.

FIGURE 2.2: NOMINAL SHARE CAPITAL WITH BREAKDOWN BETWEEN
SERVICES AND MANUFACTURING.

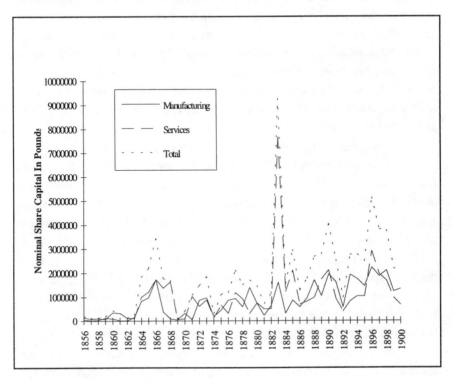

Source: Bielenberg and Burke, Chapter 3

AGRICULTURE

In a predominantly agrarian society, it is hardly surprising that land
continued to be an attractive investment proposition as a large proportion of the population had a good knowledge of agriculture. In addition, land conferred higher social status than trade and industry.
The increased supply of land coming onto the market in the immediate wake of the Great Famine and the Encumbered Estates Acts was
viewed by many as a more attractive investment option than un-
proven railway stock. Under the Encumbered Estates Acts of 1848-9
about a quarter of Irish land acreage was transferred to new owners
(Cullen, 1972, p. 138). Presumably they had much greater capital resources than their predecessors. Between October 1849 and August
1857 the amount of new land purchased amounted to almost £20.5
million. Of the 7,489 purchasers 7,180 were Irish (Larkin, 1967, p.

862). The newcomers were more eager to make a profit from their investments and tended to be greater improvers than their predecessors who had frequently been crippled by debt. O'Grada (1975) suggests that overall there was an increased investment in improvements by landlords in the period between 1850 and the 1880s, relative to the pre-famine period, while landlord investment was likely to have declined from the 1880s. More significantly, he argues that tenants accounted for the lions share of investment, even prior to the 1880s (O'Grada, 1975).

From a comparative perspective, investment in improvements by landlords in Ireland appear to have been lower than in England during the second half of the nineteenth century. Vaughan (1994) suggests that the average expenditure by landlords on all Irish estates may have been in the region of 4 to 5 per cent of rent receipts, although many were significantly higher than this; on nine of the estates he investigated, an average figure of just over 11 per cent of rent receipts were spent on improvements. According to Vaughan this compares with a figure of 20 to 27 per cent which various authorities have put forward for English estates during this period. He suggests a number of possible reasons for the lower levels of investment by landlords in Ireland; these included landlord indebtedness; customs on many estates which prevented life tenants from passing on the benefits of improvements to their own families; the small size of holdings; the predominance of livestock farming carried out in a climate with mild winters which meant that there was a lower requirement for outbuildings than in parts of Britain. Rents on average were lower in Ireland (on a ratio of 5:8 relative to England according to one authority). This would also have depressed Irish landlord investment relatively (Vaughan, 1994, pp. 82-3, 123-4, 127-8, 277-8).

Given the changing nature of Irish agricultural output whereby the relative importance of livestock increased from about 54 per cent of output in 1854 to almost 87 per cent in 1908 (O'Grada, 1988, pp. 48, 68, 129), a significant share of total tenant investment would have gone into increasing stock instead of into improvements to land, buildings etc., particularly while tenants lacked security. Cattle represented the largest single item of capital expenditure on Irish farms, the cattle population rising from 1.84 million in 1841 to 4.7 million in 1901 (Kennedy, 1978, p. 50).

As more tenants acquired the ownership of their holdings as a result of the passing of the various Land Acts, investment in Irish agriculture probably increased in the decades leading up to the First World War, especially after the Wyndham Act of 1903 (which earmarked £100 million for land purchase). Rising farmer incomes and a growth in the average size of holdings certainly increased the potential for further investment.

Is there any hard evidence which suggests that this was the case? By 1910, according to an estimate made by Feinstein and Pollard (1988, p. 275) the value of the gross stock of farm machinery, equipment and vehicles in Irish agriculture was around 25 per cent of the value of the same in Great Britain. This figure suggests that from a comparative perspective, investment in equipment, machinery and vehicles in Irish agriculture was not very far behind Great Britain. Given the greater emphasis on livestock in Irish agriculture, it is probable that investment in stock was relatively higher than in Great Britain. Feinstein suggests that it is only in investment in buildings and improvements to land that Irish agriculture was deficient relative to Great Britain (Feinstein, Pollard, 1988, p. 277).

Turner's recent work on Irish agricultural output and productivity relative to Britain also provides evidence which suggests some increase in investment. Irish agriculture contributed between about one-sixth and one-fifth of UK output in the 1860s rising to between one-fifth and one-quarter on the eve of the war (Turner, 1991). If this is the case and assuming there was some relationship between increased production and investment it seems probable that investment in Irish agriculture was growing more rapidly than in Great Britain (although Ireland was starting from a lower threshold relatively).

Vaughan has pointed out that it would be difficult to argue that landlords in post-famine Ireland were constructive in economic matters, least of all in terms of investment in agriculture. By extracting a large surplus from agriculture of about £340 million between 1850 and 1879 (a sum greater than that collected by any other agency) they could have potentially made major improvements to the agricultural economy:

> their estate management showed they did not possess complete knowledge...they neither invested, provided entrepreneurial skill,

nor maintained the agricultural interest in the state. (Vaughan, 1994, pp. 218-222.)

Their departure probably resulted in a higher level of improvement and investment in Irish agriculture. Tenants who became proprietors had a greater knowledge of agriculture and the market than their landlord predecessors, and were more likely to invest in farming stock than in government stock, even if the return was not greater. The rise in agricultural output and productivity in the first quarter of the present century (O'Grada, 1988, p. 130) must in some measure have resulted from increased capital investment in Irish agriculture, given that the labour force employed in agriculture was diminishing and the supply of land was not changing significantly.

INDUSTRY

Lee has pointed out that the capital required for most industrial firms was quite small in the mid-nineteenth century (Lee, 1969, p. 54). This was to change during the second half of the nineteenth century as the industrial sector became more capital intensive and more concentrated around a much smaller number of larger firms.

Capital for expansion purposes in the industrial sector was raised by a number of methods. Industrial firms often drew upon the resources of the family and associates of the owners. A good example of this is Harland and Wolff, the Belfast shipbuilding company; Harland who was initially taken on as a manager finally acquired the company for £5,000 in the late 1850s. By taking on Wolff as an assistant, Harland was able to raise a further £12,000 from his new partners' uncle, which was to be repaid from the company's profits. These were substantial in the following years and a significant proportion were reinvested in the company; its capital value rose from £23,000 in 1863 to £78,000 in 1872 (Moss and Hume, 1986, pp. 16-22).

A number of Irish industrial firms initially acquired fixed capital through family connections and business associates, resorting to the banks for working capital secured with the companies fixed capital assets. Industrialists engaged in processing the country's agricultural output like millers, brewers, distillers, bacon curers or flax spinners had a fairly predictable short term seasonal demand for credit which was frequently supplied by the banks. In general the Irish banks (as in Britain) were less willing to provide long term loans for fixed capital investment (Ollerenshaw, 1988, pp. 224-8). As at Harland and Wolff, further investments were usually made by ploughing profits back into the venture.

Guinness was by far the largest industrial firm in the country with regard to the value of its assets. It expanded dramatically between 1850 and 1880 simply by re-investing profits. The company became incorporated in 1886 and was sold to the public for 6 million pounds. The brewery enabled the First Earl of Iveagh to become the second wealthiest man in the United Kingdom (Gourvish and Wilson, 1994, pp. 218, 250).

The gradual concentration of the brewing industry during the second half of the nineteenth century in large capital intensive concerns like Guinness in Dublin and Beamish and Crawford's and Murphy's in Cork, displaced many of the smaller concerns located all over Ireland. A similar concentration is evident in distilling and a number of other industries. In addition to siphoning off capital from profits, many of the larger companies which survived resorted to the home share market to raise capital for expansion. This was particularly evident in linen, Ireland's premier industry. An estimate of the capital employed put the value of the assets of the industry at 20 million pounds in 1874. However, the industry's assets had been massively over-valued during the boom years and by the end of the century new estimates put the value at twelve million pounds (Lloyd Paterson, 1907).

Joint Stock Industrial Companies

Linen brought about the first major upturn in investment in joint stock manufacturing companies in the 1860s and early 1870s. Investment in joint stock industrial companies continued to rise in the 1870s and 1880s. A number of distilleries were incorporated in the 1870s. A more pronounced upturn in investment in industrial joint stock companies began around 1888, with peaks in 1896 and 1898; cycle manufacturing company shares dominated all else on the Dublin stock exchange in 1893 and again in 1895-96 (Thomas, 1986).

Mining

It is evident from the joint stock companies register that much native capital was raised for an array of mining ventures which tended to be of a more speculative nature than other investments. O'Grada (1994) has demonstrated conclusively that risk aversion was certainly not a major problem in this sector, with much native and foreign capital being invested, a large share of this yielding little or no returns to investors (O'Grada, 1994, pp. 315-321). Ireland however lacked significant mineral and coal deposits; so resource constraints rather than shy investors accounted for the very low output of the sector.

Building

Activity in the building industry perhaps more than any other sector reflects the general state of the economy. During boom periods it flourishes while in recessions activity tends to tail off. As most of Ireland's timber was imported from destinations outside the UK, it is possible to track the level of foreign timber imports which respond closely to the general level of activity in the building industry (see Figure 2.3).

FIGURE 2.3: TIMBER IMPORTS

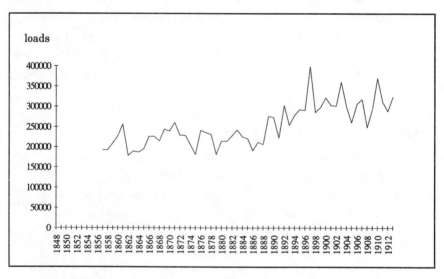

Source: Bielenberg and Burke, Chapter 3.

Between 1857 and 1888, the industry fluctuated but not dramatically, rising from the 1860s to the early 1870s, then falling until a recovery set in in the mid-1870s. The late 1870s and early 1880s were bad years with a partial recovery in the mid-1880s. The trend generally improves from 1888, peaking in 1896 but remaining strong into the new century. The upward trend over the period as a whole is impressive, given the major fall in Ireland's population; it represents an increased investment and significant improvement in Ireland's housing stock. Polak and O'Rourke who have charted an annual index of property transactions in Ireland also found a significant upturn in the late nineteenth and early twentieth century. They suggest however that this upturn was associated more with the high level of property transactions resulting from the Land Acts rather than "any new found prosperity" (Polak and O'Rourke, 1994). The evidence for the building industry above, and the general upturn in investment in the 1890s in other sectors suggest that a general increase in wealth may also have been an important factor in increasing the number of property transactions.

BRITISH GOVERNMENT STOCK AND OTHER EXTERNAL ASSETS

Before the railways began to attract a high level of investment from the mid-1840s, most of the business of the Dublin stock exchange was in government stock. A register of all the government stock held in Ireland was kept at the Bank of Ireland.

Holdings on this register reached a nineteenth century peak of £41.6 million in 1857, which represented most of the unredeemed marketable capital in the country (see Figure 2.4). Thereafter holdings of government stock experienced a fairly continuous decline for the second half of the nineteenth century with a low point of £24.2 million in 1896-97. The reason for this fall off was that better returns could be made elsewhere. *Thom's Directory* reported that the decrease of £1,249,640 in 1872 was:

> attributable to the attraction of foreign loans, especially American securities, besides increased confidence in railway securities and the larger amount of trust money in recent years held under marriage settlements authorizing investments in railway debentures and railway stock. (*Thoms Directory*, 1874, pp. 875)

Most of the rail companies paid out higher dividends than the 3 per cent or so which could be earned on government stock. In addition,

growing investment opportunities in commercial and industrial companies in Ireland whose shares were sold on the Dublin Stock Exchange, also reduced the attraction of government stock. The Catholic
Church, for example, invested in government securities, railways debentures, and first mortgages on land. Sound financial advice dis-
pensed by the archbishop of Armagh in 1896 to the rector of the Irish
College in Rome (who wished to invest in Ireland) indicates that even
land had become a more attractive investment proposition than government securities at this point. He warned the rector that:

> You have hit on a very unfortunate time for your investment. Trus-
> tee securities are so high now that you can find none which will
> pay more than 2.5 or 2.75 per cent. A few days ago I sold out near
> five thousand pounds of government stock which was left me for a
> charity, and I had to put it in the Bank to wait for some invest-
> ment. I think your best plan is to do the same for a time; but you
> should insist on the National Bank giving a special rate for it. The
> only trustee security now that will give as much as four per cent is
> first mortgage on land; but it is not every mortgage one can trust. I
> intend to look out for such a mortgage to invest my charity money.
> Mr McCann says that if it could be got in a good county, such as
> Wexford, Kildare or Meath, with a good margin of rental, it is quite
> safe (Larkin, p. 289).

FIGURE 2.4: GOVERNMENT STOCK HELD AT THE BANK OF IRELAND

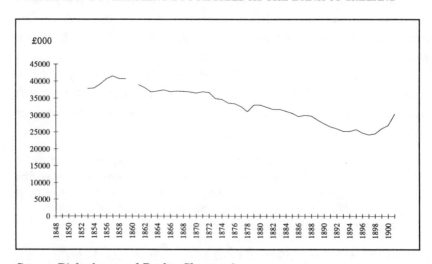

Source: Bielenberg and Burke, Chapter 3.

The poor return on government stock made it a less attractive investment as other options improved during the second half of the nineteenth century. However, the transfer of government stock between Dublin and London also provided a mechanism for stabilising the Irish financial system. Thomas (1986, p. 122) explains how this worked on the eve of the famine:

> An excess of money supply in Dublin...would lead to a fall in interest rates and a rise in stock prices above those in London. Investors would then buy stock in London for transfer to and sale in Dublin. As funds left Ireland to pay for the stock the monetary circulation would fall.... On the other hand if money was relatively scarce in Dublin....with high interest rates....then stock would be bought in Dublin for sale in London. In this case there would be a substitution of cash for stock in Dublin, thus relieving the monetary pressure.

The purchase or sale of government stock also provided other stabilising benefits. If the balance of payments was in favour of Ireland, this would lead to the importation of stock and an outflow of funds. The Bank of Ireland frequently made purchases and sales for exchange purposes rather than for profit (Thomas, pp. 122-5). Due to a balance of payments surplus during World War One, for example, there was a significant rise in British government stock held in Ireland which amounted to about £106 million in 1922. Only about 6.5 million of this was held in Northern Ireland. Investors in the more industrial 6 counties which became Northern Ireland had greater investment opportunities locally and therefore had a much lower propensity to invest in government stock or other external assets.

In regard to external assets more generally, an outflow of capital from Ireland began to become apparent in the last quarter of the nineteenth century. Much of this it seems was invested in overseas railways, notably in the US and Canada, and also in colonial stocks. Cullen surmises that it is not unlikely that the total value of Irish investment abroad was in the region of £150 million by 1914 (Cullen, 1972 p. 169. Thomas, p. 131). These external investments had risen to roughly 250 million pounds by the early 1920s, and estimates of income from external assets had risen to 12.3 million pounds by 1926 in the Free State alone. Ireland had built up substantial external assets in the period between the 1850s and the 1920s as a result of the fact that the economy was producing a large capital surplus.

CONCLUSION

In making the decision to invest in overseas assets, Irish investors (like their Scottish counterparts) were more concerned with profits than patriotism. According to Cullen, during the last quarter of the nineteenth century, the papers of Irish businessmen show a high degree of interest in overseas assets, like colonial and railway stocks, where potential returns were obviously higher than at home (Cullen, 1972, p. 169).

However, it is difficult not to conclude that a greater degree of investment and enterprise by Irish landlords in Irish agriculture in the third quarter of the nineteenth century would have increased both capital formation and agricultural output, thereby improving living standards and living conditions for those who worked in that sector. Similarly, earlier (and greater) investment in the new creamery system may have enabled Ireland to retain (or even increase) its market share for butter in Britain against the Danish incursion. Greater cooperation among Irish distillers (particularly between the large traditional pot still distillers in the south and the large patent still distillers in the north) and possible amalgamation along Scottish lines may have enabled the industry to retain its niche in British and colonial markets. Instead, after the turn of the century, the northern distillers (who had most of Ireland's British market share) were outflanked by Distillers Company Limited of Scotland in share options which resulted in the demise of most of the Ulster industry. The remaining southern pot still dynasties continued to survive on sales which were largely limited to the domestic market. There must have been other investment opportunities in food processing and fishing. These are just some examples of lost opportunities where entrepreneurial initiative could have more profitably utilised some of the surplus funds which were invested in overseas assets, thus generating incomes and profits as opposed to dividends alone.

From a wider perspective however, despite the high investment in overseas assets, the evidence in this chapter suggests that as far as economic development was concerned, a gradual but nonetheless positive shift appears to have taken place in the second half of nineteenth century towards investment in more productive fixed capital assets. A number of new industrial and commercial companies emerged, and many older ones became more consolidated and capital intensive. The shift in land ownership from landlords to tenants between the 1880s and the 1920s, if anything, probably increased investment in Irish agriculture.

The statistical trends revealed by the joint stock companies register, and the growth of the building industry conform reasonably well with the qualitative picture outlined in this chapter. All of these indicators reveal a modest rise in investment between the 1850s and the 1880s despite some fluctuations, with an upturn taking place in the late 1880s, and for most of the 1890s.

Caskey's negative verdict on the entrepreneurial performance of northern industrialists during the period seems a little harsh. Rather than isolating a few firms, it might be better to study the performance of all firms in specific sectors. In a northern context it seems likely that a study of all the firms in the linen industry, by far the most important sector, would reveal a slightly better performance from a comparative perspective given that the north was the most important linen manufacturing centre in the world (though it is not difficult to pick out a few laggard firms). Even if exogenous factors had a critical influence on the health of the industry it took a few good entrepreneurs to exploit potential opportunities, or to retain market share when the international industry experienced contraction or recession. However, these issues require more research.

From a long-term perspective, investment opportunities improved in Ireland during the second half of the nineteenth century, despite the major fall in population. There were many factors which contributed to this development, but the rise in purchasing power, the revolution in communications (which increased trade) and the extension of banking services (which improved credit) deserve special mention.

The supply and quality of entrepreneurs also probably increased with improvements in education and the emergence of a more confident rural and urban middle class. If in the mid-nineteenth century the small middle class "aped the gentry" (Hutchinson, 1972), by the eve of the First World War an expanding rural bourgeoisie was rapidly displacing the ascendancy from its pre-eminent position in regard to land ownership; the Irish middle class had effectively controlled the majority of the Irish seats in Westminster since the early 1880s. Although Unionism and Nationalism divided the Irish middle class politically, a more ambitious and self confident bourgeois culture had emerged in Ireland during the second half of the nineteenth century. One of the economic manifestations of this emerging new social order was a growth in capital accumulation and investment.

REFERENCES:

Bielenberg, A. and Burke, A.E. (1995): "A Data Set on Investment and Enterprise in Ireland 1850-1900: New Company Registrations, Timber Imports and Government Stock", in *Enterprise and the Irish Economy*, Burke, A.E. (ed.), Dublin: Oak Tree Press.

Caskey, A. (1983): "Entrepreneurs and Industrial Development in Ulster 1850-1914" M. Phil., University of Ulster.

Cullen, L. (1972): *An Economic History of Ireland from 1660*, London: Batsford.

Feinstein, C., Pollard, S. (1988): *Studies in Capital Formation*, Oxford: Clarendon Press.

Gourvish, T., Wilson, R. (1994): *The British Brewing Industry 1830-1980*, Cambridge: Cambridge University Press.

Hutchinson, R. (1972): "Study of Non Economic Factors in Irish Economic Development", *Economic and Social Review*, 1(4).

Keating, P., Desmond, D. (1993): *Culture and Capitalism in Contemporary Ireland*, Avebury: Aldershot.

Kennedy, L. (1978): "The Roman Catholic Church and Economic Growth in Nineteenth Century", *Economic and Social Review*, 10.

Larkin, E. (1967): "Economic Growth, Capital Investment and the Roman Catholic Church in the Nineteenth Century", *American History Review*, 72.

Lee, J. (1967): "Capital in the Irish Economy" in Cullen, L. (ed.) *"The Formation of the Irish Economy"*, Cork: Mercier Press.

Lee, J. (1973): "The Golden Age of Irish Railways", Nowlan, K.B. (ed.) *Travel and Transport in Ireland*, Dublin: Gill and MacMillan.

Lee, J. (1968): "The Provision of Capital for Early Irish Railways, 1830-53.", *Irish Historical Studies*, 16.

Lloyd Paterson, R. (1907): "The British Flax and Linen Industry" in Ashley, W. (ed.) *British Industries,* London: Longmans.

Mitchell, B. (1988): *British Historical Statistics*, Cambridge: Cambridge University Press.

Moss, M. and Hume, J. (1986): "Shipbuilders to the World Harland and Wolff 1861-1986", Belfast: Blackstaff.

O'Grada, C. (1975): "The Investment Behavior of Irish Landlords, 1850-1875", *Agricultural History Review,* 23(2).

O'Grada, C. (1988): *Ireland Before and After the Famine*, Manchester: Manchester University Press.

O'Grada, C. (1994): *A New Economic History of Ireland 1790-1939*, Oxford: Oxford University Press.

Ollerenshaw, P. (1988): "Aspects of Bank Lending in Post-Famine Ireland" in Mitchison, R. and Roebuck, P. (eds.) *Economy and Society in Scotland and Ireland 1500-1939*, Edinburgh: Donald.

Payne, P. (1988): "British Entrepreneurship in the Nineteenth Century", Basingstoke: MacMillan.

Polak, B., O'Rourke, K. (1994): "Property Transactions in Ireland 1788-1988", *Irish Economic and Social History Journal*, 21.

Thomas, W. (1986): *The Stock Exchanges of Ireland*, Liverpool: Cairns.

Thom's Directory, (1874).

Turner, M. (1991): in Campbell, B. and Overton, M. (eds.), *Land Labour and Livestock*, Manchester: Manchester University Press.

Vaughan, W. (1994): *Landlords and Tenants in Mid Victorian Ireland*, Oxford: Oxford University Press.

Williamson, G. (1994): "Economic Convergence; Placing Post-Famine Ireland in Comparative Perspective", *Irish Economic and Social History*, 21.

3

A DATA SET ON INVESTMENT AND ENTERPRISE IN IRELAND, 1850-1900: NEW COMPANY REGISTRATIONS, TIMBER IMPORTS AND GOVERNMENT STOCK

Andy Bielenberg and Andrew E. Burke

This brief chapter is aimed at facilitating research on the Irish economy in the second half of the nineteenth century. The chapter publishes three new data sets relating to new company registrations, timber imports and holdings of government stock at the Bank of Ireland. The chapter is divided into three sections dealing with each respective data set. Since this chapter is merely intended as a source for data, it only describes the data collection process and does not attempt an analysis.

NEW COMPANY REGISTRATIONS

New company registration data are often used as a proxy for enterprise (for example, Black et al., 1992). Under this interpretation the data represent either the creation of new firms or the expansion of existing firms who raise new capital through incorporation. An alternative view is that new company registrations may not represent enterprise but merely denote the case of an existing firm acquiring limited liability. However, if this latter interpretation were true we would expect a large number of registrations to occur in the first few years in which limited liability was available, as the stock of existing firms (who had unlimited liability) sought to reduce their risk exposure. As soon as this backlog of firms was registered one would expect the number of registrations to taper off. However, the data does not illustrate a pattern consistent with this view but even if it were to do so, the exclusion of the first decade of registrations would probably be sufficient to eliminate the backlog from the sample. Moreover, it is clear that the upturn in specific sectors resulted in an increase in the number of registrations in that sector, i.e. gas in the 1850s, linen in the 1860s, cycle manufacturing in the 1890s. Registrations, therefore, frequently took place in response to expansion, which necessitated a re-organisation of companies' finances.[1]

The data base was collected from the register of new company registrations published in the British Parliamentary Papers. These represented companies registering under the 1856 Companies Act which facilitated incorporation with limited liability. The company register provides information on the name of the company, the nature of its business activity, its nominal share capital and the address of the legal offices where it was registered. This information facilitated the collation of a data set more rich in detail than that provided by the present day Central Statistics Office.

The data is divided into manufacturing and services. There were very few companies registered in the agricultural area. Since these were generally in activities which are described today as agri-business (i.e. dairies or food processing) they were added to the manu-facturing data set.

In cases where it was clear that a company was registering in Ire-land but carrying out business abroad (e.g. South African gold min-ing), the entry was not included in the data set. These exclusions were predominantly mining operations.

The data set is presented by the number of registrations and the total value of the nominal share capital at registration. The latter is merely the amount of share capital which the company can sell with-out a new issue and does not represent paid up capital either at the registration date or indeed subsequently. On this basis, analysts often opt to use the number of company registrations (for example, see Foreman-Peck, 1985) although this methodology may only be valid if average firm size is relatively stable over the period of analysis.

Finally, the data are divided into two geographical areas repre-senting present-day Northern Ireland and the Republic of Ireland. This division has obvious analytical uses but a more detailed break-

---

[1] The issue of the survival of the new company registrations is quite another matter, as one cannot *a priori* know whether the data represent "seedcorn" or "chaff" (see Foreman-Peck (1985)).

down was prevented due to a lack of information contained within the company register. The geographical location of a company was identified on the basis of three criteria. Firstly, the name of a company often contained a reference to its market (for example, the West Clare Railway). Secondly, the legal offices through which the companies registered fell into three geographical areas, namely Belfast, Cork and Dublin. On this basis companies registered in Cork and Dublin were included in the "26 Counties" data set while those registered in Belfast were included in the "6 Counties" data set. The third criteria was based on existing Irish business history where it was possible to either recognise the name of a company or to make a reasonable guess as to where the location of the company might be (for example, linen was generally in the "6 Counties" category). Incomplete records on each firm required that the above three forms of geographical identification were necessary in order to divide the data set.

The data are presented in Tables 3.1 to 3.4. Each table contains the number and nominal share capital for each year. Tables 3.1 and 3.2 contain manufacturing company registrations for the whole of Ireland and present day Republic of Ireland respectively. It hardly deserves mention that the data for present-day Northern Ireland can be derived through subtraction. Tables 3.3 and 3.4 respectively contain the corresponding data for the services sector.

TIMBER IMPORTS

As no annual series for GNP has yet been generated for Ireland during the second half of the nineteenth century, it is useful to look at alternative indicators of the general levels of economic activity. The construction industry is a particularly good barometer as it is procyclical; when the economy is booming it experiences an upturn and during recessions it tails off. The problem then is to find a raw material used by the industry for which a series can be constructed. Timber is one of the few raw materials used by the industry from which it is possible to construct an annual series.

Ireland's native resources had been heavily depleted by the second half of the nineteenth century; by the early 1920s there were only 248,500 acres of woodland left in the country which was roughly two-thirds of the acreage which existed in the early 1840s (Neeson, 1991). The consequence of this low aforestation level was that Ireland had to import most of its timber requirements for construction, which means that imports can be used to cast some light on the amount of timber consumed. Trade data for Ireland however is incomplete between the mid-1820s and 1904. Fortunately, however, records were kept of Irish foreign imports and exports (i.e. Ireland's trade outside the UK). These returns were published annually in Thom's Directory. Since the bulk of Irelands timber requirements for construction purposes came from either the Baltic or North America the omission of the trade with Great Britain is not a major problem.

Timber was used for a range of other purposes such as shipbuilding, furniture making, barrel manufacture for food processing, and alcoholic beverages. This obviously poses problems when using foreign timber imports as a general index for the level of activity in the construction industry. To reduce this distortion, barrel staves have been excluded. To some extent furniture making would have been responsive to a rise in the amount of building activity, but shipbuilding is an example of a demand source which would have been entirely unrelated to construction. However, the much greater quantity of timber used for construction purposes should make the import series more responsive to construction than all else combined.

The timber imports were returned in "loads"; a quantity which we have assumed remained constant over time. Hewn and sawn timber have been added together for the purposes of this series. There are some minor problems with the data; the loads of hewn and sawn timber for 1872 and 1873 are identical for both years which seems improbable. Furthermore, where full returns were not made as in 1859, 1874 and 1882 the data was estimated by taking the mean of the preceding and subsequent year. These problems are not significant enough to distort the overall trend.

GOVERNMENT STOCK HELD AT THE BANK OF IRELAND

British government stock was Ireland's major external asset in the mid-nineteenth century, yielding a guaranteed dividend to investors. According to Thomas (1986), government stock prior to the railway age represented most of Ireland's unredeemed marketable capital. The transfer of government stock between Dublin and London and vice versa provided an important mechanism for stabilising the Irish financial system. If there was disequilibrium in the money market in

Dublin, the balance could be stabilised by the Bank of Ireland purchasing or selling government stock. If there was a balance of payments surplus this would generally lead to, for example, purchases of stock and an outflow of funds from Dublin. The Bank of Ireland frequently made these purchases purely for exchange purposes. Because of its responsibilities in this respect, the Bank Of Ireland was obliged to keep a register of the amount of British government stock it held, which represented most of the government stock held in Ireland. The figures published here (which originally were drawn from the bank's register) have been compiled directly from the annual returns published in *Thom's Directory* between the 1850s and the early 1900s.

TABLE 3.1: NEW MANUFACTURING COMPANY REGISTRATIONS IN THE 32
COUNTIES OF IRELAND: 1856-1900

	Number of Registrations	Nominal Share Capital in £
1856	1	50,000
1857	4	16,500
1585	3	25,500
1859	7	118,800
1860	6	87,725
1861	3	11,365
1862	3	8,500
1863	6	146,400
1864	17	833,800
1865	14	976,000
1866	19	1,724,000
1867	6	390,000
1868	5	81,360
1869	4	38,500
1870	3	332,000
1871	3	50,133
1872	12	873,000
1873	24	972,230
1874	9	182,500
1875	10	458,000
1876	18	860,700
1877	21	935,200
1878	11	587,500
1879	19	1,391,250
1880	16	728,150
1881	14	226,500
1882	18	634,000
1883	19	1,608,000
1884	18	317,400
1885	21	864,580
1886	31	585,285
1887	21	944,770
1888	30	1,696,825
1889	28	1,043,300
1890	39	1,939,500
1991	38	1,613,350
1892	37	565,000
1893	45	1,926,700
1895	40	1,447,650
1896	53	2,224,405
1897	68	1,863,650
1898	66	2,103,800
1899	52	1,230,025
1900	54	1,337,190

TABLE 3.2: NEW MANUFACTURING COMPANY REGISTRATIONS IN
THE 26 COUNTIES OF IRELAND: 1856-1900

	Number of Registrations	Nominal Share Capital in £
1856	1	50,000
1857	3	13,500
1858	2	20,500
1859	6	118,500
1860	4	34,200
1861	3	11,365
1862	3	8,500
1863	6	146,400
1864	13	241,800
1865	6	346,000
1866	3	104,000
1867	3	360,000
1868	3	26,360
1896	2	13,000
1870	3	332,000
1871	0	0
1872	9	700,000
1873	13	414,230
1874	6	165,500
1875	4	325,000
1876	13	485,700
1877	14	439,200
1878	6	225,000
1879	8	210,500
1880	9	298,150
1881	8	145,500
1882	12	532,000
1883	11	461,000
1884	8	151,000
1885	12	291,980
1886	20	212,180
1887	15	676,770
1888	17	846,325
1889	16	606,300
1890	28	1,660,500
1891	20	909,350
1892	20	245,000
1893	29	1,550,800
1894	20	1,207,005
1895	23	944,150
1896	32	882,905
1897	41	1,221,650
1898	34	1,040,300
1899	25	446,500
1900	27	538,380

TABLE 3.3: NEW SERVICES COMPANY REGISTRATIONS IN THE 32
COUNTIES OF IRELAND: 1856-1900

	Number of Registrations	Nominal Share Capital in £
1856	8	137,200
1857	15	82,500
1858	6	99,000
1859	18	69,120
1860	18	352,900
1861	16	326,000
1862	13	112,400
1863	14	103,800
1864	16	999,000
1865	24	1,214,000
1866	18	1,730,100
1867	9	1,376,800
1868	11	1,632,600
1969	9	38,600
1870	12	86,920
1871	26	1,029,650
1872	15	614,000
1873	19	886,200
1874	8	124,100
1875	15	660,300
1876	13	323,400
1877	26	1,183,250
1878	18	925,400
1879	14	315,125
1880	16	747,000
1881	15	491,600
1882	22	509,400
1883	88	7,679,950
1884	36	1,225,150
1885	32	2,105,450
1886	20	691,768
1887	26	810,500
1888	38	977,250
1889	42	1,731,240
1890	57	2,115,380
1891	44	924,000
1892	35	403,750
1893	51	824,099
1894	54	1,030,590
1895	44	1,033,705
1896	82	2,914,810
1897	76	1,954,970
1898	71	1,680,800
1899	62	972,544
1900	62	674,950

TABLE 3.4: NEW SERVICES COMPANY REGISTRATIONS IN THE 26
COUNTIES OF IRELAND: 1856-1900

	Number of Registrations	Nominal Share Capital in £
1856	6	133,000
1857	9	57,500
1858	4	89,000
1859	14	42,120
1860	11	313,400
1861	12	304,000
1862	10	103,900
1863	9	81,000
1864	13	888,000
1865	20	118,600
1866	10	559,000
1867	6	306,800
1868	7	1,518,600
1869	4	8,600
1870	8	69,320
1871	14	655,250
1872	10	542,000
1873	12	669,000
1874	4	65,000
1875	9	315,300
1876	9	286,000
1877	17	838,250
1878	12	277,400
1879	7	108,000
1880	9	695,000
1881	9	339,000
1882	15	484,000
1883	66	6,520,250
1884	23	1,040,900
1885	22	1,947,100
1886	14	653,700
1887	11	391,600
1888	24	660,750
1889	24	1,527,000
1890	32	1,301,300
1891	19	219,800
1892	18	228,750
1893	36	555,349
1894	40	893,390
1895	30	868,005
1896	48	2,468,910
1897	48	1,408,000
1898	41	860,800
1899	38	664,944
1900	37	353,950

TABLE 3.5: TIMBER IMPORTS TO IRELAND

Measured in Loads	
1857	192,568
1858	191,975
1859	209,121
1860	226,267
1861	256,184
1862	178,107
1863	189,525
1864	186,307
1865	194,761
1866	226,471
1867	225,839
1868	214,418
1869	243,686
1870	238,180
1871	260,452
1872	229,177
1873	229,177
1874	205,103
1875	181,029
1876	241,461
1877	235,513
1878	231,225
1879	180,938
1880	214,243
1881	213,907
1882	228,057
1883	242,207
1884	225,066
1885	220,995
1886	190,294
1887	211,388
1888	205,725
1889	275,931
1890	272,662
1891	222,275
1892	302,104
1893	253,939
1894	278,208
1895	292,369
1896	290,347
1897	399,040
1898	285,214
1899	298,069
1900	321,478
1901	302,161
1902	301,092
1903	360,656
1904	299,170
1905	260,427

TABLE 3.6: GOVERNMENT STOCK HELD AT THE BANK OF IRELAND (£000S)

1853	37,842.0
1854	37,982.0
1855	39,149.7
1856	40,684.8
1857	41,549.7
1858	40,712.0
1859	40,679.6
1860	N/A
1861	38,972.0
1862	38,081.0
1863	36,849.0
1864	37,115.0
1865	37,450.0
1866	36,958.0
1867	37,128.0
1868	37,023.0
1869	36,871.4
1870	36,548.0
1871	36,927.0
1872	36,756.0
1873	34,953.0
1874	34,739.0
1875	33,640.0
1876	33,424.0
1877	32,613.0
1878	31,108.0
1879	33,037.0
1880	33,113.0
1881	32,439.0
1882	31,772.0
1883	31,804.0
1884	31,280.2
1885	30,640.2
1886	29,689.0
1887	30,080.0
1888	29,839.0
1889	28,669.0
1890	27,517.0
1891	26,609.0
1892	26,042.0
1893	25,283.0
1894	25,375.0
1895	25,824.0
1896	24,776.0
1897	24,216.0
1898	24,554.0
1899	26,072.0
1900	27,021.0
1901	30,395.0

REFERENCES

Black, J., de Meza, D. and Jeffreys, D. (1992): "House Prices, the Supply of Collateral and the Enterprise Economy", manuscript University of Exeter and forthcoming in the *Economic Journal*.

Foreman-Peck, J.S. (1985): "Seedcorn or Chaff? New Firm Performance of the Interwar Economy", *Economic History Review* 38(3): 402-422.

Neeson, E. (1991): *A History of Irish Forestry*, Dublin: Lilliput Press.

Thomas, W. A. (1986): *The Stock Exchanges of Ireland*, Liverpool: Cairns.

4

IRISH ENTERPRISE IN THE 20TH CENTURY

Kieran A. Kennedy

An assessment of Irish enterprise in the 20th century must properly be set in the context of the economic environment in which enterprise has been undertaken. Section 1 of this chapter therefore gives a brief account of the overall development of the Irish economy since Independence.[1] Section 2 examines the success and failure of the industrial development strategies followed in Ireland. A major deficiency has been the generally poor performance of indigenous manufacturing industry. Section 3 considers whether this deficiency represents an entrepreneurial failure, and if so what accounts for it. Concluding remarks are made in Section 4.

THE DEVELOPMENT OF THE IRISH ECONOMY SINCE INDEPENDENCE

The partition of the island of Ireland in the early 1920s, with Northern Ireland remaining in the UK, deprived the new state of the only region which had experienced substantial industrial development. The newly Independent Ireland was heavily reliant on agriculture, with over half of total employment concentrated in that sector. Even more strikingly, food and drink amounted to over 85 per cent of total merchandise exports. Moreover, Ireland was heavily dependent on one export market, the UK, with over 90 per cent of exports going to that market. In addition, the financial, labour market, institutional and other links with the UK were extremely close — not surprisingly given that Ireland was for so long a region of the UK.

---

[1] For fuller accounts see Kennedy, Giblin and McHugh (1988) and Lee (1989).

Despite these and other indications of underdevelopment, Ireland then enjoyed a respectable level of income per capita relative to other European countries. The Irish level was between one-half and three-fifths of the UK level, and since the latter was at that time the highest in Europe, the Irish level was close to the mean of other countries of western Europe. The Irish position, however, had been reached in a most unusual way over the previous 75 years or so in the context of a massive decline in population, which had reduced the total population by more than half compared with immediate pre-Famine levels.

The overall record of economic development in Ireland since independence emerges as mediocre when set in a European context. Over the period 1926-90, real GNP grew at an average annual rate of 2.3 per cent, and real GNP per capita at 2.0 per cent. The latter figure is just slightly better than the comparable rate in the UK, so that there was only a slight reduction in the gap in living standards vis-à-vis the UK. Achieving little more than keeping pace with the UK implied a poor record, since the UK had the worst growth record in Europe over that period. All of the other small countries of western Europe did better than this, and many of them have caught up with, or exceeded, the UK level (see Table 4.1).

Ireland's economic growth rate did improve considerably in the 1960s, substantially outpacing that in the UK, and coming into line with the average for continental western Europe. Indeed estimates for the first half of the 1990s and projections for the second half suggest that Irish growth rates are now well ahead of those generally prevailing in Europe — so that by the end of the millennium Ireland should have made substantial progress in catching-up with average EU living standards. On one important count, however, the Irish record remains dismal — namely, its inability to absorb its labour surplus. This has been a perennial problem, and Ireland is altogether unique in the fact that its total level of employment is now somewhat less than it was at independence. The inadequate rate of job creation has resulted in substantial emigration, low labour force participation, and high unemployment. The current unemployment rate at 15 per cent is the highest in the EU except for Spain, and no speedy reduction is in sight.

TABLE 4.1: RELATIVE GDP PER CAPITA IN IRELAND AND SELECTED
SMALL EUROPEAN COUNTRIES (UK = 100 IN ALL YEARS)

	1913	1990
Ireland	52	68
Austria	65	105
Belgium	79	103
Denmark	73	105
Finland	41	102
Netherlands	77	100
Norway	50	101
Sweden	61	107
Greece	29	46
Portugal	23	53

Sources: Data for 1990 are from OECD *National Accounts, Main Aggregates, Vol. 1, 1960-1992* and are current PPPs based on a 1990 benchmark. Data for 1913 for all countries except Ireland are from Maddison (1992) and relate to GDP per capita at 1985 US relative prices. The derivation of the Irish figure for 1913 is given in Kennedy (1995). It should be noted that for 1990, GDP overstates the relative Irish level because it is artificially inflated by transfer pricing in multinational enterprises: GNP per capita, which provides a truer measure, would be about 10 per cent less.

Considerable progress has been made in industrialisation. The volume of manufacturing output is now 28 times greater than in the 1920s, while manufactured exports constitute two-thirds of total merchandise exports. Despite this impressive overall progress in manufacturing, however, the indigenous industrial base remains weak, and reservations have emerged about the heavy reliance on foreign enterprise.

INDUSTRIAL DEVELOPMENT STRATEGIES

Since independence in 1922, Irish manufacturing has operated under three distinct policy regimes. The first, applying during the initial decade, and for one hundred years prior to independence, was essentially a laissez-faire, non-interventionist environment. Many of the liberal prerequisites for industrialisation applied: low taxation, no national debt, large external capital reserves, an extensive banking system, a plentiful supply of labour with a high degree of literacy, an extensive rail network and good communications by contemporary standards. Yet southern Ireland remained industrially undeveloped

— if anything it had experienced a measure of de-industrialisation during the nineteenth century. The only part of the island which had experienced an industrial revolution, the northeast, remained part of the United Kingdom. In 1926, manufacturing in the South accounted for only 8 per cent of total employment, and two-thirds of manufacturing value added was concentrated in elementary food processing and drink.

A major protectionist strategy was launched in earnest in 1932, and a high level of protection continued until well into the 1960s: in 1966, the average effective tariff rate was 79 per cent compared with 28 per cent in the UK and 19 per cent in the EEC-6 (McAleese, 1971). This approach led to sizeable increases in manufacturing output and employment in the 1930s, but had little further momentum after the Second World War once the immediate post-war recovery ended. Although manufacturing employment had doubled by then, the initial base was so low that this increase was quite insufficient for Ireland's employment needs, and there was little further progress during the 1950s. Partly because of the speed and scale of protection, there had been a sudden large influx of undersized firms often engaging only in final assembly of imported components of products for which a domestic market already existed. The bulk of firms had neither the competence nor the resources to launch into export markets. Foreign enterprise was frowned on but, because of the indigenous paucity of technological, marketing and managerial capabilities needed to run larger-sized enterprises, significant numbers of foreign suppliers were allowed to establish plants to preserve their Irish sales. Such foreign subsidiaries, however, were generally precluded by their parent firms from competing in overseas markets. So while protection established an industrial base, it remained a weak and vulnerable one.

The third industrial policy regime began to evolve from the early 1950s, though it took some considerable time for this new outward-oriented strategy to reach its full flowering. It had three main elements: (a) substantial capital grants and tax concessions to encourage export-oriented manufacturing, (b) the attraction of foreign manufacturing enterprise, again aimed at exports, and (c) the dismantling of protection in return for greater access to markets abroad. The incentive package involved a large and growing exchequer subsidy, and one estimate put the annual amount involved in the early 1980s at the equivalent of nearly one-third of total manufacturing value added (Roche et al 1984).

This strategy worked quite well in the buoyant world conditions prevailing from 1960-73, but was subject to increasing questioning in the troubled economic conditions after 1973. There is no doubt that a vast increase in manufactured exports was accomplished which has continued up to the present. Most of the increase in exports, however, came from new foreign enterprises, the exports of which amounted to 86 per cent of their output in 1990 as against 33 per cent in indigenous firms, and foreign firms accounted for over three-quarters of total manufacturing exports. The share of new foreign enterprise in total employment had risen to 45 per cent in 1990 (as against 5 per cent in 1966).

The growing dependence on foreign firms gave rise to a number of concerns. A pronounced life cycle effect was observed in new foreign plants, with employment rising initially but then tapering off or declining after full capacity was reached — so that an increasing flow of new enterprises would be needed to maintain overall expansion. Because they relied heavily on their parent firms for R & D and marketing, the extent of their contribution to developing these capabilities in Ireland was questioned. Substantial and growing outflows of profits emerged in the 1980s, associated particularly with the new "sunrise" industries (notably electronics and pharmaceuticals) which have very low labour content relative to their output or exports. Whether these outflows represent genuine profits, or amortisation of investment by the parent in R & D and marketing, or just paper profits due to transfer pricing, they have highlighted the diminishing impact on domestic incomes and employment resulting from vast increases in exports.

A frequent criticism of foreign enterprise was its alleged lack of linkages with the rest of the economy, but a recent study suggests that this criticism may have been overstated. O'Malley (1995) estimated the secondary or indirect employment associated with manufacturing industry, mainly through purchases of services inputs. He found that in manufacturing as a whole there were about 84 associated services jobs per 100 direct manufacturing jobs in 1991. Dividing total manufacturing into the overseas and indigenous components, he found that the ratio for overseas industry (at 94 associated services jobs per 100 direct manufacturing jobs) was higher than in indigenous industry (at 77). The difference between the two is explained mainly by the fact that overseas industry has much higher sales per employee than indigenous industry.

If there were reservations about foreign enterprise, the situation in regard to indigenous industry was much worse. It was always recognised that the removal of protection would cause problems for indigenous firms, but it was hoped that, aided by the incentive package, many would survive and prosper by taking advantage of export opportunities. In the event, the combined effect of import penetration and the disturbed economic conditions following the oil crises was devastating. After 1966, when the dismantling of protection began in earnest, there was no further increase in employment in indigenous manufacturing employment up to the end of the 1970s, followed by a substantial fall for most of the 1980s. Effectively, indigenous firms were failing to compensate for the loss of home market share by exporting. Since they were selling largely in the home market, they could only maintain employment if domestic demand was growing sufficiently to offset their loss of home market share. That was the position up to the end of the 1970s, but when home demand slumped thereafter, a large decline in employment took place.

From 1980-88, employment in indigenous manufacturing fell continuously, by 27 per cent, or nearly 4 per cent per annum. Up to the mid-1980s there was little or no improvement in the share of gross output exported: in 1986 the figure was 26.6 per cent, much the same as the O'Malley (1989) estimate of about 26 per cent thirteen years earlier in 1973. In the next two years, however, there was a big jump in the export/output ratio to 36 per cent in 1988. This together with the revival of home demand towards the end of the 1980s, led to some recovery in indigenous manufacturing employment, though not enough by any means to restore the 1980 level.

To sum up then, since independence Ireland has tried two interventionist strategies to create an industrial base which had failed to develop of its own accord under laissez faire. Both strategies yielded quick results but in neither case did the base become self-propelling. The protectionist phase ran out of steam because of the small size of the home market and the inability of the protected enterprises to penetrate export markets. The impressive initial gains during the outward-looking phase depended heavily on attracting an increasing stream of new foreign enterprises, and when this stream declined in the 1980s, there was insufficient indigenous impetus to sustain expansion. On the contrary, indigenous industry suffered a massive decline in employment in the 1980s.

By the end of the 1970s it was officially acknowledged that a fundamental review of industrial policy was called for, and the Telesis Report (1982), commissioned by the Government, documented the limitations arising from the fragility of indigenous industry and the excessive dependence on foreign enterprise. The report recommended a modification of the outward-looking strategy to give priority to building up a limited number of large Irish companies to serve world markets. For this purpose, the report proposed that there should be a high degree of selectivity in regard to the products and firms assisted: the means used should be more *dirigiste*, using sticks as well as carrots to develop suitable corporate entities; and the approach should be comprehensive in addressing the full range of competitive disabilities, particularly in marketing and technology, which were previously neglected.

It has to be said that the Telesis prescription represented a signpost to the desired destination rather than an itinerary of how to get there — so that some time inevitably elapsed before new policies emerged in pursuit of the new directions. From the mid-1980s onwards, however, there were several changes in the content of industrial policy. The Company Development Programme first introduced on a pilot basis in 1984, directed mainly at indigenous companies, sought to assist overall company planning as opposed to individual once-off investments. The National Linkage Programme begun in 1985 aimed to develop a strong indigenous base of sub-supply firms with overseas companies operating in Ireland. These and other such measures were concentrated on achieving one or more of the key new emphases of industrial policy:

- focusing more on indigenous industry;

- adapting a more selective approach;

- addressing identified weaknesses in management, marketing and technology;

- deepening the contribution of overseas industry;

- broadening the range of assisted industry to include international services; and

- getting better value for money in relation to government incentives.

The attempt to follow these new directions of policy scarcely had time to prove themselves before a new review of industrial policy was initiated in June 1991, culminating in the Culliton Report (1992) published in January 1992. The central message of the Culliton Report was that policy for industrial development goes well beyond industrial policy as traditionally conceived (i.e. the activities of the industrial development agencies and the incentives they were empowered to offer). While proposing changes in some aspects of traditional industrial policy, it argued that the more important features lie in the broader aspects affecting the competitiveness and productivity of the economy as a whole and which form the decisive determinants of industrial performance". The Report argued for a broader approach than in the past, which "must go beyond traditional departmental demarcation lines to take account of all the major relevant factors". In this spirit, the Report placed primary emphasis on its detailed proposals for:

- wide-ranging reform of the tax system;

- the further improvement of infrastructure, especially the areas of transport, communications and energy;

- reform of the education system to secure a stronger vocational and technical orientation at second and third levels; and

- reform of the industrial training system and institutions to secure greater priority for industry-relevant training.

On industrial policy more narrowly defined, the chief recommendations of the Report were:

- a further squeezing of grant aid for foreign industry;

- a decisive switch from grants to equity in supporting indigenous industry;

- a greater focus on industry clusters;

- a clear mandate, and access to capital, for commercial state enterprises.

To give effect to these and other proposals, the Report recommended institutional changes in the state industrial development agencies. In particular, in order to give greater focus to developing indigenous industry, it recommended that a new agency should be formed with that specific mandate.

The Culliton Report did not undertake any in-depth analysis of the reasons why indigenous industry has so far resisted the various efforts of policy to develop it. Basically its stance was: policy to date has been demonstrably ineffective, but here is a better set of policies. Implied in its policies, however, is the view that what really matters for the development of indigenous industry is the general competitive environment. Unfortunately, we cannot be at all sure that defects in the general competitive environment satisfactorily explain the failure of indigenous enterprise.

POSSIBLE EXPLANATIONS

Various explanations have been put forward for the mediocre performance of the Irish economy and in particular the comparative failure of indigenous industry to develop adequately. Although none of these explanations has been established beyond question, it is important to consider their plausibility not only from an intellectual point of view, but also because different explanations imply different policy responses.

The argument is often heard that Ireland suffers from a shortage of industrial and commercial entrepreneurs, or, in economic terms, a supply deficiency. It is hardly plausible to ascribe this to innate personality characteristics of the Irish, especially since those who emigrated have not shown a similar lack of enterprise abroad. Accordingly, the defect is usually attributed to some aspect of the culture or previous history of the country. A number of writers have drawn attention to the inhibitions on Irish economic development at independence resulting from attitudes, institutions etc. inherited from the country's turbulent past. Meenan (1970) has argued that the conceptions about the economy engendered during the nationalist struggle, and which were potent in mobilising support for that struggle, were

ill-adapted to the task of economic regeneration. The major preconceptions, which he claims were widely held and took long to unlearn,
were fourfold: that Irish economic development had been retarded by
British misgovernment; that economic development depended on the
policies followed by the state; that self-government would quickly
bring prosperity; and that the future of the economy would be determined by what happens in Ireland.

A central thesis of Lee (1989) is that the insecurity of 19th century
life in Ireland engendered — quite rationally in the conditions of the
time — a "possession" mentality which carried over into the twentieth
century and stifled the emergence of a "performance" ethic so vital for
the flowering of enterprise. In regard to Olson's (1982) thesis about
the inhibiting effect of established interest groups, it may be noted
that the character of the Irish revolution was such that it did not involve any shake-up of such interests: it was a nationalist revolution
unaccompanied by an economic revolution. It has also been argued
that the incomplete settlement of the national question at independence had lasting economic repercussions. Fanning (1990) has argued
that "the Treaty split and the civil war ensured that, after the Union
as under the Union, the dynamic of Irish politics drew its energy from
the conflict of opinion about the legitimacy of the British connection"
so that "the struggle for political power hinged on the shape and form
of Irish independence, not on the economic policies best suited to a
newly independent state".

Crotty's (1986) theory about the problems of former capitalist
colonies can also be included in the catalogue of arguments suggesting that Ireland's development was constrained by its prior history.
According to Crotty, all former capitalist colonies have not only failed
to develop but have "undeveloped". The basic reason is that capitalist
colonisation imposed a social structure for the profit of the colonial
power which was inimical to indigenous development. Independence
does not remedy the situation, since independence is generally gained
by local elites benefiting from colonisation, who work to preserve the
inherited structures and institutions so as to safeguard their privileged position.

Another reason sometimes put forward to explain the shortage of
entrepreneurs is that Ireland simply did not place as high a value on
the goal of economic development as other countries did. A nation

may be conceived of as pursuing many objectives with different degrees of intensity and the fact that it scores poorly on one objective
might reflect the low priority attached to the achievement of that objective. It is probable that every country falls short of realising its full
economic potential because other goals temper, in varying degree, the
urgency with which development is pursued. Ireland's large religious
missionary effort absorbed the energies of many highly motivated
and enterprising people. De Valera articulated a vision of Ireland,
which had at least wide sentimental appeal, as "the home of a people
who valued material wealth only as the basis of right living, of a people who were satisfied with frugal comfort and devoted their leisure
to the things of the spirit" (Moynihan, 1980). According to this line of
argument, the Irish failed to hit the target of economic development,
not because they were bad shots but because they were aiming at a
different target.

One of the difficulties about the foregoing arguments based on history or culture is to explain why they have survived so long. For example, while the development of a possession mentality in nineteenth
century Ireland is plausible, Lee devotes less attention to the issue of
how such a mentality has been transmitted from generation to generation and continues to triumph over a performance ethic. Equally
the misguided preconceptions about the economy at independence,
mentioned by Meenan, or the unsettled political question, mentioned
by Fanning, may be plausible enough in relation to the first generation after independence, but surely some further explanation is
needed as to why they persisted. As to the contention that the dominant spiritual values limited entrepreneurship, there is plenty of evidence that concern for material gains was not lacking throughout the
population as a whole. Nor is it at all clear that there was in fact any
shortage of people who wanted to be entrepreneurs. In the 1930s the
imposition of tariffs and quotas elicited a vast inflow of new entrepreneurs. Equally in more recent times, the IDA Small Industry Programmes have elicited a rate of new firm formation comparable with
other countries. The deficiency in both cases was not a shortage of
people willing to be entrepreneurs, but rather the fact that so few of
them were able to develop large and sustainable businesses.

If there is little evidence that cultural-historical factors led to a
shortage of supply *per se*, it might still be argued that these factors

created an environment in which entrepreneurs could not prosper. If so, this should show up in an unfavourable price/cost environment. A variety of evidence has been adduced to demonstrate unfavourable price/cost competitiveness arising from the levels of wages, taxation, prices of support services (energy and transportation) etc. or from changes in these variables over time. Much of the evidence cited, however, relates only to the last 30 years or so and it is not at all clear that Ireland suffered the same disadvantages relative to other countries at an earlier period. For example high taxation in Ireland is a phenomenon of the past 20 years or so, which did not apply from the 1920s to the late 1960s. If low taxation is critical for the development of enterprise, why then did the comparatively low levels at earlier phases since independence not stimulate greater enterprise?

A further difficulty facing this explanation is that foreign industrial enterprise succeeded quite well and was highly profitable in the same price/cost environment. The contrast in profitability was very striking: profit as a percentage of sales in native manufacturing firms in 1986 was only 2½ per cent when it was 24 per cent in foreign firms. To some extent this gap arose from the different structural composition of the two sectors, notably the predominance of indigenous firms in the low-margin food-processing activities. Furthermore, the observed profit rate in foreign firms is probably overstated because of transfer pricing. It can also be argued that because of their very different characteristics (for example, highly developed technological and marketing capabilities), the foreign firms were less sensitive to domestic labour costs. However, this leaves unanswered the question as to why indigenous firms did not manage to develop these desirable characteristics.

It may be useful here to draw attention to the distinction made by Baumol (1990) between, on the one hand, the supply of entrepreneurs or the nature of their objectives and, on the other hand, the allocation of entrepreneurship through the *relative* reward structure prevailing in the economy. Baumol argues that while the former may vary over time or between countries, this variation is less significant than variations in the distribution of entrepreneurial talent among different activities, which is capable of being influenced by the relative reward structure. This point is particularly important in the context of policy to promote particular forms of enterprise, since it might take a long time to increase the overall supply of entrepreneurs, or to modify their goals, whereas changes in the relative reward structure are capable of being implemented more quickly.

In a similar vein, Murphy et al. (1991) argued that among the important factors influencing the occupational choice of talented people are the returns to ability and to scale in each sector. While some professions are socially more useful than others, this may not be reflected in relative compensation. In fact the authors find that the rewards to "rent-seeking" activities (e.g. security and property dealing etc.), which merely redistribute income, are greater in many countries than rewards for entrepreneurs who innovate and foster growth. This maladjustment leads to stagnation. Put pithily in the authors' own words, one of the findings is that "lawyers are indeed bad, and engineers, good for growth".

This highlights the possible disincentive effects on indigenous industrial enterprise, not of the general level of competitiveness, but rather the relative rewards to different activities or sectors. In the Irish case, the argument could be made that the attraction of high earnings in professions, such as law or medicine, or of secure, reasonably well-paid jobs, in the public service or banking, siphoned off potential industrial enterprise. Also, even when incentives were provided to encourage manufacturing enterprise they were often offset by incentives to other activities which the Irish were not slow to engage in: previous research has identified a whole plethora of such tax incentives to investment in housing, other property and financial assets.

Perhaps the most fully articulated hypothesis, advanced by O'Malley (1989) and deriving from the literature on development economics, emphasises the existence of major barriers to entry and expansion facing indigenous firms in late industrialising countries under free-trade conditions. These barriers arise from the superior competitive position of larger and longer-established foreign rivals due to economies of scale in production, technology, finance and marketing. Furthermore, external economies enjoyed by firms in big industrial concentrations — in the form of ready access to specialist supplies and services, pools of skilled labour and large adjacent markets — have been important in enabling firms to take advantage of scale economies. While part of the function of successful new entrepreneurship is to overcome such barriers, the barriers may be so great for a newly industrialising country that they cannot be overcome by the efforts of private enterprise without suitable encouragement from a stronger force, such as the state.

In fact, in Ireland, as we have seen, the state did accompany the restoration of free trade with a package of incentives, but while these measures were quite successful in attracting foreign enterprise, it is arguable that they were insufficient to address the barriers facing indigenous enterprise. The capital grants and subsidies certainly went some distance towards reducing the financial constraints, while the various advisory and training services helped to raise the efficiency of production. The export profits tax relief was not, however, adequate to encourage indigenous firms to switch to exports: while it increased the *incentive* to export, it did not improve the *ability* to do so until exporting became a profitable activity. In particular it did not meet the problem facing indigenous firms that, even if they could eventually export profitably, the initial years of building new markets were likely to be characterised by low or even negative profits. The situation was quite different for the foreign subsidiaries, which had the backing of the parent marketing organisation and often had assured markets with their overseas affiliates. The export profits tax relief may also have acted to discourage internal linkages between manufacturing firms: where foreign firms were engaged in transfer-pricing via imported inputs to maximise the tax advantage, this would tend to discourage purchases from domestic producers.[2]

The policy measures also failed to come to grips with the challenge of building an indigenous technological capability. Protection had left a legacy of undersized firms, involved mainly in the final assembly of products for sale on the small home market. These firms did not have the resources needed to engage in innovative R & D, and only from the late 1970s has the IDA shifted the emphasis to R & D, with grants for product and process development. Several studies[3] have documented the low levels of technical innovation in Irish manufacturing

---

[2] The export profits tax relief was replaced in 1981 by a new low rate of corporation tax of 10 per cent for *all* manufacturing, but full export profits tax relief continued until 1990 for those firms which qualified for it before 1981.

[3] For a review of these studies, see Kennedy and Healy (1985).

and the heavy reliance on foreign technology sources. During the 1970s real R & D expenditure in Irish manufacturing as a whole grew substantially more slowly than the volume of output, and this decline in R & D intensity was superimposed on an already low base, particularly in indigenous industry. Foreign subsidiaries were not penalised by these deficiencies since they could draw directly on the innovative capabilities of their parent firms.

The argument that the industrial policy did not address the major barriers facing indigenous industry receives support from the experience of the limited number of relatively successful indigenous enterprises. These progressed mainly in those activities that still remained in some respect sheltered from foreign competition, due to such factors as transport costs (for example, cement) or access to local raw materials (for example, food processing). The remainder which succeeded in the face of foreign competition tended to be in activities in which the technological and marketing requirements were low. A number of indigenous firms have become significant multinationals in their own right; but they have done so largely by acquiring plants abroad to cater for local markets, and their impact in developing a strong Irish industrial base has been much less than their global scale would suggest.

CONCLUSIONS

The foregoing does not exhaust the list of possible explanations of the poor record of indigenous manufacturing enterprise in the twentieth century. For example, Barry (1994) and Barry and Hannan (1995) detail various mechanisms by which foreign enterprise in Ireland may have crowded out indigenous industry e.g. by sustaining an excessively high exchange rate, or by underpinning a wage level that rendered the more labour intensive indigenous activities uncompetitive. Other hypotheses will be examined in subsequent chapters. It is fair to say, however, that we still lack a conclusive explanation as to why indigenous industry fared so poorly.

What needs to be explained is not so much a dearth of entrepreneurs *per se*, but why so few of them survived to build large and profitable manufacturing enterprises. A major difficulty in answering such a question is that while the economic literature provides a reasonable understanding of the general environmental factors bearing on competitiveness, the key dimensions of competitive advantage may be those built *within* firms. The literature is far less revealing about how these intra-firm advantages develop, or how policy can influence them where they do not develop spontaneously in an environment that is generally no less favourable than in other countries.

REFERENCES

Barry, F. (1994): "Peripherality in Economic Geography and Modern Growth Theory: Evidence From Ireland's Adjustment to Free Trade", Working Paper No. 94/13, Dublin: University College Dublin.

Barry, F. and Hannan, A. (1995): "Multinationals and Indigenous Employment: An 'Irish Disease'?", unpublished paper, May.

Baumol, W.J. (1990): "Entrepreneurship: Productive, Unproductive and Destructive", *Journal of Political Economy*, 98: 893-921.

Crotty, R. (1986): *Ireland in Crisis: A Study in Capitalist Colonial Underdevelopment*, Dingle: Brandon Books.

Culliton, J. (Chairman) (1992): "A Time for Change: Industrial Policy in the 1990s", Report of the Industrial Policy Review Group, Dublin: The Stationery Office.

Fanning, R. (1990): "The Genesis of Economic Development" in McCarthy, J.F. (ed.) *Planning Ireland's Future: The Legacy of T. K. Whitaker*, Dublin: Glendale Press.

Kennedy, K.A. and Healy, T. (1985): *Small-scale Manufacturing Industry in Ireland*, General Research Series No. 125, Dublin: Economic and Social Research Institute.

Kennedy, K.A., Giblin, T. and McHugh, D. (1988): *The Economic Development of Ireland in the Twentieth Century*, London: Routledge.

Kennedy, K.A. (1995): "The National Accounts for Ireland in the 19th and 20th Centuries", *Scandinavian Economic History Review*, Vol. XLIII No. 1: 101-114.

Lee, J. (1989): *Ireland 1912-1985: Politics and Society*, Cambridge: Cambridge University Press.

McAleese, D. (1971): "Effective Tariffs and the Structure of Industrial Protection in Ireland", General Research Series No. 62, Dublin: Economic and Social Research Institute.

Maddison, A. (1992): "Explaining the Economic Performance of Nations 1820-1989" (mimeograph).

Meenan, J.F. (1970): *The Irish Economy since 1922*, Liverpool: Liverpool University Press.

Moynihan, M. (ed.) (1980): *Speeches and Statements by Eamonn de Valera*, Dublin: Gill and Macmillan.

Murphy, K.M., Shleifer A. and Vishny, R.W. (1991): "The Allocation of Talent: Implications for Growth", *The Quarterly Journal of Economics*, Vol. CVI, No. 2, May: 507-530.

Olson, M. (1982): *The Rise and Decline of Nations,* New Haven, CT: Yale University Press.

O'Malley, E. (1989): *Industry and Economic Development: The Challenge for the Latecomer*, Dublin: Gill and Macmillan.

O'Malley, E. (1995): *An Analysis of Secondary Employment Associated with Manufacturing Industry*, General Research Series No. 167, Dublin: Economic and Social Research Institute.

Roche, F., Dowling, P., Walshe, M., Houlihan, G. and Murray, J. (1984): *The Role of the Financial System in Financing the Traded Sector*, Report No. 76, Dublin: National Economic and Social Council.

Telesis Consultancy Group (1982): *A Review of Industry Policy*, Report No. 64, Dublin: National Economic and Social Council.

5

FROM PROTECTIONISM TO ENTERPRISE: A REVIEW OF IRISH INDUSTRIAL POLICY

P.J. Drudy

INTRODUCTION

Enterprise emanates mainly from the ideas and initiatives of well-motivated individuals and groups. Such initiatives are heavily influenced by market forces (largely outside the control of the initiators) as well as by government policies which are the focus of this chapter. The nature of the policy environment can be particularly important in determining the extent of production, employment and other benefits generated. The Republic of Ireland is an interesting example of a small open and peripheral economy which has whole-heartedly changed from inward-looking, "protectionist" policies to an "outward-looking" approach, in the hope of resolving its various economic and social difficulties. Like many other countries, Ireland has in recent years also moved towards "enterprise and market-oriented" policies. For convenience, therefore, I attempt to deal with three broad policy approaches. The "protectionist" era roughly covers the period from the 1930s to the mid-1950s. The "outward-looking" era covers from the 1950s and extends up to the present day. An "enterprise and market-oriented" approach also became obvious from the early 1980s. I need hardly stress that these are not self-contained categories with clear cut-off dates. Nevertheless, they offer a convenient framework in which to review the various policy changes. This chapter briefly examines the nature of industrial change with reference to the market forces of supply and demand. It then reviews the nature of industrial policies pursued in the Republic of Ireland since Independence and attempts to assess the impact of such policies, with particular reference to employment and the location of economic activity.

MARKET FORCES AND INDUSTRIAL CHANGE

Significant changes have taken place in industrial production, organisation and employment in recent decades. The changes have occurred in all sectors — agriculture, industry and services — and can be conveniently explained in a demand and supply framework. For example, the inelastic nature of demand for food products with respect to both price and income poses special problems for farmers and regions involved in agricultural production. The pattern of demand for food products is also subject to constant change due, for example, to increased health awareness as well as national and international competition. The result is low relative incomes in the agricultural industry and a "drift from the land". On the supply side, new inputs (seeds, fertilisers and sprays) and technical change have resulted in significant increases in output with lower "labour requirements" even in relatively prosperous agricultural regions. "Marginal" agricultural regions are also faced with a range of "structural" problems such as small farm size, poor land, low levels of education and demographic imbalance which inhibit production. The end result is a movement out of agriculture. Unless alternative employment is available, increasing unemployment or out-migration must occur (Drudy, 1989).

In the case of industrial products, demand is generally more elastic than that for agricultural products and therefore more "promising". However, what has potential today may be static or declining next year due to constantly changing consumer tastes as well as competition on a national and international scale. The supply of industrial products is also heavily influenced by technical change, leading to pressure on prices, increased competition and reduced labour requirements. Unless industries adapt rapidly to such changes, a "structural" problem may again emerge where a high proportion of a particular industry is either static or in decline. If the industry is "dominant" in a country or region, a serious problem arises.

Finally, in the services sector demand is elastic but constantly changing as in industry. Competition is intense on a national and international scale and firms unable to adapt go out of business. The supply of services is heavily influenced by technical change, where a substitution effect often leads to pressure to reduce employment. Despite this, the services sector overall has displayed significant growth in employment over the last few decades and it is in this latter sector that the main opportunities are likely to occur in the future.

A spatial dimension should be noted here, namely, that the impact of market forces is not locationally neutral. Some regions, whether for "structural" or "locational" reasons, suffer more than others and the operation of the market is unlikely to ensure "convergence" of incomes and employment opportunities, as the neoclassical model would imply (Armstrong and Taylor, 1993). As a result, government policies have usually contained a strong "regional orientation". With this framework in mind, we turn now to review the three policy approaches outlined earlier.

IRELAND IN THE PROTECTIONIST ERA

The newly-independent state, established in 1922, inherited an economic structure which was largely under-developed during the British rule. In order to protect British commercial interests, Irish industry had been suppressed during the seventeenth and eighteenth centuries. During the nineteenth and early twentieth centuries, when a pattern of free trade was imposed, Ireland was likewise unable to compete on equal terms with Britain in most areas of industrial activity and it was only in the Northeast of the country that any significant industrial development took place. The Republic thus remained heavily dependent on the agricultural industry throughout this extended period and (despite a significant change in the pattern of land ownership) the structure of agriculture left much to be desired at Independence. In view of the problematic nature of demand for food products mentioned earlier, any country or region dependent on agriculture is at a clear disadvantage. When coupled with a "structural" problem, it was inevitable that there would be a slow pattern of development and high levels of out-migration.

Ireland at Independence was a predominantly small farm economy with two-thirds of the agricultural holdings having less than 30 acres. This situation was accompanied (particularly in the western areas of the country) by certain physical difficulties such as fragmentation of holdings and high proportions of poor land. In such "marginal" areas a pattern of late inheritance, an unbalanced demographic structure and slow progress in improving the structure of land holdings subsequently resulted in retarded agricultural development, low-relative

incomes and poor employment prospects. In relatively prosperous agricultural areas in the south and south east of the country the structure of agriculture was rather better but in such areas increased
mechanisation reduced the demand for labour. This reduction in
"labour requirements" meant that there was little incentive for young
people to remain on farms in any part of Ireland. The exodus from
agriculture was not of course confined to Ireland; it was occurring in
all European countries during this period and it continues. Such a
trend need not necessarily be regarded as undesirable if those leaving
agriculture can be absorbed into non-agricultural employment. However, for the majority in Ireland this was not to be.

In addition to Ireland's dependence on a problematic agricultural
industry, it should be noted that there was no extended period in the
decades after independence, even up to the 1950s, which could be regarded as "normal" in any meaningful sense. Civil war in the 1920s
was followed closely by a world recession, the widespread erection of
trade barriers, an "economic war" with Britain on which Ireland depended for an export market, and the Second World War in which
Ireland chose to remain neutral. These various events influenced, and
perhaps compelled, successive Irish governments towards policies
which, however well-intentioned, had not always the desired domestic
effects. Thus, in order to build up native Irish industry the government embarked on a programme of selective tariff imposition from
the mid-1920s and a strong protectionist approach was emphasised
from the early 1930s. One of the most significant pieces of legislation
was the Control of Manufactures Acts of 1932 and 1934. These placed
considerable constraints on foreign ownership or control of Irish
manufacturing industry. This control over foreign ownership lasted,
with the exception of the War period, right up to the 1960s. Furthermore, a range of tariff barriers were introduced in the 1930s to curb
imports and these resulted in a significant reduction in the imports of
various products. These policies proved effective in protecting and
developing new industries, as well as expanding older ones in Ireland
and helped to secure substantial growth of employment during particular periods. Thus, manufacturing employment grew by 40,000 between 1931 and 1939 and by a further 41,000 by 1953. However, employment growth was to be short-lived and the numbers employed in
manufacturing fell between 1953 and 1958. A strong import propen-

sity, accompanied by poor export performance, therefore resulted in recurrent balance of payments difficulties in the late 1940s and 1950s (see O'Hagan and McStay, 1981).

The overall employment record during the protectionist era may be noted. As an indication, the number of people employed in agriculture over the period 1926-61 declined by over 272,300. During the same period only 101,800 non-agricultural jobs (provided either by the state or private enterprise) became available. The net loss of jobs was thus 170,500 and about half this loss was accounted for by areas in the West and Northwest — Galway, Mayo, Sligo, Leitrim and Donegal. This absence of sufficient opportunities to earn a livelihood, especially in rural Ireland, was a crucial factor in influencing people to migrate to the main urban centres with better employment prospects. However, the vast majority chose (or were compelled) to emigrate — and emigrate they did in their thousands. The average net emigration from Ireland increased from 16,600 per annum in the 1926-36 period to 42,400 in the 1950s. Something was seriously wrong.

TOWARDS OUTWARD-LOOKING AND INCENTIVE POLICIES

From the early 1950s there was a recognition of the difficulties of relying unduly on protectionist and self-sufficiency policies which characterised the post-independence decades. Whatever the advantages of such policies, they were not creating sufficient jobs to stem the tide of emigration. Therefore, a number of agencies, which were to assume significant roles in later years, were established at this time. These were the Industrial Development Authority, An Foras Tionscal, Coras Trachtala and Bord Fáilte. The Capital Investment Advisory Committee (appointed in 1956) strongly argued for a change of direction and laid particular emphasis on productive capital investment which encouraged exports. One of the most important early changes was the introduction in 1956 of the Export Profits Tax Relief Scheme, whereby manufacturing firms were to be freed from taxation on profits earned on export sales. In 1957 Ireland joined the International Monetary Fund and the World Bank. The White Paper on *Economic Development* in 1958 and, arising from this, the *First Programme for Economic Expansion* (1959-64) gave details of the future approach which would be pursued in relation to employment creation, particularly in the manufacturing sector. The emphasis in the future was to be on outward-looking and export-oriented policies which attempted to attract foreign companies to Ireland and the abandonment of protectionism. During subsequent decades, this approach was to continue and included the cutting of tariffs, the signing of the Anglo-Irish Free Trade Agreement, joining GATT and the European Community. Table 5.1 summarises the progress in this direction over the period since 1952.

TABLE 5.1: EVIDENCE OF OUTWARD-LOOKING APPROACH IN IRELAND

1952	Córas Tráchtála (Irish Exports Board) established
1956	Exports Profits Tax Relief Scheme
1957	Joined IMF and World Bank
1958	Exports Profits Tax Relief Scheme extended
1958/59	Economic Development and First Programme
1961	Sought membership of European Community.
1963/64	Tariff cuts
1964	Repeal of Control of Manufactures Act
1965	Anglo-Irish Free Trade Agreement
1967	Joined GATT
1973	Joined European Community
1979	Joined EMS
1986	Supported Single European Act
1992	Supported Treaty on European Union

From the early 1950s, incentives to manufacturing industries in the "undeveloped" areas of the west of Ireland were also available. The Undeveloped Areas Act of 1952 was passed in order to persuade Irish industrial concerns to locate in the Designated Areas in the western half of the country. This Act established Foras Tionscal as an industrial promotion agency which had powers to assist industrialists with grant aid for land, buildings and machinery as well as the training of workers. This agency was to be joined later in the 1950s by the Shannon Free Airport Development Company (now re-named Shannon Development) and Gaeltarra Éireann (now Údaras Na Gaeltachta), designed to support initiatives at Shannon Airport and the Gaeltacht areas respectively. During the 1960s these agencies were to be supplemented by the establishment of County Development Teams in the Designated Areas and Regional Development Organisations for nine Planning Regions around the country. The concern to give special assistance to the Designated Areas was well justified in view of the range of special difficulties in agriculture in these areas and the failure to provide sufficient alternative employment opportunities to counteract losses from that industry. This assistance was to continue in the years ahead.

The 1969 Industrial Development Act dissolved An Foras Tionscal and transferred its powers to the Industrial Development Authority (IDA). Under the Act, the IDA could give grants towards the purchase of fixed assets of up to 60 per cent of the cost in the Designated Areas and up to 45 per cent elsewhere, although grants were to be given only if the Authority was satisfied that "employment of a reasonably permanent nature" would be provided. In addition, the Authority could give grants towards re-equipment, modernisation, improvements or expansion of up to 35 per cent in the Designated Areas and 25 per cent elsewhere. It had powers to give grants towards the reduction of interest on loans, towards loan guarantees, training, and reduction of factory rents. It could also purchase or construct industrial buildings and estates. The powers granted to the IDA under the legislation were thus extensive. A number of points may be noted. First, the policy could be argued to have a "capital bias" in that it emphasised — and the vast brunt of its expenditure went to fund — investment in land, buildings and machinery. This was of course in line with the philosophy that such investment would increase output and that employment growth would inevitably follow. In retrospect, we know that the association between the two is weak. Secondly, the Act continued the regional orientation of earlier policies. One of the Authority's new functions was to "foster the national objective of regional development" and, as mentioned above, to give special assistance to the Designated Areas under the Act. Thirdly, it could be contended that insufficient "conditions" were attached to the giving of state funds over an extended period of this particular legislation up to 1986. A wide range of enterprises, whether promising or not, were eligible for assistance and it was not always easy to distinguish between them. Similarly, it was inevitable that, despite the best intentions of the Authority, not all promised "targets" for employment could or would be met. In cases of this kind, there were few real powers to retrieve substantial grants.

The policy emphasis on areas in the west of the country was again exemplified in the 1973/77 and 1978/82 Regional Industrial Plans (Industrial Development Authority, 1973 and 1978). The former Plans specified target growth rates in manufacturing employment of between 30 and 50 per cent for four "less-developed regions" (Donegal, the Northwest, the West and Midlands). The general thrust of this policy was continued in the 1978/82 Plans, although it was acknowledged that serious problems of industrial decline were emerging in other parts of the country and particularly in the East region.

One of the most fundamental changes to occur in Ireland during this outward-looking era was entry to the European Community. With the United Kingdom, Ireland had sought to join the Community in 1961. The simultaneous application to join made sense in view of the close economic links between the two countries. When the United Kingdom's application was vetoed at that time, however, Ireland decided to remain outside. Ten years later, membership was more firmly on the agenda and both countries, together with Denmark, joined the Community in 1973. A White Paper produced by the Government in 1972 had high expectations of membership and predicted that Community policy would be directed in a positive way to helping economic expansion and the raising of living standards in the less-favoured regions of Ireland, as well as assisting our national industrial development with Community funds (Government of Ireland, 1972).

An assessment of the impact of entry to the Community is beyond the scope of this chapter. However, a small number of comments are of relevance. First, while entry to the Community could be expected to bring substantial net financial transfers to Ireland, it also clearly involved accepting greater formal competition and market-oriented rules than applied previously. Indeed, within a decade the Export Profits Tax Relief Scheme was under scrutiny in view of its alleged conflict with European competition policy. Secondly, the Community policies placed considerable emphasis on price supports to agricultural production and the vast brunt of the transfers to Ireland during the first two decades of membership were channelled to that purpose. Much less attention was given to structural problems of agriculture or industry. The Community impact on industries and matters of concern other than agriculture could therefore only be modest or even neutral. It is only in recent years that serious attention has been given to redressing this difficulty in the light of serious emerging industrial, regional and social difficulties (see Drudy, 1994). Thirdly, and most important, Ireland's entry to the European Community opened up an ideal base from which multinational companies could export their products to a rich and varied market in Europe. Taken together with the significant national and regional incentives already outlined, entry to the Community made Ireland a most attractive industrial location.

How effective was this extensive range of outward-looking and incentive policies, including membership of the Community? There is of course no easy answer. It is always problematic to separate out the impact of particular policies from the impact of other policies or market factors. Our comments must be indicative rather than conclusive. During the period 1971 to 1981 overall employment in industry in Ireland grew from 326,000 to 366,000 — a net increase of 39,000 which took place primarily in manufacturing. This net increase must be regarded as modest in view of the significant incentives available. It compares with a net increase of almost 129,000 in services during the same period where virtually no incentives were available. One explanation is that the level of *gross* manufacturing employment creation was significant, but that it was being seriously counteracted by *gross* losses, thus resulting in modest net change. In a study covering the period 1973/80, the author showed that gross manufacturing employment gains of 142,600 were in fact counteracted by gross losses of almost 110,000. There was an impressive performance in relation to *new* employment; the record in maintaining *existing* jobs was less creditable (Drudy, 1991). The same study illustrated a significant difference between manufacturing employment gains in the "Eastern Core" — consisting of the East, the Northeast and Southeast regions of Ireland — and the "Western Periphery" containing the remaining regions. It also pinpointed a notable difference between the impact of foreign and indigenous firms. Thus, during the period in question, gross gains exceeded losses for both Irish and foreign firms and overall net gains were recorded in the Eastern Core and in the Western Periphery. However, the foreign firms indicated a superior performance, with a ratio of gains to losses of 1.6 to 1 compared to 1.1 to 1 in the case of Irish firms. Second, the periphery fared about three times better than the core, with foreign firms also performing three times better than their Irish counterparts. The foreign net gains were significant in the Midwest, the West, the Midlands and Donegal — these latter three regions had been designated for special treatment in the 1973/77 IDA Regional Industrial Plans. O'Farrell also provides confirmation of the success of the rural regions and small towns during this period (O'Farrell, 1986). The East region was the only region to register net manufacturing losses in the indigenous sector during the period up to 1980. It was a signal for the 1980s.

ENTERPRISE AND MARKET-ORIENTATED APPROACHES

The year 1980 represented a peak in manufacturing employment numbers and, as we shall see, significant declines were to occur in subsequent years. By the early 1980s serious concern was being expressed at our failure to provide sufficient jobs to prevent further rises in unemployment and a resurgence in emigration. In response, a major study was commissioned from the Telesis Consultancy Group and in 1982 *A Review of Industrial Policy* was published (NESC, 1982). This study made a wide range of recommendations for change. These included a significant reduction in the level of grant aid to foreign firms, a re-allocation of expenditure in favour of internationally trading indigenous industry and sub-supply firms and a far greater "control" over the process of industrial development by the government and relevant agencies. The Group was critical of the nature of foreign investment attracted. For example, in relation to electronics firms it stated :

> One must look carefully at the extent to which the electronics industry is really rooted in Ireland and can contribute to rising incomes. Of the 60 companies we surveyed, none have a truly stand-alone operation in Ireland, and only three have operations in Ireland which embody the key competitive elements of the company's business. All the others are manufacturing satellites, performing partial steps in the manufacturing process. Most of the operations surveyed performed only assembly, test, packaging and simple machining or coating functions (p. 139).

Mechanical engineering firms were described as follows :

> Ireland's foreign-owned mechanical engineering companies consist mainly of sub-assembly shops of the sort commonly found in newly industrialising countries. They are limited in complexity and as-

sembly forms the basis for most employment. Of the 34 shops surveyed, about half had only one or two skilled blue-collar workers and one or two engineers. Most of the rest have a small pool of skilled workers and designers for modification of products, but together they represent less than 1-2 per cent of the workers in the plant (p. 144).

In relation to chemicals and pharmaceuticals the study contended :

Only two of the companies surveyed carry on research and development in Ireland. Thus, the key activities which determine success in this industry are not carried out in Ireland. None of the Irish operations could easily operate independently of their parent companies (p. 146).

The Telesis Group laid considerable emphasis on the development of indigenous industry and urged that "the development effort aimed towards new indigenous industry must be re-organised to emphasise the building of structurally strong Irish companies." The main thrust of the study was given government support in the Industrial Policy White Paper in 1984. A number of new measures were introduced in 1985 and a new Industrial Development Act was passed in 1986. The 1985 Company Development Programme probably reflected the view that Ireland should be "picking winners". This Programme was designed to provide support for the specific requirements of Irish companies with "growth potential" and involved the integrated assistance of a number of key agencies such as the IDA, Córas Tráchtála and Eolas. In 1985 also the National Linkage Programme was established in order to "maximise local purchases of Irish materials, components and services by overseas firms" based in Ireland. This was in response to the finding that overseas companies were purchasing a relatively low proportion of raw materials in Ireland. A Market Entry and Development Scheme was also initiated in the same year to assist companies with loans to develop new export markets.

The Industrial Development Act of 1986 introduced a range of fundamental changes to the earlier approaches. First, the criteria for eligibility for grants were tightened up considerably. In future, there would be an increased emphasis on exports, appropriate products and ability to compete on an international scale. Supported firms would require an adequate equity base; they must provide new employment and increase local value added. Second, incentives were introduced for internationally traded services. This was a new and important departure. Third, the legislation shifted the emphasis somewhat from funding fixed assets towards developing export markets, the acquisition of technology and research and development. Ireland's past record in relation to research and development had been particularly poor and this latter move was overdue (O'Brien, 1985). Fourth, employment grants were introduced. In a country where labour surplus was a recurring issue, it may seem surprising that capital subsidies were favoured over labour for so long. This "factor-price distortion" was now being addressed to some extent. Fifth, the legislation specified that more careful monitoring of public expenditure would be required. Thus, the cost per job, the viability of the employment and the spin-off effects should be assessed in regular "reviews". Sixth, more rigorous regulations were introduced regarding the repayment of grants by enterprises which failed to meet employment targets. Finally, the distinction between the grant levels for large industrial enterprises in the Designated and Non-Designated Areas was terminated. This latter measure was introduced in view of the heavy orientation of previous policies towards the western half of the country, despite the fact that serious manufacturing losses had been evident for some time in other parts of the country and especially in the East region.

Under the new legislation, the IDA administered a range of new measures to reflect the requirements given above. In the case of "large" industry, these included a reduction in capital grants to a maximum of 25 per cent, product development grants, and management development grants. As regards "small" industry, employment grants were introduced, as well as management and product development grants and a range of incentives for firms in an "Enterprise Development Programme". Prior to this, it could be argued that small companies had received little attention. They were apparently being "crowded out" by the large firms with more political and financial clout, despite the growing literature indicating the significance of the former in terms of employment, linkages with indigenous and overseas firms, skill development and regional dispersal (See O'Farrell 1986 and Ruane, 1991). A special "International Services Programme" was also initiated which included grants for employment, management, feasibility studies, training, research and development and the purchase of computers, equipment and buildings. Separate legislation established an International Financial Services Centre in the Custom House Docks area of Dublin, where generous incentives were made available in the form of rates remission as well as tax and rent allowances.[1]

In 1990 a Marketing Consultancy Programme replaced the earlier Market Entry Scheme. The new Programme provided grants (as opposed to loans) to draw up marketing strategies for eligible companies and further performance-related grants to pursue approved projects. By 1990 also there seemed to be a recognition of the critical need for a Science and Technology policy which endeavoured to upgrade the level of technology and skills of indigenous firms (Government of Ireland, 1990).

The culmination of the enterprise and market-oriented approach occurred with the appointment in 1991 by the Government of a further Committee on industrial policy chaired by Mr Jim Culliton. In January 1992 this Committee produced the much-quoted Culliton Report, *A Time for Change: Industrial Policy for the 1990s*. This Report re-affirmed much of the analysis of the Telesis Report ten years earlier. It argued for an approach based on "market-oriented enterprise" and called for a much broader set of policies rather than those directly related to industry. These included areas such as taxation, infrastructural provision, education and training, competition policy as well as monetary, fiscal and government budgetary policies which influence the environment within which business enterprise can operate. While much of the analysis was helpful and indicative of needed change, it was not — and could not — be accepted without qualification. We refer to only two issues here. First, the Report appears to be pre-occupied with manufacturing industry, despite the obvious trends, both in Ireland and internationally, in relation to employment in this sector. Little explicit attention is given to services which have shown enormous growth and would appear to have most

---

[1] It may be noted that in addition to the above changes, a new maximum tax rate of 10 per cent was in operation for some time for manufacturing. This had replaced the Export Profits Tax Relief Scheme which was being phased out from the early 1980s under advice from the Competition Directorate of the European Commission. This rate was to also apply to a small number of non-manufacturing services.

potential for growth in the decades ahead. Some of the general principles outlined in the Culliton Report may well apply to services, but
this matter should have been explicitly examined and evaluated. Secondly, the Report attempts to draw a distinction between what it describes as "academic" and "vocationally-oriented" education and argues for much more emphasis on the latter at second level on the
grounds that there is a "skills shortage" in Irish industry. The basis
for this contention is not clear in the brief section on education and
training in the Report. The supporting background study provides no
serious evidence to support it (Roche and Tansey, 1992) and some of
the leading experts in the field of education refute it (See, for example, Lynch, 1992 and Sheehan, 1992). As Lynch puts it :

> There is nothing intrinsic to the different forms of knowledge
> which makes some vocational and others not. One cannot conse-
> quently draw a clear and fast distinction between subjects which
> are practical and those which are academic. It is patent nonsense
> to suggest that subjects such as Engineering and Technical Draw-
> ing are entirely practical subjects. While they do have practical
> elements, there are areas in which these subjects are highly aca-
> demic. The assumption that certain subjects are entirely voca-
> tional and practical while others are academic and non-practical is
> false. Subjects cannot be neatly divided in this way (Lynch, 1992).

Even if the distinction could be made, one would have serious reservations about an undue focus on vocational and technical education
at an early stage in the educational system. This is particularly relevant at a time when employers seek a broad-based education which
combines some technical skills with critical appraisal, an ability to
assess and solve problems, as well as good communications and social
skills. It is this latter range of skills that is most required in the expanding services sector. A narrowly-based technical education at second level would unwisely cater for a manufacturing sector with declining employment opportunities. Furthermore, the alleged "academic drift" in third level institutions in the Report is simply inaccu-
rate. For example, the "market share" of Business, Engineering and
Science categories have increased from 31 per cent of the total in
1980 to 42 per cent in 1988, while the share of Arts and the professions has declined from 55 per cent to 41 per cent (Sheehan, 1992)

Although reservations can be raised regarding certain elements of
the Culliton Report, the broad thrust of its recommendations was ac-

cepted by the Government. A Task Force was subsequently established to advise on how its recommendations could be implemented and a Ministerial Group was formed in January 1993 to take decisions on the report of the Task Force. In a Progress Report in mid-1994, the Minister for Enterprise and Employment (in a new Department of Enterprise and Employment instead of the former Department of Industry and Commerce) reported "real progress" in relation to many of these recommendations. He affirmed that the government was engaged in a systematic reform of enterprise support and development which would reap dividends over time in increased levels of sustainable jobs and improved living standards (Government of Ireland, 1994). At a local level, the setting up of Enterprise Boards on a county basis as well as Enterprise Areas in a number of urban areas reflects the new approach.

Bearing in mind the caveat mentioned earlier regarding the difficulty of isolating the "policy effect", what has the record been in relation to employment creation? In stark contrast to the 1970s, the 1980s recorded severe losses in employment, despite the new orientation of policy. Over the period 1981 to 1991, the number employed in industry fell by 43,000 persons and in the period between 1991 and 1993, there was a further loss of 11,000 jobs. The vast bulk of these losses were in manufacturing. During the 1980s, the job gains, though significant, were insufficient to counteract the scale of job losses. Taking the period 1981-89 as an example, the total gross gains of 178,600 were counteracted by gross losses of 220,000, resulting in a net loss of 41,000 manufacturing jobs. The bulk of these losses were from indigenous firms and were concentrated in the formerly prosperous Eastern Core (Drudy, 1991). It appears that, as during the 1970s, we have been far more successful in generating *new* jobs than in maintaining *existing* ones. This point is also stressed in recent research on new firm formation in the Republic. As a result of this, Hart and Gudgin (1994) argue that special attention should be paid to the growth of existing firms as an integral part of any development strategy. The manufacturing record is in contrast with the services sector which showed a net increase of 65,000 between 1981 and 1991 and a further increase of 44,000 up to 1993 (Central Statistics Office, 1993). During this same period, the numbers unemployed in Ireland increased from 133,000 in 1981 (10.5 per cent) to 230,000 (16.7 per cent) in 1993 indicating that a much greater level of net job creation is required.

Finally, what were the costs involved? If we take 1991 as an example, we find that budgeted expenditure on industrial policy (and this was almost exclusively related to manufacturing) for the former Department of Industry and Commerce was £292 million in that year. If we add related expenditures from other Departments, the total could increase to about £460 million. In addition, it can be estimated that a sum of about £150 million can be attributed to the costs of tax relief, even after the phasing out of the Export Profits Tax Relief Scheme. The total cost could therefore be in excess of £600 million per annum and this figure probably held for typical years during the 1980s (see Culliton Report, 1992 and Government of Ireland, 1990).

CONCLUSION

This chapter has provided a review of industrial policy in Ireland covering the period from protectionism to the current orientation to enterprise and markets. We commenced by pointing to the importance of market forces. While government intervention can influence change — and intervention can be justified on economic grounds — it would be unwise to ignore constant changes in the market for goods and services and to fail to make appropriate policy adjustments (see Burke, 1995). In the 1950s, the move towards outward-looking policies seemed justified in view of the failure of protectionist policies and on the basis of benefits to be generated by foreign manufacturing investment. The generous grants and tax incentives to foreign firms also seemed justified in order to reduce the "savings gap", to increase output and hence employment and to improve indigenous technology and management. This was in line with the new economic thinking at the time. Ireland's entry to the European Community was also expected to have a positive influence on employment and standards of living in all parts of the country.

By the late 1970s, however, serious questions were being raised concerning the extent and nature of the manufacturing generated as well as the capital bias of the incentive system and indeed concerning the efficacy of foreign investment together with the continuing weakness of indigenous industry. The apparent dependence on manufacturing (which showed relatively modest increases in employment) was in contrast to the limited attention given to the growing services sector.

The emphasis during the 1980s has been on an enterprise and market-oriented approach, designed to pick winners. This involved a re-orientation of policy in favour of internationally traded industry, an emphasis on value for money, local value added and greater account-ability by those who received grant aid. Unfortunately, the new ap-proach coincided with a dramatic reduction in employment both in indigenous and foreign manufacturing in Ireland at a time of reces-sion — and this occurred despite continuing and significant grant levels and tax incentives. While support to the services sector in-creased during this period, it was still modest in comparison with its manufacturing counterpart. Much recent research suggests that vi-able service activities showing potential for employment growth must receive increasing attention in the future (see, for example, Bannon and Ward, 1985, Commission of the European Communities, 1993 and O'Farrell, 1993). The establishment of a Small Business and Services Division in the Department of Enterprise and Employment is a rec-ognition of this need.

In the past, both Irish and European policies have given special at-tention to the problems of agricultural and rural areas and particu-larly those in the western half of Ireland. While the needs of such ar-eas are not in question, serious difficulties of urban unemployment and multiple deprivation have become obvious during the last few decades (see, for example, Drudy and MacLaran, 1994). This matter deserves far more attention than it has received to date.

In recent years, the approach has broadened to include taxation and infrastructure as well as monetary and budgetary policies. Whether "getting the environment right" in this way will have a fa-vourable impact in stabilising employment in manufacturing, maxi-mising growth in services and reducing unemployment in the future remains to be seen. In any case, the new emerging "enterprise cul-ture" must not lose sight of the growing problem of unemployment (including substantial long-term unemployment) and poverty which persists in Ireland. Inability to deal with these fundamental problems would represent a failure to achieve one of the most basic objectives of any caring society.

REFERENCES

Armstrong, H. and Taylor, J. (1993): *Regional Economics and Policy*, London: Harvester Wheatsheaf.

Burke, A.E. (1995): "Economic Integration and New Firm Formation: Britain's Influence on Irish Enterprise", forthcoming *Review of Industrial Organization*.

Bannon, M.J. and Ward, S. (1985): "Services and the New Economy: Implications for National and Regional Development", Dublin: Regional Studies Association.

Central Statistics Office (1993): "Labour Force Survey 1993", Dublin: The Stationery Office.

Commission of the European Communities (1993): "Market Services and European Integration", *European Economy,* Report and Studies No. 3, Luxembourg.

Culliton, J. (Chairman) (1992): *A Time for Change: Industrial Policy in the 1990s, Report of the Industrial Policy Review Group*, Dublin: The Stationery Office.

Drudy, P.J. (1989): "Problems and Priorities in the Development of Rural Regions" in Albrecht, L. et al (eds.) *Regional Policy at the Crossroads*, London: Kingsley.

Drudy, P.J. (1991): "The Regional Impact of Overseas Industry" in Foley, A. and McAleese, D. *Overseas Industry in Ireland*, Dublin: Gill and Macmillan.

Drudy, P.J. (1994): "Ireland: A Region of the European Union", European Commission, Luxembourg.

Drudy, P.J. and MacLaran, A. (1994): "Dublin: Economic and Social Trends", Trinity College Dublin: Centre for Urban and Regional Studies.

Government of Ireland (1972): "The Accession of Ireland to the European Community", Dublin: The Stationery Office.

Government of Ireland (1990): "A Review of Industrial Performance 1990", Dublin: The Stationery Office.

Government of Ireland (1994): "Employment Through Enterprise", Dublin: The Stationery Office.

Hart, M. and Gudgin, G. (1994): "Spatial Variations in New Firm Formation in the Republic of Ireland, 1980/90", *Regional Studies,* 28(4): 367-380.

Industrial Development Authority (1973): "Regional Industrial Plans 1973/77", Dublin: IDA.

Industrial Development Authority (1978): "Regional Industrial Plans 1978/82", Dublin: IDA.

Lynch, K. (1992): "Education and the Paid Labour Market", *Irish Educational Studies*, 11: 13-33.

NESC (1982): "A Review of Industrial Policy", Dublin.

O'Brien, R. (1985): "Technology and Industrial Development: The Irish Electronics Industry in an International Context", in Fitzpatrick, J., *Perspectives on Irish Industry*, Dublin: Irish Management Institute.

O'Farrell, P. (1986): *Entrepreneurs and Industrial Change*, Dublin: Irish Management Institute.

O'Farrell, P. (1993): "The Competitive Advantage of Business Service Firms", *The Services Industry Journal*, 13(1).

O'Hagan, J. and McStay, K. (1981): "The Evolution of Manufacturing Industry in Ireland", Dublin: Confederation of Irish Industry.

Roche, F. and Tansey, P. (1992): "Industrial Training in Ireland", A Study prepared for the Industrial Policy Review Group, Dublin: The Stationery Office.

Ruane, F. (1991): "The Traded Sector: Industry", in O'Hagan, J. (ed.) *The Economy of Ireland: Policy and Performance*, Dublin: Irish Management Institute.

Sheehan, J. (1992): "Education, Training and the Culliton Report", Policy Paper Series, Centre for Economic Research, University College, Dublin.

II

FIRM CREATION AND DYNAMICS

6

THE SUPPLY OF SELF-EMPLOYED AND EMPLOYED ENTREPRENEURS

Andrew E. Burke

In Chapter 1 we chided purely neoclassical economists for their over-reliance on the assumption that "all profit opportunities are exploited". On this basis we noted that neoclassical methodology has derived a predictive theory based on an analysis of the level of profit opportunities. Economic shocks are viewed, therefore, to alter the level of profit opportunities hence directly affecting economic performance. Thus, for example, a fall in wages is seen to increase the level of profit opportunities which are automatically assumed to be exploited by entrepreneurs, resulting in an increase in employment and output. In terms of the supply and demand framework for enterprise (which is outlined in Chapter 1) the neoclassical approach may be viewed as a rigorous analysis of the demand for enterprise while simultaneously making an assumption that the demand for enterprise will generate its own supply. In other words, one simply takes the view that the supply of enterprise doesn't matter!

Despite decades (actually centuries if one delves into the history of economic thought) of objections to this approach by both the Austrian School and a peripheral group of mainstream economists, it has only been in recent years that an analysis of the supply of enterprise has permeated mainstream economic thought. This new approach explicitly assumes that all profit opportunities are *not always* exploited due to various economic and sociological factors that may cause the supply of entrepreneurs to vary across time.

The initial proliferation of this literature focused on a framework which equated entrepreneurship with self-employment (for example, see Kihlstrom and Laffont, 1979; Evans and Jovanovic, 1989; Holmes and Schmitz, 1990; and Blanchflower and Oswald, 1991). Since it was commonly accepted that entrepreneurship was also carried out by individuals in employment, this approach was merely adopted to initiate theoretical analysis and facilitate empirical research (the self-employed are observable in longitudinal labour surveys and most employment data). Subsequent papers, such as Holtz-Eakin (1994) and Jovanovic (1994) considered entrepreneurial employment in analyses of firm survival and skill allocation respectively. This chapter continues along this trajectory and develops a model of the supply of employed and self-employed entrepreneurs. The model aims to illustrate the impact of various economic shocks and policy actions on the *effective* supply of enterprise i.e. distinguishing between seedcorn and chaff (see Chapter 1). In this manner, the chapter illustrates the means through which economic factors affect the supply of enterprise and hence the extent to which profit opportunities are exploited. The model derives important lessons for the implementation of enterprise policy and also raises some pertinent research questions.

The chapter is divided into two sections. Section one models the supply of entrepreneurs. The "bones" of this model are taken from the author's D.Phil. thesis (Burke, 1994a) and an earlier version appeared as Burke (1992). It develops the self-employment model of Evans and Jovanovic (1989) to include the option of entrepreneurial employment. Section two then utilises the model to evaluate the impact of various economic shocks on the supply of entrepreneurship. The conclusion discusses the ramifications of the analysis for research on enterprise and other areas of economics.

THE MODEL

We start by assuming that an individual's utility function is solely dependent on income, ignoring the desire for independence cited in the empirical literature.[1] The individual has a choice of income from three sources:

---

[1] Augmenting the results of the model to cater for "utility from independence" is simple and has obvious implications — essentially an "independence wage wedge" is driven between employed and self-employed entrepreneurship.

1. *Self-employed entrepreneurship*: income (Y) includes a return on enterprise and capital.

2. *Employed entrepreneurship*: income (Y_e) includes a fixed wage and enterprise related pay. For example, managers receiving payment in the form of a fixed wage and performance related pay. The incentive component of the wage being related to the worker's innovative input to the firm, while the fixed wage relates to routine non-entrepreneurial duties.

3. *Non-Entrepreneurial Employment*: Workers receive a fixed wage (W_l), they are required to fulfil a defined task and not expected to innovate, (in an economic sense), in any significant manner.

To avoid tedious cross reference, we provide the reader with a brief review of the fundamental equations of Evans and Jovanovics' self-employment model. They assume that an individual has a choice between non-entrepreneurial employment and self-employment. We reproduce their wage equation in general form as:

$$W_l = g(x_1, x_2): \qquad (1)$$

$$\partial g / \partial x_1, \partial g / \partial x_2 > 0.$$
$$\partial^2 g / \partial x_1^2, \partial^2 g / \partial x_2^2 < 0$$

where x_1 is work experience and x_2 is education.

Evans and Jovanovic assume an individual is certain of her entrepreneurial ability (Q). We drop this assumption in order to include uncertainty and related asymmetries of information relating to entrepreneurial ability as factors determining career choice. Therefore, moving from certainty to uncertainty we replace Q by E(Q). Thus, self-employed income is defined as:

$$Y_g = E(Q)k^d \qquad (2)$$

k=capital invested

An entrepreneur in self-employment will have to find her own capital and Evans and Jovanovic assume that she can borrow up to a proportion "b-1" (b≥1) of her initial wealth "Z".[2] They assert that an individual can raise capital up to a maximum of bZ, where Z = initial wealth. Hence capital k ≤ initial wealth + any borrowing:

$$i.e.\ k \le Z+(b-1)Z = bZ$$

$$so\ 0 \le k \le bZ \qquad (3)$$

Thus, a self-employed entrepreneur's net income is:

$$Y = E(Q)k^d + r(Z-k) \qquad (4)$$

where r = 1 + the interest rate. Maximising (4) to find optimal "k" gives:

$$k^* = (\frac{dE(Q)}{r})^{\frac{1}{1-d}} \qquad (5)$$

If the self employed individual is not constrained then:

$$k \le bZ \qquad (6)$$

Substituting (5) into (6) and solving for E(Q) yields:

$$E(Q) \le (\frac{r}{d})(bZ)^{1-d} \qquad (7)$$

This defines a locus in E(Q) and Z space where a self-employed individual is constrained above, but not below. However, if an entrepreneur is indeed constrained then this optimal level of k is not attained and

$$k=bZ \qquad (8)$$

---

[2] Evans and Jovanovic do not identify the cause of the capital constraint. Possible explanations include an asymmetry of information between borrower and lender (see Blanchflower and Oswald, 1991) or high fixed costs of a stock market flotation (see ACOST, 1990).

Thus, substituting the constrained (8) and the unconstrained (5) values for k into the self-employed gross income (2), defines constrained and unconstrained self employment gross incomes.

$$Constrained\ Y_g = E(Q)(bZ)^d \qquad (9)$$

$$Unconstrained\ Y_g = E(Q)^{1/1-d}(\frac{d}{r})^{d/1-d} \qquad (10)$$

Hence in the constrained region an indifference locus between E(Q) and Z can be derived which has a slope of -(dE(Q))/Z from (9). In the unconstrained region this becomes a horizontal line as an increase in initial wealth no longer increases gross income as is apparent from (10). This allows Evans and Jovanovic to make a distinction between non-entrepreneurial employment and self-employed entrepreneurs which splits into 3 divisions: (a) constrained self-employment, (b) unconstrained self-employment and (c) non-entrepreneurial employment. This is represented in Figure 6.1.[3]

---

[3] We persist with Evans and Jovanovics' methodology in dividing the diagram using gross incomes as the more realistic means of composing net incomes, (which allow for negative entrepreneurial incomes) derives the same sign and general direction of flows as gross incomes in the comparative static analysis.

FIGURE 6.1: EVANS AND JOVANOVICS' SELF-EMPLOYMENT MODEL

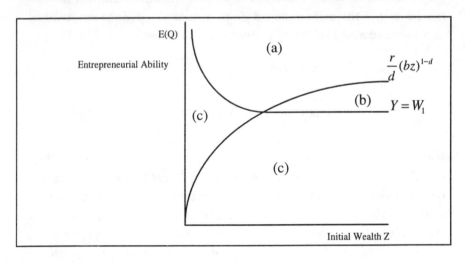

(a) Constrained Self-Employment
(b) Unconstrained Self-Employment
(c) Non Entrepreneurial Employment

FIGURE 6.2: EMPLOYED AND UNCOSTRAINED SELF-EMPLOYED ENTREPRENEURIAL INCOMES

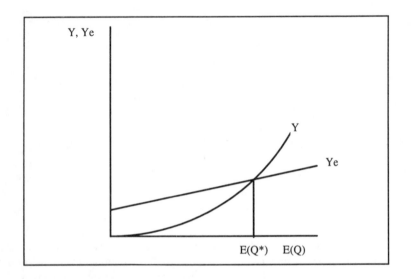

Now we want to further augment Evans and Jovanovics' model to allow for some entrepreneurial endeavours to be imputed by the employed. Therefore, we define the income of employed entrepreneurs (Y_e) as being made up of two components: that related to entrepreneurial ability (QA^β) and that related to certain routine tasks which do not involve entrepreneurship (D).

$$Y_e = D + E(Q)A^\beta \qquad A, \beta \geq 0 \qquad (11)^4$$

To model an individual's expanded career choice, we will first clarify relative income between employed entrepreneurship and self-employment. With this relationship specified, we can then use the indifference curve in Figure 6.1 to compare all four possible income sources. Noting that rZ is constant for a given individual, we can graph the relative income of employed entrepreneurship and unconstrained self-employment in Figure 6.2. The slope of employed entrepreneurial income is given by equation (11) while the slope of unconstrained self-employment income is given by equation (10). Assuming there are diminishing returns to capital ($0 < d < 1$), entrepreneurial ability causes unconstrained self-employed income to increase at an increasing rate. In Figure 6.2 for all entrepreneurial ability up to demarcation $E(Q^*)$ (where the income of both forms of entrepreneurship are equal) an individual secures more income in employment than self-employment. Above $E(Q^*)$, an unconstrained individual is better off in self-employment.

Linking Figures 6.1 and 6.2 we derive Figure 6.3. Using the equation for unconstrained self-employment as numeraire, we are able to compare incomes in indifference curve space. By tracing an income level from the horizontal axis of the left hand panel through

$$Y_{unconstrained} = [E(Q)^{(1/(1-d))}][(d/r)^{(d/(1-d))}]$$

we are able to ascertain the E(Q) level that would have secured the same income if the individual was self-employed and unconstrained by capital. This derived E(Q) value links our original income to an indifference curve in the right hand panel, (which represents the same income level). To find this indifference curve we simply trace the derived E(Q) value across horizontally until it intersects

---

[4] We expect $D = f(x_1, x_2); f'() > 0, f''() < 0$

$(r/d)(bZ)^{(1-d)}$; thereby linking it to the indifference curve which represents the same unconstrained self-employed entrepreneur's income.

FIGURE 6.3: THE SUPPLY OF EMPLOYED AND SELF-EMPLOYED
ENTREPRENEURS

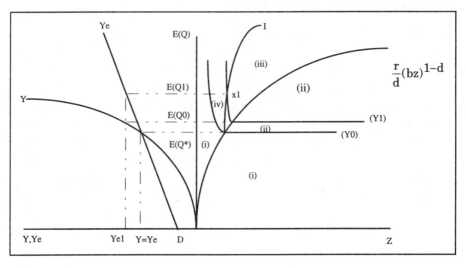

(i)   Employment as an entrepreneur
(ii)   Unconstrained Self-employment
(iii) Constrained Self-Employment
(iv)   Employment as an Entrepreneur

Thus, for example, tracing the income level $Y=Y_e$ at $E(Q^*)$ across to the right hand panel in Figure 6.3, we find it is represented by indifference curve Y_0. Initially ignoring the option of employment in non-entrepreneurial labour, we can divide the right hand panel into forms of entrepreneurship. On all utility curves below Y_0, employment as an entrepreneur derives a superior income source to both constrained and unconstrained self-employment, as is apparent from the left hand panel. Therefore, this area is made up exclusively of employed entrepreneurs and is represented by area (i) in Figure 6.3. Also from the left hand panel we know that unconstrained self-employed entrepreneurs earn more than their employed counterparts for all levels of $E(Q)$ above $E(Q^*)$. This generates area (ii) in Figure 6.3 which is solely comprised of unconstrained self-employed entrepreneurs.

The remaining area, (formerly devoted to constrained self-employed entrepreneurs in Evans and Jovanovics' framework), is now divided between employed and constrained self-employed entrepreneurs. We demonstrate this by choosing $E(Q_1) > E(Q^*)$ which is associated with employed entrepreneurial income Y_{e1}. We can find the indifference curve corresponding to Y_{e1} by tracing it through

$$Y_{\text{unconstrained}} = [E(Q)^{(1/(1-d))}][(d/r)^{(d/(1-d))}]$$

in the left hand panel. This provides us with $E(Q_0)$ which corresponds to utility curve Y_1. Therefore, the income of an employed entrepreneur with entrepreneurial ability $E(Q_1)$ is represented by the point "x" on indifference curve Y_1. This allows us to compare the income derived from employed entrepreneurship and constrained self-employment.

Supposing an individual is initially at point "x" where she is indifferent between employed entrepreneurship and constrained self-employment. If we were to increase her initial wealth "Z" above that at "x", her income from self-employment would increase while that of employment would remain unchanged (since Y_e is independent of "Z"). Hence she would choose to become self-employed. If on the other hand we were to reduce her initial wealth below that at point "x", this would diminish her income derived from self-employment but again leave her income from employed entrepreneurship unchanged. Therefore, in this case, she would choose to become an employed entrepreneur. Thus, by locating corresponding points to "x" for each $E(Q)$ above $E(Q^*)$, we are able to derive an indifference locus "I" where the individual is indifferent between employed and constrained self-employed entrepreneurship. To the right of "I", (denoted (iii)), the individual chooses to become a self-employed entrepreneur and to the left of "I", (denoted (iv)), she opts for entrepreneurial employment.

In the forgoing analysis we adopt the assumption that $(bZ)^d < A^\beta$ so that the "I" locus is presented with a positive concave slope. The slope of "I" is easily ascertained. Along "I" the income from constrained self-employment is equal to the income from employed entrepreneurship i.e. $E(Q)(bZ)^d = D + E(Q)A^\beta$. The first derivatives of these incomes with respect to $E(Q)$ are $(bZ)^d$ and A^β, respectively. The second derivatives are both equal to zero. If $(bZ)^d < A^\beta$, then as $E(Q)$ rises income from employed entrepreneurship will rise faster than that of constrained self-employed entrepreneurship. Consequently, in order to reduce this differential so that incomes are equal, we must give (take) an increasing (decreasing) amount of initial wealth Z to (from) the constrained self-employed, as E(Q) increases (decreases), in order to maintain equality between employed and self-employed entrepreneurial incomes. This implies that if $(bZ)^d < A^\beta$ then the "I" locus will have a concave slope.

We make this assumption on the grounds that it appears to be more likely at an empirical level. The adoption of either assumption does not change the conclusions of the analysis except in one area. This is where we increase E(Q) in the limit and where the adoption of the assumption $(bZ)^d < A^\beta$ implies that the probability of the individual choosing employed entrepreneurship as a career approaches 1. If we assume $(bZ)^d > A^\beta$ then as E(Q) increases in the limit the probability of the individual choosing self-employment approaches 1. The first outcome seems more realistic, entrepreneurs such as James Hanson of Hanson PLC, and Tony O'Reilly of Heinz initiate ventures that require a level of capital investment that cannot generally be supplied within the constraints of their own initial wealth. They either become employed entrepreneurs or, if already self-employed, become semi-employed by selling shares and/or merging with other companies.

Thus, if an individual is self-employed and endowed with an initial wealth Z, then as her entrepreneurial ability increases, she becomes increasingly constrained. On the other hand, an employed entrepreneur is unlikely to be constrained by capital (as her entrepreneurial ability increases), since this is being provided by the firm. Therefore, as E(Q) increases in the limit, the wealth generating capacity of the employed entrepreneur will exceed that of the self-employed entrepreneur (who will eventually become capital constrained) as long as the firm continues to supply capital for the employed entrepreneur's projects. Hence, we see an area that was formerly defined as constrained self-employment under Evans and Jovanovics' schema now being split between employed and constrained self-employed entrepreneurship.

Now re-introducing the option of employment in non-entrepreneurial employment we can model the supply of enterprise in Figure 6.3. If the routine wage rate is equal to Y_0 then it can be represented by income indifference curve Y_0. This implies that individuals whose $E(Q)$ and Z characteristics are represented within the area to the southwest of Y_0 (i.e. area (i)) maximise their income by becoming employed in the non-entrepreneurial employment sector. Thus, the availability of a wage equal to $Y = Y_e$ at $E(Q^*)$ reduces the supply of employed entrepreneurs. As the wage increases above this level to say, Y_1 (represented by indifference curve Y_1) it reduces the supply of entrepreneurs from all sectors i.e. (iv), (iii) and (ii). Therefore, the model is consistent with self-employment models of entrepreneurship supply to the extent that the supply of entrepreneurs is negatively affected by the wage rate. It does, however, caution the use of average wages to represent this effect in empirical analyses, as they include employed entrepreneurial income.

FACTORS AFFECTING THE SUPPLY OF ENTREPRENEURSHIP

The previous section demonstrated how a rise in the wage rate for non-entrepreneurial employment can affect the supply of entrepreneurs. In other words, it depicts a process whereby economic performance is negatively related to the wage rate through a reduction in the *supply* of enterprise. This is interesting as the neoclassical model also demonstrates a negative relationship between the wage rate and economic performance. The only difference, however, is that in the neoclassical model unemployment and output are affected through *demand* for enterprise i.e. a fall in wages increases the range of profit opportunities. Consideration of the supply of enterprise, therefore, qualifies the neoclassical result to the extent that an increase in the demand for enterprise *is not a sufficient condition* for an increase in output but rather a *necessary condition*. An increase in the demand for enterprise will only enhance output performance when it is matched by an effective supply of productive entrepreneurs who are willing to exploit the available profit opportunities. In a nutshell, consideration of the supply of entrepreneurs necessitates a reappraisal of the role of wages in mainstream economic analysis in two important directions. Firstly, wages play two roles rather than one, namely all forms of wage costs negatively affect profit opportunities (apart, possibly, from efficiency wage effects) while the relatively of non-entrepreneurial wages to entrepreneurial incomes affects the supply of entrepreneurs. Thus, although (non-entrepreneurial) wages are expected to negatively affect economic performance in both instances, the fact that the relevant wage in each case is not the same implies that traditional empirical analysis using an aggregate wage rate is unlikely to account for both effects. Moreover, given that other economic shocks are likely to affect the supply of entrepreneurs over time, it is extremely unlikely that one would capture this influence (the supply of entrepreneurs) by a single explanatory variable, wages.

The second point for consideration is the fact that relative wages play a central role as a determinant of both the supply and distribution of entrepreneurs. Therefore, an aggregate approach towards the description of economic performance through composite wage indices cannot realistically explain the evolution and dynamics of industrial performance, and is therefore unlikely to accurately account for overall performance at an aggregate level.

The model identified a capital constraint as a central factor which was likely to affect the supply of enterprise. In addition, there is a significant body of research that verifies this finding at an empirical level. Most studies (for example, ACOST, 1989, Blanchflower and Oswald, 1991 and Black et al, 1992, Burke 1994b to mention just a few) find evidence indicating that a capital constraint is decreasing in firm size as larger firms have access to more sources of finance and generally have a greater number of assets to act as collateral. Therefore, the recent rise in the importance of small firms internationally is likely to increase the degree to which a lack of capital constrains the supply of enterprise. In addition, the model also indicates that a more uneven distribution of wealth in an economy is likely to increase the extent to which a lack of capital constrains the supply of enterprise. This is especially likely in cases where small firms account for a significant share of GNP and where capital market imperfections exist.

The characteristics of the recent literature on the supply of entrepreneurs provide justification for government intervention to ease the capital constraint among aspiring and existing entrepreneurs. As documented in this volume by both Kennedy and Drudy, Irish government policy has led mainstream economic thought on this issue. Since the foundation of the state, various governments have played an active role in supplying capital to entrepreneurs.

One of the more common forms of government aid has been through the provision of capital grants to firms. We know that capital grants to new firms undoubtedly stimulate the numbers of self-employed entrepreneurs, but do they achieve their desired objective of increasing the level of enterprise? Using the augmented model of section 1 we assume that the introduction of capital grants are of amount Z_0 and are made available to the self-employed. This has the same effect as increasing an individual's initial wealth and hence, increases the area in "E(Q) and Z" space classified as unconstrained by capital, in other words it shifts the $(r/d)(bZ)^{(1-d)}$ locus up by the amount $(r/d)(bZ_0)^{(1-d)}$. The supply of self-employed entrepreneurs increases as self-employment income is enhanced through the increased availability of free capital, rZ_0. However, only in the case of constrained self-employment is there a *real* increase in entrepreneurial income:[5]

$$Y = Q(bZ)^d + r(Z - k)$$

$$\partial Y / \partial Z = dQ(b^d)(Z^{d-1}) + r$$

So $$\frac{\partial Y}{\partial Z} Z_0 = dQb^2 Z^{d-1} Z_0 + rZ_0 \qquad (12)$$

i.e.=(income increase)+(wealth distribution)

This real increase in income is due to the fact that the capital grant allows constrained entrepreneurs to move towards, and sometimes attain, the optimal level of capital required.

The introduction of capital grants causes a redistribution of entrepreneurs from the employed sector to self-employment. A proportion of this movement represents individuals who are moving from (capital unconstrained) employment as an entrepreneur, to capital constrained self-employment. It is possible, therefore, that the incidence of entrepreneurs who are constrained by capital may be higher after the introduction of capital grants, than before.

---

[5] "rZ_0" is not a real increase in entrepreneurial income since it is merely a redistribution of wealth from taxpayers to self-employed entrepreneurs.

FIGURE 6.4: THE IMPACT OF CAPITAL GRANTS ON THE SUPPLY OF
ENTREPRENEURS

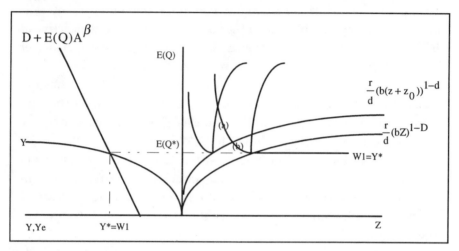

(a) Former Employed Entrepreneurs who now become Constrained Self-
employed Entrepreneurs

(b) Former Employed Entrepreneurs who now become Unconstrained Self-
employed Entrepreneurs

This is illustrated in Figure 6.4 by the area marked (a). Figure 6.4
represents the case where the non-entrepreneurial employment wage
rate W_1 is equal to entrepreneurial income Y_e at $E(Q_*)$. The capital
grant causes the constraint locus to shift upwards in the right hand
panel. The new "I" locus, (I_1), and the downward sloping portion of the
indifference curve are thereby shifted to the left. They are now located on the new constraint locus. Since the "I" locus denotes the division between employed and self-employed entrepreneurs, the shift
to the left of the "I" locus causes a movement of entrepreneurs from
employment to self-employment. The portion of the new self-
employed entrepreneurs who are located above the new constraint
locus will be constrained by capital.

Thus, in this setting the provision of capital grants to alleviate
capital constraints are seen to have a number of undesirable side-
effects. Firstly, it is possible that capital grants may have the paradoxical effect of increasing the capital constraint by drawing unconstrained employed entrepreneurs into the constrained self-employed
sector. This effect is most likely to retard enterprise in cases where an

entrepreneur's skills are heterogeneous to an extent that it is difficult to replace her. Secondly, the wealth distribution effect is likely to have two negative impacts. In the first instance, its financing causes a standard tax distortion effect and in the second place it creates rent-seeking opportunities. The latter is represented by rZ_0 and is likely to cause a degree of misallocation of entrepreneurial skills within the economy. Whether these negative effects are sufficient to negate, or even overwhelm, any possible positive effects generated through the provision of capital grants can, however, be only assessed at an empirical level.

However, a general distaste for capital grants has mounted over the last decade and government policy has now tended to favour the scaling down of capital grant assistance with a new emphasis on "capital for equity" and the provision of loan guarantees. In terms of the model, these policies have the effect of increasing the value of "b" which causes the constraint locus in the right hand panel to swivel upwards. The net effect is to increase the supply of entrepreneurs without generating rent seeking opportunities. To this extent these policies are more desirable than the capital grant approach.

But the provision of rent-seeking rewards as a part of a financial package to encourage the supply of enterprise may be justifiable in certain instances in Ireland's case where, (a) the supply of entrepreneurs is internationally mobile, and (b) the domestic supply of enterprise is viewed as inadequate. In this setting, capital grants by providing a reward over and above that generated by purely productive enterprise, may entice enterprise to Ireland that would otherwise have opted to locate elsewhere. In cases where such firms have acquired first mover and learning advantages, the policy not only reallocates the supply of enterprise in Ireland's favour but also enhances the demand for enterprise in the Irish economy as the importation of foreign firms who already have first mover advantages effectively expands the level of profit opportunities located in Ireland. Of course, as has often happened, foreign enterprise which has located in Ireland often chooses to leave when financial incentives disappear. However, the main point here is merely the fact that when entrepreneurship and capital are internationally mobile and markets are not purely competitive, there may be some justification for distorting the allocation of enterprise in the international arena in order to favour the "region" of interest.

Interestingly, the provision of unemployment assistance and benefit acts in the same manner in the informal economy as capital grants affect the supply and distribution of entrepreneurs in the formal economy. Therefore, returning to Figure 6.4 one can view the flows into constrained and unconstrained self-employment as movements into informal self-employment where individuals collect social welfare payments and simultaneously earn untaxed income. The extent of this phenomenon among measured unemployment is extremely difficult to gauge but its existence cannot be denied. For example, Burke (1995) found that roughly a quarter of Irish composers in receipt of music royalties also claimed some form of social welfare payment. Due to the costs associated with social unrest and the sometime existence of positive externalities, the economic ramifications of examples such as these are by no means obvious and are certainly worthy of further research.

If one assumes that there is an asymmetry of information between employer and a prospective employee regarding the abilities of the latter, then the model exemplifies the kernel of the "seedcorn" and "chaff" perspective on new firm formation. The idea here is that the *estimate* of an individuals entrepreneurial ability, E(Q), may differ between employer and employee. If this is due to an asymmetry of information where the employee possesses more relevant information than the employer, then a proportion of applicants who are rejected by employed sector are likely to enter self-employment. As long as significant barriers to entry do not exist, these new enterprises may expect to prosper, i.e. seedcorn. On the other hand, if the prospective employee possesses less relevant information than the employer then individuals who are "pushed" into self-employment are likely to represent those with low entrepreneurial ability and hence poor growth prospects i.e. chaff. Therefore, an evaluation of enterprise within a particular industry which uses new firm formation as a measure of entrepreneurship, ought to consider this issue of the quality of enterprise in addition to an evaluation of whether new firms are constrained by capital. In the case of the Irish music industry Burke (1994c) finds that most record companies set up by composers represent chaff rather than seedcorn.

The role of emigration as well as education and training are fairly transparent in terms of their affect on the supply of entrepreneurs. If one wished, one could illustrate these influences through the model in section one. For example, we could represent the highest outside option to a prospective entrepreneur in Ireland (i.e. domestic non-entrepreneurial income and all forms of foreign income) while specific forms of education and training could be gauged through the extent to which they affect $E(Q)$ and W_1.

SUMMARY AND CONCLUSION

The chapter identifies at the conceptual level the factors that have potential to affect the supply for enterprise. Through an augmentation of the model of Evans and Jovanovic (1989) the chapter derives a model of the supply of employed and self-employed entrepreneurs. This analysis identifies economic factors that are likely to cause the supply of entrepreneurs to vary and hence indirectly identifies the extent to which profit opportunities are likely to be exploited. In particular, wages are seen to play a more complex role in the economy than is allowed for in the neoclassical framework and capital grants are found to have some potentially paradoxical influences on the incidence of liquidity constraints among entrepreneurs. The model also highlights the importance (from a policy perspective in particular) and conceptual difficulties of separating new firm formation into "seedcorn" and "chaff".

Although general, the discussion in this chapter is by no means comprehensive. It is intended to clarify and provide a reference point for the identification of influences that can affect enterprise. In fact, research in this area is ongoing and is still in its early stages so this author by no means desires to give the impression of a final word on the topic. However, there are a few areas that have been researched and deserve a mention before closing the chapter. Firstly, the model of Evans and Jovanovic (1989) is Schumpeterarian in emphasis to the extent that it assumes risk neutrality and places entrepreneurial ability (or in the Schumpeterarian framework, innovative ability) as the pivotal factor. Readers who are more sympathetic to the Knightian (1921) perspective of entrepreneurship might prefer to include (impure) risk-taking within the analysis. In this regard, it seems plausible that the model of Kihlstrom and Laffont (1979) provides the best potential to expand a model of the supply of entrepreneurs (where risk-taking is the key variable) to include the option of entrepreneurial employment. In addition, the model of section one defined entrepreneurial income as being independent of the wage rate (i.e. as wages increased the return on entrepreneurship was unaffected) and again the model of Kihlstrom and Laffont (1979) provides a suitable framework for development, as its general equilibrium approach allows the wage rate to affect both the supply *and* the demand for entrepreneurs. It is interesting to note that if one incorporates the capital constraint (bZ) within the Kihlstrom and Laffont general equilibrium model that the number of possible equilibria increases monotonically with the number of wealth distributions with which one cares to experiment. There are, without doubt, numerous research projects that deserve future attention in this area.

Other areas that deserve a mention include the often cited "desire for independence" that has been found to be an important stimulus in encouraging self-employment (for example, see Scase and Goffee, 1980 or Burke, 1994c). If one allows for utility from independence, then it is quite plausible that many self-employed entrepreneurs may be *voluntarily* constrained by capital due to an unwillingness to trade off independence (i.e. less ownership of the firm) for more capital. This point has been made explicitly by Burke (1992) and documented in a historical context by Lazonick (1986). Its key analytical implication indicates that an identification of a capital constraint among smaller firms does not necessarily imply (and is likely to overestimate the extent of) capital market imperfections.

Finally, the model of section one did not allow for intertemporal effects. In terms of Irish enterprise, two research papers are particularity relevant in this sphere. Firstly, the work of Gladstone and Lane-Lee (1995) indicate that the British insolvency system mitigates against initially unsuccessful enterprises attempting further enterprise initiatives. Gladstone and Lane-Lee argue that as a result (and in contrast to the United States), failure for a British entrepreneur usually means the end of her (entrepreneurial) career. This has the additional effect of increasing the risks involved in enterprise. Since Irish company law is based on that of Britain these effects would also be expected to apply. In addition, a fear of being the focus point of attention among "Irish begrudgers" may be a further mitigating factor in Ireland's case. Secondly, the paper by Schmitz (1989) identifies the supply of entrepreneurs as a crucial vehicle for the generation of learning and information externalities in a process of endogenous growth. An interesting adoption and application of his model to Ireland may indicate that the significant amount of rent seeking opportunities within the economy (see the chapters by Kingston and Barrett) may be sufficient to ensure that the learning and information externalities generated in Ireland are such that Irish rent seeking activity is itself endogenously determined!

REFERENCES

ACOST — Advisory Council on Science and Technology (1990): *The Enterprise Challenge: Overcoming Barriers to Growth in Small Firms*, London: HMSO.

Black, J., de Meza, D. and Jeffrys, D. (1992): "House Prices: the Supply, Collateral and the Enterprise Economy", mimeo, Exeter University, 1992 and forthcoming in *The Economic Journal*.

Blanchflower, D.G. and Oswald, A.J. (1991): "What Makes an Entrepreneur?", manuscript, Dartmouth College, NBER. and Centre for Economic Performance, LSE. London.

Burke, A.E. (1992): "The Impact of Capital Grants on Entrepreneurship: A Model of the Supply of General Entrepreneurs", University College, Dublin, Centre for Economic Research, Working Paper 92/16. Dublin.

Burke, A.E. (1994a): "An Economic Analysis of Enterprise in the Music Industry", D.Phil. Thesis, University of Oxford.

Burke, A.E. (1994b): "Economic Integration and New Firm Formation: Evidence from the UK and Ireland". Trinity Economic Papers, Technical Paper 94/3 and forthcoming in the *Review of Industrial Organization*, 1996.

Burke, A.E. (1994c): "Small Firm Start-up in the Record Industry", Trinity Economic Papers, Technical Paper 94/6 and forthcoming in *Small Business Economics*.

Burke, A.E. (1995): "Employment Prospects in the Music Industry", forthcoming in the *Journal of the Statistical and Social Inquiry Society Of Ireland*.

Evans D.S. and Jovanovic, B. (1989): "An Estimated Model of Entrepreneurial Choice Under Liquidity Constraints", *Journal of Political Economy*, 97, August: 809-827.

Gladstone, B. and Lane-Lee, J. (1995): "The Operation of the Insolvency System in the UK, Some Implications for Entrepreneurialism", *Small Business Economics*, 7, February: 55-67.

Holmes, T.J. and Schmitz, J.A. (1990): "A Theory of Entrepreneurship and its Application to Business Transfers", *Journal of Political Economy*, 98, April: 265-294.

Holtz-Eakin, D., Joulfaian, D. and Roesn, H.S. (1994): "Sticking It Out: Entrepreneurial Survival and Liquidity Constraints", *Journal of Political Economy*, 102: 53-75.

Jovanovic, B. (1994): "Firm Formation with Heterogeneous Management and Labour Skills" *Small Business Economics*, 6, June: 185-193.

Kihlstrom, R.E. and Laffont, J.J. (1979): "A General Equilibrium Theory of Firm Formation Based on Risk Aversion", *Journal of Political Economy*, 84(4): 719-748.

Lazonick, W. (1986): "The Cotton Industry" in Elbaum, B. and Lazonick, W. (eds.) *The Decline of the British Economy* Oxford: The Clarendon Press.

Scase, R. and Goffee, R. (1980): *The Real World of the Small Business Owner*, London: Croom Helm.

Schmitz, J.A. Jr. (1989): "Imitation, Entrepreneurship and Long Term Growth", *Journal of Political Economy*, 97, June: 721-739.

7

ECONOMIC INTEGRATION AND NEW FIRM FORMATION: BRITAIN'S IMPACT ON IRISH ENTERPRISE[1]

Andrew E. Burke

INTRODUCTION

This chapter sets out to examine the determinants of new firm formation in the Republic of Ireland. It aims to generate two contributions to the literature on the economics of enterprise. Firstly, it seeks to assess the impact of economic integration on new firm formation in the Republic. To this end, this chapter focuses on two forms of international market spill-over: from the labour market and the product market. From an international perspective Ireland is an interesting case study of the impact of economic integration on new firm formation, as it is a small open economy which exhibits a relatively high level of international labour mobility.

Secondly, the chapter aims to test existing propositions relating to the determinants of new firm creation by focusing on a previously unutilised data set on new company registrations. This latter contribution is only noteworthy because the paucity of new company registration data implies that most analyses are based on a statistically small number of observations. In this setting, an extra data set, albeit small, may shed significant light on earlier deductions.

Since independence, both the Irish labour and product markets have been effectively integrated with the United Kingdom. Emigra-

---

[1] The material for this chapter is taken from Burke (1994), "Integration and New Firm Formation: Evidence for the United Kingdom and Ireland", Trinity Economic Papers, Technical Paper No. 3 and forthcoming in *The Review of Industrial Organisation*, 1996.

tion is one of the hallmarks of Irish labour history, and the United Kingdom has been the destination for the overwhelming majority of these emigrants. Geographical proximity, free movement of labour between Ireland and Britain, a common language and to a large extent a common culture, have all contributed to a highly integrated Irish and British labour market.

The data set in this chapter spans 1964 to 1991. Over this period average net emigration from Ireland accounted for 1.3 per cent of the Irish labour force per annum. The United Kingdom was the destination for 78 per cent of these emigrants. In this light, it is not surprising that real wage increases in United Kingdom are quickly transmitted to Ireland. It is also likely that such labour market spill-overs do not flow from Ireland to the United Kingdom, as the Irish labour force is small in comparison to that of the United Kingdom; 4.7 per cent in 1991.

A similar picture emerges in terms of international product market spill-overs. Ireland is unambiguously an open economy with exports accounting for a significant and increasing proportion of Ireland's GDP: the exports to GDP ratio has risen from 32 per cent in 1960 to 62 per cent in 1990. The United Kingdom has always been the main market for Irish exports. However, Ireland's reliance on the British market has weakened with exports to the United Kingdom falling from 75 per cent of total Irish exports in 1960 to 34 per cent in 1990. These characteristics imply that product market developments in the United Kingdom are likely to have an impact on the Irish product market, and hence on firm formation in Ireland. It is unlikely that such international product market spill-overs would also flow from Ireland to the United Kingdom, as Ireland's GDP is small in comparison to that of the United Kingdom: 5.4 per cent in 1991.

The structure of this chapter is as follows: section one outlines the theoretical framework, section two describes the data and section three conducts econometric analysis using a general to specific framework.

THEORETICAL BACKGROUND

The choice of most of the independent variables in this analysis stems from models of the supply of entrepreneurs such as that of Evans and Jovanovic (1989), Blanchflower and Oswald (1991), and Kihlstrom and Laffont (1979). These models are generally consistent and may be nested within a supply and demand framework for enterprise (outlined in chapter one) akin to that of both Casson (1982) and Schultz (1975 and 1980). In general, the level of new firm formation is generated by the number of individuals who choose to set up a firm rather than accept wage-work. An individual's expected utility is assumed to be dependent on income and hence an individual will set-up a firm if

$$EU(\pi) > U(w) \qquad (1)$$

where π is income from enterprise and w is the income from wage-work.

$$\pi = \pi (Q,W,R,Z,D) \qquad (2)$$

where:
Q = entrepreneurial ability
R = vector of capital good prices
Z = monetary value of initial wealth
D = income/business conditions
W = actual wage rate
w = (1-u)W
u = rate of unemployment

Income from enterprise is decreasing in W and R, increasing in Q, and non decreasing in Z. If an individual is constrained by capital, an increase in Z will increase π, while if an individual is unconstrained by capital an increase in Z will not affect π. An increase in income will affect π depending on whether the output is a normal or inferior good.

Applying Equation 1 to new firm formation in the Republic of Ireland requires recognition of the integration of Irish and United Kingdom labour markets, and therefore the condition for firm start-up in Ireland becomes:

$$U (\pi_{IR}) > \{ \begin{matrix} U(w_{UK}) \\ \\ U(w_{IR}) \end{matrix} \qquad (3)$$

and through labour market integration:

$$w_{IR} = f(w_{UK}) \quad f'(w_{UK}) > 0 \qquad (4)$$

Equation (4) has been estimated extensively by Irish economists. The most recent estimates are those by Curtis and FitzGerald (1994) and Walsh (1994). The former estimate an error correction model of Irish industrial wages and find a short-run elasticity of 0.91 per cent between Irish and British real wages. Walsh (1994) runs a co-integrating wage equation for Irish industrial wages and derives evidence of a one to one relationship between Irish and UK wages, "provided an adjustment is made for the differences in purchasing power in the two countries".

Since these results are consistent with earlier research, we will employ an average (0.96) of these estimates in quantifying the spill-over effect from the UK labour market to Irish firm foundation. Irish and UK real manufacturing wage rates are plotted in Figure 7.1.

FIGURE 7.1: IRISH AND UK MANUFACTURING WAGES

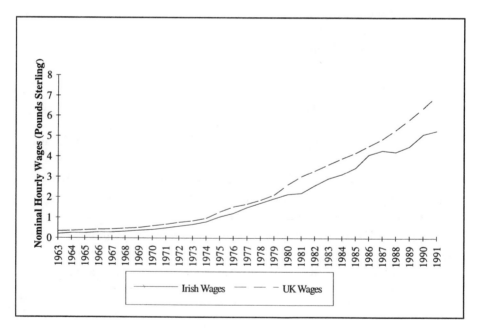

THE DATA

The analysis of section three carries out general to specific regressions where all potential determinants are nested in a general model. The variables employed in this analysis are listed below.

Dependent Variables

New Company Registrations (CSO Ireland): New company registrations in the Republic of Ireland are listed in the Annual Statistical Abstract published by the Central Statistics Office (CSO) of Ireland. Since new company registrations are also listed according to initial share capital, it is possible to sub-divide the data set into relatively small and large firms. In Table 7.1, we have denoted the percentage of firms accounted for by the various size categories of initial nominal capital from 1964 to 1968. Over the period it is apparent that over half of the new companies registered had a nominal capital base of less than £5,000. Given the significant drop in the percentage of new companies registered with a capital base of £5,000 or above (i.e. to 12 per cent), it seems reasonable to conclude that at the time £5,000 was a significant capital threshold. On this basis it is possible to sort the data according to initial firm size using the 1964 value of £5,000 as a demarcation value. By the end of the sample period (1991), £50,583 was the equivalent value of £5,000 in 1964.

Two dependent variables were created by indexing £5,000 to the retail price index (with 1964 set as the base year), and using this index to divide new company registrations into large and small firms. When the actual value of the index fell within the range of an initial capital category, the number of firms within this category were divided between large and small firms in direct proportion to the share of that category accounted for by the index. For example, if the index was equal to £6,000 in year X then 20 per cent of the new firms registered in the £5,000-£10,000 category in year X would have been counted as small firms. Figure 7.2 plots "total", "large" and "small" company registrations. It is apparent from these figures that the dramatic rise in new company registrations in the latter 1980s is *not* due to a rise in small company share. Therefore, it does not merely represent a static rate of enterprise creation in the presence of a fall in minimum efficient scale.

TABLE 7.1: NEW COMPANY REGISTRATIONS IN IRELAND

Percentage of new company registrations categorised by nominal share
capital investment. The data refer to nominal share capital up to, but not
including, respective amounts. "Total number of New Company
Registrations" refers to the actual quantity.

IR £	1964	1965	1966	1967	1968	Average
< 1,000	19.23	25.53	31.93	29.09	31.08	27.37
1,000 — 5,000	23.53	21.74	20.56	23.81	23.50	22.63
5,000 — 10,000	10.92	11.71	14.00	12.72	11.29	12.13
10,000 — 20,000	17.74	16.81	15.75	16.37	15.46	16.43
20,000 — 50,000	11.11	11.36	10.06	9.90	9.97	10.48
50,000 — 200,000	14.38	10.83	6.30	6.47	7.07	9.01
200,000 >	3.08	2.02	1.40	1.64	1.63	1.95
Total Number of New Companies Registered	1,071	1,136	1,143	1,344	1,966	

FIGURE 7.2: NEW COMPANY REGISTRATIONS

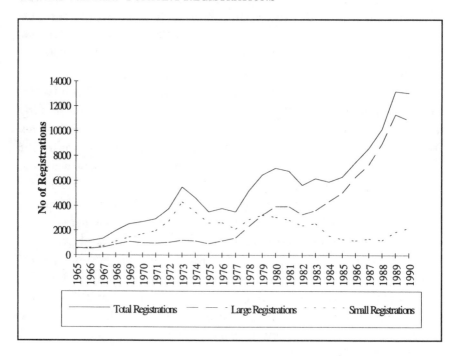

Independent Variables

Unemployment (OECD): Irish unemployment may positively affect the supply of entrepreneurs through three channels. Firstly, by reducing the prospect of employment it diminishes the expected wage, and thereby increases the probability of self-employment. Secondly, it reduces the value of time to an individual and hence in certain cases may increase investment in human capital relevant for enterprise. Thirdly, if the event of becoming unemployed is associated with the receipt of a lump-sum redundancy payment, it may provide an individual with seed venture capital. However, as is sometimes the case in empirical studies, unemployment may materialise as a proxy for business conditions with a negative co-efficient (for example, see Blanchflower and Oswald 1991).

Wages (Manufacturing, OECD): A real wage increase in Ireland would be expected to have a negative impact on enterprise. A rise in real wages, by depleting profit opportunities, would reduce the demand for enterprise. On the supply side, a rise in wages increases the attraction of wage-work, thereby reducing the supply of entrepreneurs.

Irish GDP (OECD): Irish GDP is used as a proxy for business conditions.

Migration (ESRI): Integrated labour markets, while ensuring spillover effects in terms of an equalisation of wages, also cause a reallocation of human capital. If it turns out that the more enterprising individuals emigrate, then the extensive emigration from Ireland to the UK may reduce new company registrations. To test for this effect we use net migration data from the Economic and Social Research Institute's database. However since the data is prone to measurement error, (passports are not required for travel between Ireland and the UK), we also use another proxy, namely Irish and British relative real expected wages: WREL.[2]

---

[2] WREL $= ((1-U_B)W_B)/(e(1-U_I)W_I)$. W_B = UK real manufacturing wages (OECD); W_I = Irish real manufacturing wages (OECD); e = Punt-Sterling exchange rate (Central Bank of Ireland); U_B = rate of unemployment in the UK (OECD); U_I = rate of unemployment in Ireland (OECD).

Cost of Capital (Central Bank of Ireland and Frain, 1990): The Irish fiscal system offers an extensive range of tax incentives and subsidies for capital investment. For this reason, it is often argued that the real rate of interest is not an accurate measure of the cost of capital in Ireland. To account for this we employ the "five-year full cost of capital index" derived by Frain (1990) which accounts for incentives faced by a firm liable for full profit taxes. In addition, we also utilise the more traditional measure of the cost of capital, namely the real rate of interest (Central Bank of Ireland).

Education (CSO Ireland): It is often argued that the Irish education system does not stimulate enterprise. Over the sample period secondary schooling did not change a great deal, while the number of students who attended universities rose dramatically. With a rise in the number of graduates in the labour market it is possible to gauge what affect, if any, this may have had on new company registrations. A negative impact would support the hypothesis of an "anti-enterprise culture in Irish education" — at least at a university level. On the other hand, a positive impact could be due to either supply or demand influences. On the supply side university education may increase entrepreneurial ability, thereby increasing the effective supply of entrepreneurs. On the demand side, it may increase business opportunities through its impact on labour productivity. To search for possible evidence of the effects of graduates in the labour force, we use a four-year moving average of the number of university graduates in Ireland.

Collateral (OECD): Stemming from the seminal work of Evans and Jovanovic (1989), a plethora of research chapters have identified collateral as an important factor in determining firm start-ups. With these results as a foundation, Black et al (1992) offered evidence to suggest that house prices may potentially affect new company registrations: the rise in real house prices increasing the value of collateral. In Ireland, home ownership is relatively high by international standards and hence we are afforded an opportunity to test this hypothesis further. The nominal house price index is sourced from the OECD's Main Economic Indicators, and is converted into real terms using the consumer price index (OECD).

Capital Grants (ESRI): Promoting new industry through the provision of capital grants has been a feature of Irish government policy for the last four decades, and specifically the main concern of the Irish Industrial Development Authority (IDA). These grants have been generous and in many cases have contributed to well over 50 per cent of total capital expenditure. In order to test whether capital grants have genuinely encouraged enterprise, we include total IDA capital grants to industry as an explanatory variable. It should be noted that the possible significance of this variable does not eliminate the possibility of rent seeking behaviour. As pointed out by Burke (1992), new firms created with the aid of capital grants may entail a re-allocation of enterprise from existing to new firms.

Irish Exports to the United Kingdom (CSO Ireland): Given the importance of the United Kingdom product market to the Irish economy, the relative buoyancy of this market would be expected to affect new company registrations in Ireland. To measure this possible market spill-over we use the CSO's real value of Irish exports to the United Kingdom (excluding Northern Ireland). This data is plotted in Figure 7.3.

FIGURE 7.3: EXPORTS TO THE UK

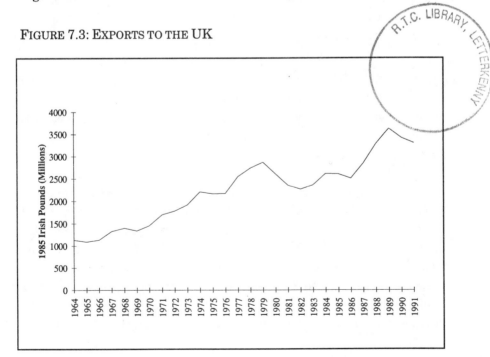

ANALYSIS

In this section we conduct a general to specific analysis of small, large and total new company registrations. The data set is small, (21 – 24 observations) and so deserves modesty in the interpretation of diagnostic tests. All of the variables appear to have a unit root as identified by the Augmented Dickey-Fuller test. Therefore, our methodology entails an estimation of a general to specific co-integrated equation, proceeding to estimate an error correction model (ECM). The economic interpretation of the ECM is as follows: if the number of new companies registered in a particular year are above (below) the long-run equilibrium/sustainable level, given the level of available profit opportunities and the ability (skill and financial capacity) of entrepreneurs to exploit these opportunities, then in subsequent years the number of company registrations will have to adjust below (above) the then long-run sustainable level in order to allow for the over (under) supply of enterprise being carried over from a previous period.

However, since the sample size is small, we will also proceed as if the relationship between the dependent and independent variables is not I(1) and hence estimate a general to specific model in first differences. In this case an ECM is not relevant since we are estimating a short-run relationship.

Total New Company Registrations

The estimates for total new company registrations are presented in tables 2 and 3. The specific equation (Specific 1), identifies business conditions (GDP [+] and unemployment [-]), real wages [-], university graduates [+], and Frain's cost of capital [-], as the determinants of new company registrations. If one was to accept this equation at face value one would unambiguously claim that labour market spill-overs dominate product market spill-overs, since real wages are significant while exports to Britain are insignificant. However, it may be possible that either of the business conditions variables (GDP or unemployment), may be accounting for this influence. Therefore, we enter Irish exports to the United Kingdom (lagged) into the specific equation. This gives us Specific 2, and removing GDP from this equation results in Specific 3. The corresponding error correction model of Specific 3 is

ECM 3, where Irish exports to the United Kingdom are only significant at the 90 per cent level.

TABLE 7.2: TOTAL IRISH COMPANY REGISTRATIONS — ERROR
CORRECTION MODEL

Dependant Variable: The log of total company registrations 1969-1989. For ECM equations the variables are in first differences, except for lagged residuals.					
Variables:	*Specific 1*	*ECM 1*	*Specific 2*	*Specific 3*	*ECM 3*
Constant	-22.0		-24.7	-21.1	
	(-8.2)		(-8.1)	(-5.1)	
GDP	2.2	2.1	2.0		
	(-4.3)	(5.8)	(4.1)		
Unemp	-0.6	-0.44	-0.57	-0.54	-0.63
	(-8.8)	(-5.2)	(-8.7)	(-5.9)	(-5.1)
R Wage	-1.4	-1.99	-1.9	-0.9	-1.6
	(-3.8)	(-5.3)	(-4.1)	(-1.7)	(-2.8)
Graduates	2.1	2.2	2.1	3.2	3.8
	(5.8)	(6.2)	(6.3)	(10.1)	(8.8)
K Cost	-0.008	-0.006	-0.009	-0.02	-0.01
	(-2.9)	(-2.9)	(-3.3)	(-3.4)	(-3.7)
X's UK (-1)			0.38	0.56	0.48
			(1.65)	(1.8)	(1.8)
Residuals		-1.4			-1.3
(-1)		(-5.7)			(-4.7)
Adj — R^2	0.98	0.92	0.99	0.97	0.83
DW	2.25	1.8	2.5	2.2	2.0

Although the above regressions pass the co-integrating regression
Durbin-Watson test, the small sample prevents application of the
Engle-Granger Augmented Dickey-Fuller tests. Therefore, given the
small sample, it is prudent to investigate a general to specific model
in first differences. The results are presented in Table 7.3 and again
the specific equation rejects exports to the United Kingdom as an explanatory variable. The inclusion of Irish exports to the United Kingdom was never found to be significant, even when either of the
"business conditions" variables were omitted. (In Table 7.3 we report
the better fit of these tests i.e. the case of deleting the unemployment
variable). Thus, even a first differences approach would seem to imply
that negative labour market spill-overs from the United Kingdom

outweigh any possible positive market spill-overs. It is also interesting to note that while the error correction models of Table 7.2 find the cost of capital (i.e. Frain's measure) to be significant, the short-run estimates of Table 7.3 find the cost of capital to be insignificant and replace it by collateral factors, namely house prices and IDA capital grants.

TABLE 7.3: TOTAL IRISH COMPANY REGISTRATIONS — FIRST DIFFERENCES REGRESSIONS

Dependent Variable: First difference of the log of all new company registrations 1969 — 1990. All independent variables are in first differences.

Variables	Specific	A	B
d GDP	2.65	2.56	2.48
	(4.4)	(4.15)	(2.72)
d Unemp	-0.62	-0.60	
	(04.78)	(-4.48)	
d R Wage	-2.33	-2.57	-2.88
	(-3.83)	(-3.79)	(-2.89)
d Graduates	2.06	2.05	1.86
	(3.76)	(3.72)	(2.29)
d P Houses	-0.66	-0.63	-0.39
	(-2.25)	(-2.10)	(-0.89)
d K Grants	0.18	0.18	0.15
	(2.1)	(2.05)	(1.20)
d X's UK(-1)		0.23	0.47
		(0.83)	(1.16)
Adj - R^2	0.85	0.85	0.55
DW	2.13	2.10	1.37

The short-run elasticities from ECM 3 may be used to estimate labour and product market spill-overs from the United Kingdom to Irish firm formation. These estimates are presented in Table 7.4. Over the sample period, Ireland's labour and product market integration with the United Kingdom appears to have had a net negative impact on Irish firm start-ups: an average of 2.3 per cent per annum decline in the change in the percentage change of new firms created. This negative impact has apparently strengthened over the period with the comparable losses estimated as -0.6 per cent in the period 1969-79 and -3.9 per cent in the period 1980-89.

TABLE 7.4: UNITED KINGDOM PRODUCT AND LABOUR MARKET SPILL-OVER EFFECTS ON TOTAL IRISH COMPANY REGISTRATIONS

UK product and labour market spill-over effects on total Irish new company registrations.

Spill-overs	Product Market	Labour Market	Net Effect
1969	2.58	-2.97	-0.39
1970	-2.17	-13.90	-16.07
1971	3.97	-4.95	-0.98
1972	7.47	-7.79	-0.33
1973	2.20	0.05	2.25
1974	3.58	1.34	4.92
1975	6.74	-8.70	-1.96
1976	-0.92	-3.96	-4.88
1977	0.18	9.41	9.58
1978	7.66	-5.38	2.28
1979	3.47	-4.90	-1.43
1980	2.18	-19.22	-17.04
1981	-4.53	-18.72	-23.26
1982	-4.93	0.84	-4.09
1983	-1.84	-4.53	-6.37
1984	2.04	-6.20	-4.16
1985	4.79	0.60	5.39
1986	-0.12	8.67	8.55
1987	-1.83	-5.49	-7.32
1988	5.99	-14.23	-8.23
1989	6.93	-0.95	5.98
1990	4.69	10.04	14.73
1991	-2.79	-8.16	-10.95
Averages			
1969-91	1.97	-4.31	-2.34
1969-79	3.16	-3.80	-0.6
1980-1991	0.88	-4.78	-3.90

Product Market Spill-over = 0.48 * change in the log of Irish exports to the UK (lagged by one year) * 100

Labour Market Spill-over = -1.6 * 0.96 * change in the log of UK wages in IR£, * 100.

Net Effect = Product market + labour market.

As is evident from the table, this rise is due to a slight strengthening in negative labour market spill-overs (up from -3.8 per cent in the period 1969-79 to -4.8 per cent in the period 1980-91), and substantial reductions in positive product market spill-overs (down from 3.2 per cent in 1969-1979 to 0.9 per cent in 1980-91). Notable among the years with net positive labour market spill-overs are both the United Kingdom's incomes policy in 1977, and the 1973-74 oil shock; real wages falling in the latter period due to high inflation. The net negative impact of market spill-overs from the United Kingdom are fairly strong, to an extent that it is possible to halve the real wage coefficient in ECM 3 and still derive a net negative spill-over for the period. In order to derive a net positive effect, it is necessary to reduce the real wage coefficient to 48 per cent of its value.

Large Company Registrations

The "co-integrating" specific equation for large company registrations is represented in Table 7.5. Both real wages and lagged exports to the United Kingdom are significant. In the resulting error correction model (ECM 4) the respective short term elasticities of these variables are -5.3 and 0.63. Table 7.6 represents the results using a first differences approach. Here lagged exports to the United Kingdom are not found to be significant, and this remains the case even when a "business conditions" variable is excluded. However, it is noteworthy that the value of the lagged exports variable is found to be virtually identical in Tables 7.5 and 7.6, i.e. 0.63 and 0.64.

The remaining explanatory variables in Tables 7.5 and 7.6 suggest that house prices negatively affect large firm start-ups. IDA capital grants and graduates appear as positive determinants in Table 7.5. However, in Table 7.6, graduates did not survive to the specific form and IDA capital grants did so with a t-ratio just below the 90 per cent significance level. The significance of the positive coefficient on the lagged dependent variable in Table 7.6 appears to represent evidence of a multiplier effect similar to that examined by Carree and Thurik (1994) and Johnson and Parker (1994). However, it is also plausible that it represents a degree of inertia in the level of business opportunities over time.

In terms of the theory of new firm formation the specific equation in Table 7.5 seems most comprehensive: business conditions are accounted for by real GDP and current unemployment, the push effect of unemployment seems to take a two year period (which could be due either to time spent acquiring human and financial capital, or an increase in the "push" factor over time if the individual only gradually discovers it difficult/impossible to become re-employed), a negative wage effect, human capital represented by graduates, significant capital grants, a negative impact of property prices and a positive impact of exports.

TABLE 7.5: LARGE IRISH COMPANY REGISTRATIONS — ERROR CORRECTION MODEL

Dependant Variable: The log of large company registrations 1968-1990. For the ECM equation the independent variables are in first differences, except for lagged residuals.

Variables	Specific 4	ECM 4
Constant	-50.2	
	(-8.6)	
GDP	2.4	3.2
	(2.4)	(4.2)
Unemp	-0.75	-0.65
	(-4.6)	(-4.6)
Unemp (-2)	1.0	0.75
	(5.0)	(4.2)
X's UK (-1)	0.97	0.63
	(2.4)	(2.1)
R Wage	-6.3	-5.3
	(-7.0)	(-5.1)
Graduates	2.5	1.9
	(3.5)	(3.2)
K Grants	0.46	0.4
	(3.2)	(3.7)
P Houses	-1.99	-1.4
	(-5.78)	(-4.2)
Residuals (-1)		-0.91
		(-3.0)
ADJ — R^2	0.99	0.76
DW	2.04	1.65

TABLE 7.6: LARGE IRISH COMPANY REGISTRATIONS — FIRST
DIFFERENCES REGRESSIONS

Dependent Variable: First difference of the log of large company registrations 1967-1990. Independent variables are in
first differences

Variables:	Specific	A	B
d GDP	2.62	2.35	2.13
	(3.89)	(3.35)	(2.70)
d Unemp	-0.52	-0.49	
	(-2.56)	(-2.43)	
d Unemp (-2)	0.48	0.54	0.41
	(2.0)	(2.23)	(1.55)
d R Wage	-1.43	-1.95	-2.03
	(-1.76)	(-2.17)	(-1.99)
d K Grants	0.23	0.22	0.16
	(1.70)	(1.70)	(1.10)
d House Prices	-0.92	-0.85	-0.73
	(-2.23)	(-1.99)	(-1.50)
d Dependent (-1)	0.30	0.28	0.32
	(2.23)	(2.12)	(2.13)
d X's UK (-1)		0.52	0.64
		(1.62)	(1.37)
ADJ R^2	0.49	0.51	0.37
DW	1.9	1.86	1.87

Since the coefficient of real wages in ECM 4 is significantly higher in
absolute value than that estimated through the first differences approach, it is worth tracing the spill-over effects from both equations.
These are presented in Table 7.7. By definition, the pattern of the results must be similar to those derived for all company registrations:
the labour market spill-overs dominate product spill-overs and this
effect seems to have become more pronounced over time. The scale of
this net result is dramatically higher in the case of ECM 4 due to the
high coefficient on the real wage variable. In virtually every year with
positive net spill-overs, there is a positive spill-over from the United
Kingdom labour market.

TABLE 7.7: UNITED KINGDOM PRODUCT AND LABOUR MARKET
SPILL-OVER EFFECTS ON LARGE IRISH COMPANY REGISTRATIONS

Year	Error Correction Model			First Differences Approach		
	Product Market	Labour Market	Net Effect	Product Market	Labour Market	Net Effect
1969	3.39	-9.85	-6.45	3.44	-3.77	-0.38
1970	-2.29	-46.05	-48.90	-2.89	-17.64	-20.49
1971	5.21	-16.40	-11.19	5.29	-6.28	-1.07
1972	9.80	-25.82	-16.02	9.95	-9.89	-0.09
1973	2.89	0.15	3.05	2.93	0.06	2.95
1974	4.69	4.44	9.13	4.77	1.70	6.40
1975	8.85	-28.82	-19.97	8.99	-11.04	-2.19
1976	-1.21	-13.13	-14.33	-1.22	-5.03	-6.23
1977	0.23	31.16	31.39	0.24	11.94	12.17
1978	10.05	-17.80	-7.75	10.21	-6.82	3.23
1979	4.56	-16.23	-11.67	4.63	-6.22	-1.66
1980	2.86	-63.66	-60.81	2.91	-24.39	-21.53
1981	-5.95	-62.02	-67.97	-6.04	-23.76	-29.71
1982	-6.47	2.80	-3.67	-6.57	1.07	-5.40
1983	-2.41	-15.01	-17.43	-2.45	-5.75	-8.17
1984	2.68	-2.05	-17.85	2.72	-7.86	-5.18
1985	6.29	2.00	8.28	6.38	0.77	7.05
1986	-0.15	28.70	28.55	-0.15	10.99	10.84
1987	-2.40	-18.19	-20.59	-2.43	-6.96	-9.37
1988	7.86	-47.14	-39.27	7.99	-18.06	-10.19
1989	9.09	-3.16	5.94	9.24	-1.21	7.89
1990	6.15	33.24	39.40	6.25	12.73	18.89
1991	-3.66	-27.02	-30.68	-3.72	-10.35	-14.01
Average:						
1969 — 91	2.59	-14.28	-11.69	2.63	-5.47	-2.88
1969 — 79	4.15	-12.58	-8.43	4.21	-4.82	-0.67
1980 — 91	1.16	-15.83	-14.67	1.18	-6.06	-4.91

ECM labour market spill-over = -5.3 * 0.96 * the change in the log of UK wages in Punts * 100.

ECM product market spill-over = 0.63 * the change in the log of Irish exports to the UK (lagged by one year) * 100.

First differences labour market spill-over = -2.03 * 0.96 * the change in the log of UK wages in Punts * 100.

First differences product market spill-over = 0.64 * the change in the log of Irish exports to the UK (lagged by one year) * 100.

Small Company Registrations

The specific equations for the small company registrations are presented in Tables 7.8 and 7.9, where wages and exports to the United Kingdom do not appear due to insignificance; even when business conditions variables were omitted. In Table 7.9 the results are not very satisfactory, as apart from "business conditions" variables, the cost of capital is the only "theory of firm start-up" variable that appears significant. In Table 7.9 we report the insignificant estimates of wages and exports to the United Kingdom.

TABLE 7.8: SMALL IRISH COMPANY REGISTRATIONS — ERROR CORRECTION MODEL

Dependant Variable: The log of small Irish company registrations 1965-1989. For the ECM regression all variables apart from the error correction mechanism are in first differences

Dependant Variables	Specific	ECM
Constant	-5.81	
	(-5.20)	
GDP	3.66	3.04
	(11.66)	(6.02)
Unemp (-1)	-1.06	-0.87
	(-6.20)	(-4.22)
House Prices	1.36	0.56
	(4.27)	(1.11)
Migration	-0.01	-0.01
	(-3.08)	(-2.23)
K Cost	-0.02	-0.20
	(-3.55)	(-3.84)
Residuals (-1)		-1.27
		(-5.40)
ADJ - R^2	0.95	0.83
DW	2.37	1.92

TABLE 7.9: SMALL IRISH COMPANY REGISTRATIONS — FIRST
DIFFERENCES REGRESSIONS

Dependent Variable: First difference of the log of small Irish company registrations. All independent variables are in first differences.			
Variables	*Specific*	*A*	*B*
GDP	3.42	4.35	2.68
	(4.50)	(3.77)	(2.24)
Unemp (-1)	-0.91	-1.09	
	(-2.77)	(-3.00)	
K Cost	-0.02	-0.17	-0.01
	(-2.14)	(-2.17)	(-1.27)
R Wage		0.07	-0.19
		(0.07)	(-0.15)
X's UK (-1)		-0.77	0.02
		(-1.19)	(0.03)
ADJ - R^2	0.50	0.44	0.21
DW	2.23	2.31	1.47

We offer two possible interpretations for these results. Firstly, the
sample size may be too small to allow the small firm start-up data to
exhibit its true dynamics. Secondly, small firms may be less responsive to macroeconomic variables, especially since factors such as "a
desire for independence" and individual entrepreneurial ability may
play a significant role in the variation of small firm start-ups. Larger
firms, requiring more financial and human capital would tend to have
a smaller variance (and hence a more stable mean), in entrepreneurial ability and at the same time might be too large to satisfy a "desire
for independence".

Therefore, it may be the case that influences such as these may
"cloud" small firm data to an extent that economic variables find it
difficult to exhibit their true impact. In terms of this analysis this
would seem to be supported by the more pleasant theoretical characteristics of the estimates derived from large firms exclusively, than
estimates based on large and small firms together, or small firms exclusively.

SUMMARY AND CONCLUSIONS

The chapter examined the determinants of, total, large and small firm formation in Ireland. The main focus of the study was to assess the impact on Irish enterprise of the economic integration between the Republic of Ireland and the United Kingdom. To this end the chapter analysed two international market spill-overs from the United Kingdom to Ireland, namely labour and product market spill-overs.

The chapter found that labour market spill-overs generally had a negative impact on Irish enterprise while the product market spill-overs were on average positive. In terms of the net effect, negative labour market spill-overs were seen to outweigh the positive product market spill-overs. This effect seems to have strengthened over time due to an accentuation of labour market spill-overs and a decline in product market spill-overs.

In terms of dynamics, the spill-overs are transmitted at a faster rate through the labour market than through the product market. The general to specific estimates allowed for lagged effects in independent variables and found that product market spill-overs occurred after a one year lag, whereas the labour market spill-overs were found to pass through in the same year.

Summarising the spill-over effects, the evidence from the chapter would suggest that the Irish enterprise economy has suffered as a result of economic integration with the United Kingdom. With a net negative impact on new company registrations in Ireland, the British economy seems to have generated a degree of inertia in Irish enterprise. In terms of possible policy conclusions for economic integration in general, the results may imply that a small developing economy would generate more enterprise if product market integration was implemented *before* the introduction of free movement of labour.[3]

In terms of the remaining explanatory variables, the chapter found weak support for Black et al's (1993) hypothesis that house prices may stimulate enterprise among small firms. However, the chapter found that in the case of both large company registrations and total

---

[3] A logical extension of this argument is that the enterprise component of an ecomony outside the EU, which has access to EU product market but not the labour market, is likely to benefit more from market spill-overs than if the same economy was inside the EU with access to both the EU labour and product markets.

company registrations house prices have a negative effect on enterprise. Since Black et al also use new company registrations data (finding a positive impact) this result is strongly at odds with their analysis. We offer two possible explanations. Firstly, many house buyers regard the purchase of a house as an investment; often with a view to providing wealth for retirement. In this respect housing investment may be a substitute for enterprise investment and hence a rise in house prices, driven by a flow of investment funds into the housing sector, may be associated with a reduction of investment finance available for enterprise. This argument is consistent with the existence of collateral constraints since house "owners" who are already heavily mortgaged will have restricted scope in using their home as collateral. Secondly, since both the residential and commercial property markets are influenced by similar macroeconomic factors and often compete for the same resources (particularly land), a negative coefficient on the house price variable may in fact be "capturing" the likely negative influence of a rise in commercial property prices on the level of profit opportunities. Further research is required, (particularly assessing the interaction between commercial and residential property prices), to resolve this issue but in the meantime the significance of the negative coefficient on the house price variable indicates that Black et al's policy recommendation to subsidise house buyers in order to stimulate enterprise is premature and may even be misguided.

The chapter also finds that the number of university graduates in the labour force plays a significant role in large company registrations.[4] It is not clear, however, whether this is due to increased entrepreneurial ability or increased business opportunities generated by a plentiful supply of "cheap" graduate labour.

Finally, the chapter found weak evidence to support the hypothesis that Ireland is losing her entrepreneurs through emigration. Only among small company registration did net migration appear significant.

---

[4] A positive and significant education variable is fairly unusual in the literature on enterprise but this finding is also consistent with the analyses of the determinents of US self-employment by both Evans and Leighton (1989) and Blanchflower and Meyer (1994).

Key to Variables in the Tables:

GDP:	log of Irish GDP
Unemp:	log of Irish unemployment
R Wage:	log of real hourly manufacturing earnings
Graduates:	log of a four-year moving average of university graduates
K Cost:	Frain's (1990) "five year full cost of capital index"
X's UK:	log of the real value of Irish exports to the UK (excluding Northern Ireland)
Residuals:	residuals from respective co-integrating regressions
P Houses:	log of an index of the real price of houses
K Grants:	IDA capital grants to industry
Real R:	the real rate of interest (discount rate)
Migration:	net migration from Ireland (ESRI database)
Dependent:	dependent variable

REFERENCES

Black, J., de Meza, D., and Jefferys, D. (1992): "House Prices, the Supply of Collateral and the Enterprise Economy", manuscript University of Exeter and forthcoming in *The Economic Journal*.

Blanchflower, D. and Meyer, B. (1994): "A Longitudinal Analysis of the Young Self-Employed in Australia and the United States", *Small Business Economics: An International Journal*, 6(1): 1-19.

Blanchflower, D. and Oswald, A. (1991): "What Makes an Entrepreneur?", Manuscript, Dartmouth College, NBER and Centre for Economic Performance, LSE.

Burke, A.E. (1992): "The Impact of Capital Grants on Entrepreneurship: A Model of the Supply of General Entrepreneurs", Working Paper 92/16, Centre for Economic Research, University College, Dublin.

Carree, M. and Thurik, R. (1994): "The Dynamics of Entry, Exit and Profitability: An Error Correction Approach for the Retail Industry", *Small Business Economics: An International Journal*, 6(2): 107-116.

Casson, M. (1982): *The Entrepreneur: An Economic Theory*, Oxford: Martin Robertson & Company.

Curtis, J. and FitzGerald, J. (1994): "Convergence in an Open Labour Market", Working Paper 45, The Economic and Social Research Institute.

Evans, D.S. and Jovanovic, B. (1989): "An Estimated Model of Entrepreneurial Choice Under Liquidity Constraints", *Journal of Political Economy,* 97: 808-827.

Evans, D.S. and Leighton, L.S. (1989): "Some Empirical Aspects of Entrepreneurship", *American Economic Review,* 79(3): 519-535.

Frain, J. (1990): "Borrow or Prosper? Notes on the User Cost of Capital", Technical Paper 3/RT/90, Central Bank of Ireland Research Department.

Johnson, P. and Parker, S. (1994): "The Interrelationships between Births and Deaths", *Small Business Economics: An International Journal,* 6(4): 283-290.

Kihlstrom, R.E. and Laffont, J.J. (1979): "A General Equilibrium Theory of Firm Foundation Based on Risk Aversion", *Journal of Political Economy,* 87(4): 719-748.

Schultz, T.W. (1975): "The Value of the Ability to Deal with Disequilibrium", *Journal of Economic Literature,* 13: 827-846.

Schultz, T.W. (1980): "Investment in Entrepreneurial Ability", *Scandinavian Journal of Economics,* 82(4): 437-448.

Walsh, B. (1994): "Wage Convergence and Integrated Labour Markets: Ireland and Britain 1841-1991", Working Paper WP94/6, Centre for Economic Research, University College, Dublin.

8

ENTERPRISE IN IRISH BUSINESS SERVICE COMPANIES: AN INTERNATIONAL COMPARISON

P.N. O'Farrell and D.M. Hitchens

INTRODUCTION

William Baumol (1990, p. 893) has suggested that:

> while the total supply of entrepreneurs varies among societies, the productive contribution of the society's entrepreneurial activities varies much more because of their allocation between productive activities, such as innovation, and largely unproductive activities such as rent seeking or organised crime.

He goes on to argue that the relative payoffs to different entrepreneurial activities will play a key role in determining whether entrepreneurship will be allocated in productive or unproductive directions and this can significantly affect the vigour of the economy's productivity growth. This chapter is concerned with one expression of productive entrepreneurship, specifically small and medium sized indigenous firms (SMEs) in business services. The aim is to evaluate the relative competitiveness of Irish business service enterprises with those in a comparable peripheral area, Scotland, rather than to examine the process of new firm formation which has been considered elsewhere (O'Farrell, 1986). However, it is important to set this analysis in the context of a consideration of the key role of services in the economy. Services are embodied in all products of an economy, whether these supply the needs of producers or, as they ultimately must, of consumers. Service activities are implicated in every process of economic change whether of restructuring, growth or decline, at local, national and international level; yet they have been seriously neglected by economists. This is partly because many economists treat services as a residual, analogous to the "non-production" functions of extractive and manufacturing firms. Such a view of services is misleading since many are involved with material processing and the quality of such services directly influences the competitiveness of production (Marshall, 1988 and O'Farrell and Hitchens, 1990a). While there is not a complete consensus on the definition of services, most authorities consider the services sector to include all economic activities whose output (a) is not a product or construction, (b) is generally consumed at the time it is produced, and (c) provides added value in forms (such as convenience, assurance, comfort, knowledge, or health) that are essentially intangible concerns of the purchaser. A key characteristic of services is that they offer the expertise necessary to support other economic activities. This expertise may take a wide variety of forms: knowledge of financial markets, research and development in manufacturing, maintenance and repair services, marketing skills, provision for leisure, or support for educational and health needs. This view of services is demand orientated stressing the worth of materials handling or information services to other production or consumption activities (Marshall et al., 1987).

The notion that the service sector is primarily dependent upon the demands of the "wealth" creating manufacturing goods sector for its prosperity, and that it is the non basic component of the national or regional economy incapable of autonomous growth dates from the thinking of Adam Smith. He distinguished between "productive" and "unproductive" labour: "the labour of a manufacturer adds generally to the value of the materials which he works upon . . . The labour of a menial servant, on the other hand, adds to the value of nothing" (Smith, 1976, p. 314). In Smith's classification, not only menial servants were unproductive but also the sovereign, the army and navy, churchmen, lawyers, physicians and men of letters of all kinds "like the declamation of the actor, the harangue of the orator, or the tune of the musicians, the work of all of them perishes in the instant of its production" (Ibid., p. 315). Hence, Smith made tangibility, with its associated quality of durability of the economic activity, the criterion of productiveness (O'Farrell and Hitchens, 1990b, p. 164). It was Smith's disciple, J.B. Say, who realised Smith's error and who accepted that "the professor, the doctor and the actor had claims to be regarded as producers" (Gide and Rist, 1948, p. 35). Despite Alfred Marshall's dictum to the effect that "there is not in real life a clear line of division between labour that is or is not productive" (1961, p. ix), much of the conventional thinking on the subject of goods and services is based on the assumption of a clear cut distinction between the two.

THE ROLE OF SERVICES IN DEVELOPMENT

Does the apparent increased domination by services of employment in late twentieth century developed economies imply that services are less capable of triggering productivity gains, technological advances, tradable exports and inter-industry multipliers than are manufacturing industries? Can services be considered "basic", to be a prime mover and exist without prior goods production, or must services always follow and be dependent upon goods production? Do business services play a peripheral, or supportive, role *vis-à-vis* goods production, or do they lie at the heart of any economy and provide the facilitative milieu in which other, especially market-orientated production activities, become possible? We shall consider these questions by considering the role of services in production.

First, many services, such as medical, legal, entertainment, banking, consultancy and education do not necessitate prior goods production. Such service activities require that there be income for individuals to buy the services; the source of that income can be either a goods or a services producing industry, or other income such as rent, interest, savings, or dividends. Second, the status of many services as intermediate inputs into industrial production has long been recognised. A substantial proportion of what is characterised as the service sector — distribution, transport, construction, utilities, business or producer and many government services — is linked to an evolving division of labour within primary and secondary industries. Data for the UK, Australia, Canada and the USA in the 1970s showed that one-third (22-38 per cent) of tertiary sector output (share of GDP) took the form of intermediate services to the "productive" sectors (Gershuny and Miles, 1983, p. 30). More recently, the OECD analysed GDP data for eight member countries by classifying services (i.e. excluding "goods" and "government") into those "directly linked to goods production", those which "are a necessary adjunct to the process of producing goods", and "free-standing services" which are "bought by households in their capacity as final consumers" (Blade, 1987, pp. 164-165). It was found that on average production-related services contributed 25 per cent of GDP and "free-standing services" 20 per cent.

Other studies have also demonstrated the vital function of services within manufacturing: approximately 75 per cent of the total value-added in the US goods sector is created by service activities within that sector (Quinn and Gagnon, 1986, p. 101); about 25 per cent of US GNP was accounted for (in 1980) by services used as inputs by goods-producing industries — more than the total value-added to GNP by the manufacturing sector (Riddle, 1986, p. 21). The ability to compete for many firms — both manufacturing and service — is increasingly dependent on the quality of knowledge (information services) at the disposal of management. There has been a rapid increase in demand for advice and information on merger and take-over options, portfolio investments, product design, computer aided manufacturing systems, quality control, commercial and international law, market research, corporate strategy and advertising. To an increasing degree, therefore, it is the services end of the production chain — design, research, quality, style, marketing, delivery, packaging, and advertising — which determines the competitiveness of agricultural and manufacturing investment. Services are responsible for a growing share of value-added to products. All the evidence therefore points to manufacturing, other service firms and the public sector being important sources of demand for service inputs.

There are two patterns which appear at odds with the notion of services being intermediate inputs to goods production. First, all service groups serve both intermediate and final demand markets; second, a substantial volume of transactions are generated within and between service industries themselves such as links between finance institutions and legal and accountancy services, or between advertising agencies, market consultants and other service firms. The traditional relationship of manufacturing "demand" determining service "supply" is therefore no longer applicable for important parts of the two sectors because of various interdependencies between them. Furthermore, there are circumstances where the demand from services had led manufacturing investment. Many goods-producing industries manufacture items such as printing, computer systems and IT that are inputs to service industries i.e. services are the prime movers. Also technological breakthroughs in certain services have stimulated the expansion of important manufacturing industries, as for example with research and development (scientific instruments), health care (medical equipment), and information processing (typewriters, photocopiers, computers). Similarly the transformation of the form of provision and consumption of some services has led to major surges in demand for a variety of goods such as household appliances, leisure equipment, and home improvement supplies. There is no basis for the belief that goods production is more necessary to an economy, more income-generating, or more wealth-enhancing than services.

The Competitiveness and Performance of Indigenous Business Service Enterprises: Issues to be Investigated

We have argued that business services are central to the economic base of a nation, are at the leading edge of growth in service employment, and generally conform to Baumol's definition of "productive" entrepreneurial activity. There are clearly some exceptions and Baumol (1990), for example, views a significant proportion of the output of the legal profession as being unproductive if not destructive. The key to the dynamics of service growth and uneven spatial development lies in growing intermediate demands for services, frequently operating at an international scale. It has been argued that a number of mechanisms have contributed to the rapid recent growth in demand for business services: (a) the increasingly complex competitive environment; (b) the accelerated internationalisation of production and trade; (c) greater non-price competition in product and service markets; and (d) the development of new information technology (Moulaert and Daniels, 1991, p. 1; O'Farrell et al., 1992b). Moreover, business services are increasingly recognised as a crucial element in economic development and as a factor that significantly influences the dynamics of growth, innovation diffusion, productivity increases and competitiveness across firms, sectors and regions (Martinelli, 1991, p. 21). Business services satisfy intermediate demand by supplying expertise which adds value to other sectors' output at various stages in the production process. They are traded within companies and on the open market; but their demand and supply need not be spatially coincident and, therefore, they influence the process of uneven development.

It is well known that business services are very unevenly distributed within Ireland. Some 62.6 per cent of all producer service jobs were in the East region — dominated by Dublin — in 1981 (Bannon, et al., 1989, p. 29). Similarly in the UK the South East in 1989 accounted for 58.8 per cent of total, national, other business service employment (8395 of the Standard Industrial Classification), with the North West (8.2 per cent), West Midlands (6.5 per cent), Scotland (5.6 per cent) and the South West (5.6 per cent) constituting secondary concentrations (Keeble et al., 1991, p. 449). Business service employment is highly concentrated spatially *within* Scotland: for example, Glasgow and Edinburgh account for 86 per cent of advertising agencies and 64 per cent of management consultancies (O'Farrell and Hitchens, 1990a, p. 1147). Does it matter therefore that business service supply is so unevenly distributed within developed economies such as the UK and Ireland? The ability of industry and major service organisations in the regions to adapt to market changes is partly dependent upon the availability and quality of local services and, hence, users in peripheral regions may be disadvantaged if their local economy has an uncompetitive service sector (Marshall, 1982, p. 1523). Furthermore, as has been argued elsewhere (O'Farrell and Hitchens, 1990b) "there is an implicit assumption that firms in peripheral regions will deliver services to their local clients of an equivalent quality and price to those available in the South East". Hence, a crucial issue is the way in which either the absence of business services in a region (gaps) or insufficient price and quality competitiveness of those available (deficiencies), impedes local competitiveness and exacerbates spatial economic differentials (O'Farrell and Hitchens, 1990a).

This prompts several important research questions. What are the major demand and supply factors constraining the competitiveness of business services and their capacity to generate extra-regional sales? What is the potential of this form of productive enterprise for contributing to the regional and national export base? Does this vary by type, size and ownership of business? Do the local business service suppliers avoid competition by targeting specific market segments in the regions — such as SMEs — where the large multi-office firms do not compete? A related research question is whether indigenous business service firms in Ireland are as capable of penetrating extra-regional and export markets as those in a comparable peripheral country, Scotland? This will provide evidence as to whether entrepreneurship in Irish business services has created companies which are competitive on both regional and foreign markets.

THE SAMPLE

The analysis in this chapter is conducted at office level. Offices in Scotland and Ireland were sampled from relevant professional directories, supplemented by regional directories and yellow pages. Since the population of offices varies considerably by industry, different sampling fractions were used. The offices interviewed in the survey totalled 40 in Ireland and 41 in Scotland and were drawn from five industries — product design, graphic design, management consultancy, advertising and market research. The Scottish offices were interviewed first in 1990-91 and the Irish sample in 1992, using a matched pairs design attempting to match the offices as closely as possible with respect to age, employment size, ownership, and nature of service(s) supplied (O'Farrell and Hitchens, 1988). The matching of services focused upon the core service provided since some Scottish and Irish firms were likely to offer additional peripheral service offerings. A close matching of the offices in the two regions was not possible. In both graphic design and product design it was only possible to identify 5 matches in Ireland for the 8 Scottish offices. Sample sizes in some industries are small either because there are very few firms in the industry (e.g. product design in Ireland and market research) or because of the inability to match firms according to the criteria specified. A total of 70 per cent of the sample in Scotland and 80 per cent in Ireland are indigenous. Hence, the two samples are not differentiated by ownership structure with entrepreneurial single office businesses predominant in both Scotland and Ireland. The distribution of the matched sample of offices by business service sector in the two regions is outlined in Table 8.1. Some 46 per cent of the Scottish sample were located in Edinburgh (partly because of the heavy concentration of market research firms in the capital), 34 per cent in Glasgow and 20 per cent elsewhere in Scotland, principally in Fife and the Borders. Some 85 per cent of the offices sampled in Ireland were in the Dublin conurbation and 15 per cent in the Limerick-Shannon area.

TABLE 8.1: PERCENTAGE GROWTH IN SAMPLE OFFICES, 1986-91

Industry	Growth of Nominal Sales		Employment Growth		Sample Size	
	Ireland	Scotland	Ireland	Scotland	Ireland	Scotland
Advertising and Marketing	100	78	13	55	11	8
Management Consultancy	178	133	75	43	13	9
Market Research	117	181	36	112	6	8
Graphic Design	118	169	85	73	5	8
Product Design*	—	62	—	44	5	8
All Firms	122	103	35	57	40	41

Source: O'Farrell et al., 1995

* Too few Irish Offices to calculate average growth.

The median employment size of the sample of Scottish offices was 11 compared with 10 for the Irish sample and a Wilcoxon matched pairs signed ranks statistic shows that this difference is not significant (O'Farrell et al., 1995). Similarly the median ages of the two samples — Ireland 9 and Scotland 8.5 are not statistically significant. Hence, the two samples are well matched by size and age. However, the inability to match all the Scottish graphic design and product design offices suggests that it would not be valid to focus any statistical analysis upon differences in performance between each matched pair of offices as has been done elsewhere (O'Farrell et al., 1992a). Therefore, it is necessary to analyse the data as two random stratified samples with the Irish offices assumed to have been chosen on the basis that they are similar as a group to the Scottish sample.

COMPARATIVE PERFORMANCE OF IRISH AND SCOTTISH COMPANIES

Competitiveness is a relative concept which, therefore, needs to be defined with respect to some other state of the world (Buckley, et al., 1988). This might be relative to a comparator firm, as in this analysis, or to a different time, or relative to a defined counter-factual position.

We shall evaluate performance using several performance measures at the level of the firm including employment growth, sales growth, export dependency, value-added per person and extra-regional sales. The data for two variables in the analysis — employment and sales change — refer to 1985-90 for the Scottish sample and 1986-91 for the Irish one. There is the possibility that unspecified business cycle effects may be incorporated, although Scotland was entering a recession in 1990 and Ireland somewhat later in 1991.

Total employment at the sampled Irish offices increased by 35 per cent between 1985 and 1990 compared with an increase of 57 per cent at the Scottish firms, and the difference is significant (P<0.01). These overall employment trends are not influenced disproportionately by rapid growth in a few exceptional firms which would have biased the overall result. Aggregate employment performance masks marked differences between industries in the two regions (Table 8.1). In general, Scottish companies displayed superior growth in advertising and marketing and market research; the performance of the latter being primarily due to the youthfulness of this industry in Scotland. The Irish companies recorded faster employment growth in management consultancy and graphic design. The pattern of sales growth presents a contrasting picture. Whereas employment expanded more rapidly in Scotland, sales in Ireland grew at a faster rate (122 per cent) between 1985-90 than their Scottish counterparts (103 per cent). However, there were substantial industry differences between the two areas in the growth of nominal sales with the Irish offices growing faster in advertising and management consultancy; and the Scottish offices recording superior growth in market research and graphic design. Overall the rate of employment growth relative to sales growth is lower in Ireland than in Scotland, where offices are more likely to respond to growing sales by recruiting more staff.

Value-added per person (sales minus purchases of materials and services) is a more useful measure of competitive potential in business services than in manufacturing since the level of capital employed per person varies considerably more between firms and industries in manufacturing than in services. To analyse value-added per person a sensitivity analysis was conducted converting Irish punts into sterling at exchange rates of 0.90 per pound, 0.95 per pound and

1.0. Mean value-added per person across all offices[1] surveyed in Ireland is 1.3 per cent higher than in Scotland at an exchange rate of 1.0; but 9 per cent lower at an exchange rate of 0.90. At industry level, Ireland, at an exchange rate of 1.0, recorded advantages of over 25 per cent in market research and 18 per cent in product design; while Scottish offices registered advantages of 8 per cent in management consultancy and 68 per cent in graphic design (see Table 8.2). The data for the advertising industry is not sufficiently reliable to yield accurate value-added figures and, therefore, is not quoted. Hence, overall there is little difference in value-added per person between the two areas but this aggregate result masks considerable between-industry variations. Previous research has shown that value-added per person in the South East of England is 23 per cent higher than in Scotland (O'Farrell et al., 1992a). To set the Irish Republic/Scottish comparison in the wider context, it is useful to compare the value-added figures for peripheral regional economies with that of the South East of England, the major European concentration of business services. This shows that value-added per person for a sample of Northern Ireland business service companies in 1991 was only one half of the South East England level while the Irish Republic firms attained levels equivalent to three quarters of their counterparts in South East England (Hitchens, O'Farrell and Conway, 1992).

DEMAND SIDE FACTORS AND COMPETITIVENESS

Markets

It is necessary to examine contrasts in demand and key supply factors facing offices in the two countries in an attempt to explain the observed differences in performance. The ability of firms to survive and grow is partially dependent upon access to a suitable market and, in this context, a key question arises concerning the extent to which the considerable geographical separation of Scotland and Ireland from major European markets is a significant constraint upon competitiveness? Two features of relative isolation are considered: (a) the spatial structure of the market; and (b) its qualitative characteristics

---

[1] The terms office and consultancy are used interchangeably to avoid tedious repetition.

TABLE 8.2: SELECTED PERFORMANCE MEASURES

Industry	Export Dependency Mean % Sales Due to Exports		Value-added Per Person*			
	Ireland	Scotland	Ireland at Exchange Rates:			Scotland
			0.90	0.95	1.00	
Advertising and Marketing	14	2	-	-	-	-
Management Consultancy	18	7	47.0	49.6	52.2	56.6
Market Research	21	0.2	41.8	44.1	46.4	36.9
Graphic Design	0	3	20.9	22.0	23.2	38.9
Product Design	33	23	27.8	25.8	28.7	24.4
All Offices**	16	4	36	38	40	39.5

Source: O'Farrell et al., 1995

* Sales minus bought in services and materials and are expressed as medians.

** The measure for all offices in the mean percentage of all exports and total sales for offices; value-added per person is the mean overall sampled offices.

Spatial Structure of Markets

The geographical structure of markets was analysed at three spatial scales: local (within a 40 mile radius of the office), sales to the rest of the country, and exports. The Irish offices derive two-thirds of their business from local customers compared with 56 per cent for their Scottish counterparts. Hence, the Irish businesses are more dependent upon their local area markets. Sales to the rest of the UK accounted for a mean of 41 per cent of the turnover of Scottish offices, while the rest of the Irish Republic accounted for 11 per cent of Irish sales (Table 8.3). Hence, Scottish businesses generated a healthy 45 per cent of their sales turnover from extra- regional markets beyond a 40-mile radius of the office compared with 35 per cent for the Irish consultancies. The Irish service business achieved a much greater degree of export penetration — 16 per cent of sales — than the Scottish firms (4 per cent). Similarly matched business service firms in Northern Ireland only generated 5 per cent of turnover from exports, including sales to the Republic (Hitchens, O'Farrell and Conway

1992). The greater export sales of the Irish offices is largely due to the
size of the country which limits the scope for expansion based upon
domestic demand. The Irish offices, therefore, need to export at an
earlier stage in their development than Scottish ones in order to sustain their growth. The major differentials between the two countries
are the larger export dependency of the Irish service businesses
combined, paradoxically, with a larger local area market dependency.
For all but a few Scottish offices, exporting was reactive, responding
to orders from abroad on an ad hoc basis. It is also apparent that
business services in the Republic, probably benefiting from a larger
market promoting more specialisation, are more competitive than in
Northern Ireland generating higher value-added and more exports
(Hitchens, O'Farrell and Conway 1992).

TABLE 8.3: SPATIAL STRUCTURE OF MARKETS*

Industry	Ireland			Scotland		
	% Local Area<40 Miles	% Rest of Republic	% Exports**	% Local Area<40 Miles	% Rest of UK	% Exports
Advertising and Marketing	76 (89)	10 (10)	14 (5)	58 (69)	40 (30)	2 (0)
Management Consultancy	53 (60)	28 (25)	18 (10)	51 (65)	43 (35)	7 (0)
Market Research	66 (64)	14 (10)	21 (22)	35 (43)	59 (43)	0.2 (0)
Graphic Design	89 (90)	11 (10)	0 (0)	61 (60)	36 (40)	3 (0)
Product Design	30 (30)	38 (30)	33 (31)	24 (30)	53 (40)	23 (15)
All Offices	66 (65)	19 (21)	16 (18)	56 (60)	41 (35)	4 (0)

Source: O'Farrell et al., 1995

* Data in parenthesis represent median values. Totals may not sum to 100
due to rounding errors.

** Exports include sales to Northern Ireland which account for 3 per cent of
sales while other exports total 13 per cent of sales.

When market structures are examined by industry both similarities
and strong contrasts emerge. First, in both nations, the advertising
and graphic design industries are most dependent upon their local

area market; while product design is least tied to local sales with management consultancy and market research in the middle. The product design, market research and management consultancy industries in Ireland were the most export orientated, with advertising and graphic design firms displaying the lowest export penetration. In Scotland, only the product design companies and, to a lesser extent, management consultants achieved a significant degree of export business. Hence, the degree of export dependency varies systematically both by industry and regional location.

Qualitative Characteristics of the Markets

The Scottish and Irish markets for business services are somewhat softer than the South East of England which is the region with the most discriminating clients and greatest competition on the supply side. First, there is less competition than in the South East, an issue to be discussed later. Second, much of the growth of business service demand is derived from indigenous Irish and Scottish firms which, on the basis of questioning both service suppliers in Ireland and Scotland are more likely to require a generalised rather than specialised service and to expect their suppliers, therefore, to provide them with a range of ancillary services in addition to a core offering. Third, Irish and Scottish firms are further disadvantaged on the demand side by the growing external control of the two economies, especially the manufacturing sector. Inevitably when firms in peripheral areas are taken over by companies headquartered elsewhere, decisions on the purchasing of business service inputs are made at head office and consequently few, if any, regionally based firms are invited to tender. Also multinational branch plants in peripheral areas make few demands for strategic business services. Several Irish businesses reported that there was an increasing trend for multinationals not to commission as much market research in Ireland as in the past but to centralise their market research purchasing at head office as more multi-country studies are required. Also, multinationals are tending to co-ordinate their advertising budgets transnationally by using perhaps one or two advertisers to cover the whole EU. A product designer stated that multinationals in Ireland "have little autonomy in product development and limited independence to commission work here". Furthermore, a proportion of the Scottish business service proprietors perceive the South East of England as an export market; this is partly a cultural problem, perhaps arising from an inferiority complex believing it to be more difficult to sell in the South East than it really is. There is a tendency for some Scottish proprietors to use remoteness as an excuse not to attack the South East market; and to combine this rationalisation with a policy of confining their activity to the Scottish market. Their strategic marketing perspective is, therefore, largely defensive; most Scottish firms are not psychologically integrated into the South East market. Fourth, on the basis of questioning the offices sampled in both areas, it is apparent that demand for business services in Ireland and Scotland is less discriminating and sophisticated than in the South East of England. In the interviews we invited service suppliers to state whether there were systematic differences in the nature of demand from similar types of clients in the South East and Scotland (O'Farrell et al., 1995). It is clear that most categories of business service users in the peripheral regions, especially SMEs, display less expertise in using consultants and make fewer complex demands upon them. This is a South East/rest of UK differential in which Scotland is no different than any other region such as the North West, North East or West Midlands.

A Scottish graphic design consultancy which sells successfully in the South East stated that their London clients have "clearly defined the job required" and "understand what they see"; while those commissioning in Scotland "have no design background . . . are less visually aware" and "they can tell Scottish firms what they need". A London agency expressed the view that South East clients were "more aware of quality standards than their Scottish ones" and needed a "quicker service". A London management consultant stated that they need to "sell the concept of service more in Scotland" where clients are "less international", and "demand was more price sensitive". A management consultant who relocated to Scotland from the South East, with direct experience of working with clients in both regions, admitted that "skills and solutions used several years ago in London were now applied in Scotland" and that clients north of the border were "more conservative" and "most do not want leading edge technical excellence". In market research a London partner said that local clients were "more demanding on delivery time"; that provincial clients "needed assistance to re-define their objectives and the brief and generally required more hand holding" they want to "commission findings rather than research", while their conception of market research is "management consultancy, market research, crystal ball gazing, and God the Father rolled into one". A Scottish-based market research firm argued that "clients don't appreciate quality so much in Scotland" and there is "a need to educate potential clients in the benefits of qualitative research".

There are two important exceptions to this trend. First, blue chip Scottish and Irish companies in financial services (e.g. Royal Bank of Scotland and Bank of Scotland, Bank of Ireland and Allied Irish Banks), insurance (Standard Life, Scottish Provident, Scottish Widows, etc.), and manufacturing (e.g. Scottish and Newcastle, Weir's, Guinness, etc.) require the same performance and delivery standards from consultants as firms in the South East; the quality demanded by blue chip companies, unlike other firms, does not vary spatially. Second, both the Scottish Development Agency (now Scottish Enterprise) and the Industrial Development Authority in Dublin have acted as a major stimulus to enhancing the quality of management consultancy supply in both countries. By setting very high standards and monitoring performance of consultants during assignments, they have been a key influence on the demand side in helping consultancies to become internationally competitive.

Turning to the Irish market, it appears that, unlike the UK, there is no significant spatial variation in the qualitative aspects of demand within the country. The country is too small and the majority of jobs are conducted for clients in the Dublin region. However, there is a difference by type of firm if not by location. With the exception of large Irish companies (for example, the banks which are sophisticated users of consultants, as are the Industrial Development Authority but less so government departments) indigenous firms are less discriminating users of business services than the MNE branches. MNEs were described as "more professional concerning specification and fees" while "Irish firms are more financially oriented and cost conscious"; but "the gap is closing". An advertising executive argued that "Irish firms require hand holding all the way ... they need more services ... a one stop shop". Irish firms are "more reliant upon market researchers for interpretation". A London advertising agency with a branch in Dublin reported that they had to be "more generalist in Ireland ... the market being smaller and less segmented". Overall the evidence suggests that there is a remarkable similarity between the two regions in the characteristics of local demand and also that *variability in quality on the supply side in both Ireland and Scotland is partly demand-determined.*

Customer Dominance

The degree to which business service suppliers are dependent upon, and potentially dominated by, their largest customer is an important issue which may retard profitability and growth. Overall there is little difference between the two countries in customer dominance: companies in Scotland depend upon their major customer for one-quarter of their fee income compared with one-fifth in Ireland. Scottish consultancies display greater dependency in all industries except advertising. However, in contrast, the median number of clients served during the previous year by Scottish offices (35) is marginally greater than the equivalent number (30) for Ireland. The Irish organisations had fewer clients in each industry except market research and product design. There is little difference in the proportions of fee income accounted for by repeat business.

Extent of Competition

A crucial factor in promoting price competitiveness, new service innovation, increases in value-added and quality is competition, especially from other similar suppliers in the same region. Successful firms arise from strong competition in their regional and national market which pressures business to upgrade, innovate and improve efficiency. Domestic rivalry also creates advantages for the entire industry that are external to any specific company; good ideas are initiated by local competitors, raising the overall rate of industry innovation (Porter, 1990, p. 120). The extent and nature of competition is assessed in three ways: (a) the number of competitors in the major marker; (b) competition from public sector organisations; and (c) whether the office faces overseas competition or not. In order to examine the relationship between the extent of competition (i.e. number of competitors faced by each company) and regional location it is necessary to control for industry. Research evidence shows that the median number of offices in competition with the Scottish consultancies (25) is almost double the number identified by their Irish counterparts (14). The number of competitors located within the home region of the sampled respondents is very similar in the two areas; the major difference is that the Scottish offices face far more competition from outside the region (a median of 17 firms) than do Irish ones (4 firms).

In Ireland some 58 per cent of independent single office firms and 55 per cent of branch offices reported that they faced competition from overseas while the proportions in Scotland were 18 per cent and 25 per cent respectively. There is little difference between ownership categories within countries in the extent of foreign competition; but major differences between countries. The degree to which individual business service offices in Scotland face competition from abroad varies from a maximum of 63 per cent of product design consultancies, 41 per cent in market research, 33 per cent of management consultants, 18 per cent of graphic design offices, to a minimum of 13 per cent in advertising. The extent to which Irish offices have to cope with foreign competition varies from 100 per cent in market research, 80 per cent of product design consultancies, 70 per cent of management consultants, 46 per cent of graphic designers, and 10 per cent of advertising agencies. Hence, Irish offices are much more likely to face foreign competition in all industries than their Scottish counterparts. However, 78 per cent of the foreign competitors identified by the Irish offices were located in the UK, principally London, which is equivalent to extra-regional competition in the Scottish case.

However, many global business service companies — such as Saatchi and Saatchi, Hay Management Consultants, McCann Erickson, Nielsen's and so on, have branch offices in Dublin. Other leading management consultants notably Arthur D. Little, Booze Allen and Mckinsey win strategic contracts in Ireland from their London base without an office in Dublin. Conversely advertisers "need a local presence to operate on the Irish market"; but London market research firms conduct qualitative work for clients in Ireland despite having no office presence in Dublin. As one Dublin market researcher candidly conceded: "qualitative market research here is not great". Also the executive recruitment industry tends to be segmented: at chief executive level there is considerable competition in the Irish market from London based consultancies but not for middle management positions. Some English graphic designers are targeting the Irish market as in the view of one multinational consultant "graphic design is not as good here because it is not exposed to leading edge ideas".

One potential source of competition faced by business services is that provided by various public sector organisations such as universities, polytechnics, local enterprise organisations, and development agencies. Some 22 per cent of the Irish respondents reported that they faced some form of public sector competition compared with 35 per cent of Scottish ones. It is clear that there are marked interindustry differences in the likelihood of encountering competition from public organisations: in Scotland over 40 per cent of both market research and management consultancies face such rivalry compared with only 15 per cent, 12 per cent and 8 per cent in the cases of advertising, product design and graphic design, respectively. Similarly, in Ireland 44 per cent of management consultants face public sector competition, 20 per cent of market research and product design consultancies, 10 per cent of advertising agencies and no graphic design firms. The major source of public sector competition in Scotland is from the higher education sector; but enterprise agencies were also an important competitive source. In Ireland the major source of public sector competition is also the university sector with state agencies also competing in market research and management consultancy. The responding entrepreneurs were asked to rank on a five point scale the relative importance of criteria by which firms compete in their market segments. Unsurprisingly, in both Scotland and Ireland, quality was ranked first in every industry; while delivery was classified second and price third by management consultancy firms and product design consultancies in the two areas. Moreover, the judgement of market research agencies in the two areas was also identical: price was ranked second before delivery, reflecting the price sensitive nature of the industry. The only differences between the two countries occurred in advertising and market research: Scottish respondents ranked delivery second in the former and price second in the latter; for Irish businesses this rank ordering was reversed. It is important to emphasise that similar rankings of the competitive criteria by offices in the two regions reveals nothing about the intensity of the competition.

Sources of Growth, Dynamics of Market and Marketing Methods

The entrepreneurs were asked to identify those strategies which had yielded the largest increments to increased turnover during the previous 5 years. For 30 per cent of the Irish consultancies and 28 per cent of the Scottish offices the major source of growth was increasing sales to clients already supplied. The most important strategy for securing growth implemented by 62 per cent of Scottish offices and 65 per cent of Irish ones was selling the same services to new clients. The results indicate a strong similarity between the two countries in contrast to the South East of England, where the most important growth strategy of business service firms was to increase sales to clients already supplied.

The dynamics of both the spatial and industrial structure of markets were investigated by identifying any changes in the previous 5 years. Again between-country differentials were more substantial than those between-industries. Some 60 per cent of Scottish businesses reported no change in the spatial structure of their markets over the previous 5 years compared with 74 per cent of Irish ones. The degree of change in the sectoral mix of markets was virtually identical: 60 per cent of Irish respondents reported no change in the past 5 years compared with 62 per cent of Scottish ones. Hence, there is more turbulence in the spatial structure of the Scottish business service markets than the Irish ones possibly due to greater competitive pressure. The marketing methods used by offices in the two regions are very similar with word of mouth recommendations being the most important followed by mail shots and presentations, specific targeting of clients, seminars, advertising in the trade press, networking, and winning awards (in advertising and graphic design).

SUPPLY SIDE FACTORS AND COMPETITIVENESS

We shall now turn to the examination of the key supply side factors potentially constraining the competitiveness of business services in Ireland and Scotland. These include office rents, costs of labour, charge out rates, training and quality of sub-contract suppliers, i.e. those supply side factors most likely to impact upon the performance of business service companies. The comparative cost and quality of each office's physical assets was examined in relation to their competitive performance. First, the average square footage of floor space available to each employee is almost 20 per cent greater in Ireland. Rents per square foot average £9 in Ireland at an exchange rate of 1.00 which is 4 per cent lower than in Scotland. Since the median size of office in the sample is 2450 square feet, the average rent payment for an office in Ireland is £22,050 compared with £23,000 in Scotland. The difference of £1,000 represents only 0.4 per cent of the median value-added of £281,000 for the Scottish offices and, therefore, rents as a proportion of value-added do not contribute significantly to any differences in competitiveness between the two countries.

The cost of labour and a number of qualitative characteristics of the personnel employed by the matched samples of businesses in the two regions was compared. In analysing gross annual pay rates, the seniority level of the jobs was matched as closely as possible. The evidence in Table 8.4 is unequivocal: salary differentials between the Ireland and Scotland vary both by grade and by industry. Senior personnel and partners are paid 33 per cent more in Ireland than in Scotland at an exchange rate of 1.0 and middle management 10 per cent more; while salaries for recent graduates in Ireland are 12 per cent higher. However, in addition to variations by grade, there is a major industry effect largely accounting for these between-country differences. Pay differentials between senior personnel in advertising and management consultancy are considerable: Irish firms pay senior advertising executives 79 per cent more and in management consultancy 50 per cent more than in Scotland. Conversely, senior staff in market research and graphic design are more highly rewarded in Scotland (Table 8.4). Variations in pay rates between Scotland and Ireland at middle management and graduate levels are considerably less than at senior level.

TABLE 8.4: MEDIAN GROSS ANNUAL PAY RATES BY GRADE, INDUSTRY
AND REGION (000S)

	*Ireland**			*Scotland*		
Industry	Senior Personnel	Middle Managers	Recent Graduates	Senior Personnel	Middle Manager	Recent Graduates
Advertising	50 (45)	24 (21.6)	15 (13.5)	28	23	12
Management Consultancy	45 (40.5)	30 (27)	15 (13.5)	30	23	15
Market Research	30 (27)	20 (18)	13 (11.7)	33	20	12
Graphic Design	20 (18)	14 (12.6)	9 (8.1)	30	18	8
Product Design	25 (22.5)	17.5 (15.8)	10.5 (9.5)	25	20	14
All Offices**	40 (36)	22 (19.8)	14 (12.6)	30	20	12.5

Source: O'Farrell et al., 1995

* Figures in parenthesis are Irish pay rates at an exchange rate of 0.90.

** The measure for all offices represents the median pay rates by grade for
all offices in the sample.

Data on charge out rates was collected for three grades of staff —
senior personnel/partners, middle managers and junior staff/recent
graduates. The analysis of median charge out rates in Table 8.5 shows
that there is considerable variation between industries, areas and
grades. Management consultancy commands the highest charge out
rates within all grades in both countries while product design consultancies generally have the lowest rates. At both partner and middle
management levels, the charge out rates of product designers in Ireland and Scotland are less than half of their management consultancy equivalents. Advertising rates are second only to management
consultants in Ireland; but market research is, perhaps unexpectedly,
an industry which commands relatively low charge out rates in both
Ireland and Scotland, reflecting its greater price sensitivity. The rates
which are charged out on the Scottish market are 16 per cent higher
at senior level than those obtainable in Ireland. Conversely, Scottish
rates are 8 per cent and 19 per cent lower, respectively, at middle
management and junior levels. The higher Scottish charge out rates
at senior level are somewhat anomalous given that salaries are lower
than in Ireland.

TABLE 8.5: MEDIAN CHARGE OUT RATES BY GRADE, INDUSTRY AND
REGION

Industry	*Ireland at Exchange Rate 1.00**			*Scotland***		
	Senior Personnel/ Partners	Middle Managers	Junior Staff/ Recent Graduates	Senior Personnel /Partners	Middle Managers	Junior Staff/ Recent Graduates
Advertising	410 (369)	305 (275)	235 (212)	435	263	158
Management Consultancy	750 (675)	500 (450)	304 (274)	770	510	255
Market Research	250 (225)	200 (180)	100 (90)	350	280	182
Graphic Design	350 (315)	300 (270)	260 (234)	420	350	210
Product Design	300 (270)	240 (216)	220 (198)	250	240	-
All Offices	363 (327)	325 (293)	250 (225)	420	300	210

Source: O' Farrell et al., 1995.

* Figures in parenthesis are Irish figure at an exchange rate of 0.9.

** Measures for all offices represent median charge-out rates by grade for all offices in the sample.

The presence of high quality competitive supplier industries such as typesetting, illustration, data processing, photography and so on, is important to the competitiveness of business service suppliers. The consensus view of the 40 Irish business service entrepreneurs was that local sub-contractors were competent but "if specialisms are required then it's necessary to go to London". However, several advertisers argued that "London is cheaper than Dublin for printing" while a graphic designer said that "the printing service in Dublin is poor — the quality is OK but delivery is terrible". A number of market researchers sub-contract their data processing to London "which is both cheaper and higher quality". Similarly advertisers and graphic designers tend to use London for specialised photographic requirements.

The business service supply infrastructure in Scotland is smaller and less specialised than in London. Hence, many business service firms, especially the best-practice companies, buy in some service inputs from outside the region, overwhelmingly from London. The Scottish printing industry is clearly characterised by quality variability: at best two respondents regarded it as "good but poor on delivery". One respondent spoke of the "need to go to London for perfection ... it can't be done here ... they attempt jobs they are not technically competent to do". Typesetting was categorised as "not brilliant" because of a "skills problem ... one needs to go to London for specialised work". Photography was also characterised by variability: one advertising executive said there were "no problems with his local suppliers" who were "more dedicated although not as skilled"; a product design proprietor firm stated that Scottish photographers were "not as good as in London" where it was necessary to go "for exceptional quality". In film making, an advertising executive said Edinburgh suppliers provided a "basic film service" but "London is best for creative flair and a more specialised and professional job". One Scotsman who had recently returned from London to establish a market research firm was unimpressed by the local field agencies; the quantitative research was "indifferent characterised by interviewer bias" while the "qualitative work was not as good as in London".

Hence, the quality variability and less reliable delivery performance of the sub-supply industries in both Scotland and Dublin has some detrimental effect upon the efficiency of the business service sector in the countries, although the introduction of new technology, especially the FAX, has made it easier for firms to mobilise such service inputs from outside. All the evidence suggests that there is little difference between Scotland and Ireland in terms of the quality of sub-supply industries. Firms in both countries need to use London suppliers if specialised high quality services are required.

CONCLUSIONS

This chapter has investigated one component of what Baumol (1990) has defined as productive entrepreneurship by examining the role of business services in regional and national development. The focus of the analysis has been an international comparison, using a common methodology, of the performance of predominantly indigenous business service companies in two peripheral countries, Ireland and Scotland. A fairly consistent picture has emerged of the relative position of local business services in Scotland and Ireland, reflecting their peripherality and small market size despite being in separate EU countries. Location and market size appear to be more important factors influencing business service performance than the national economic policy content. However, there are also some important differences. First, employment growth of the sampled Scottish offices has been greater than in Ireland; but, conversely, sales in Ireland grew faster (122 per cent) than in Scotland (103 per cent) over the five year period. Second, Irish offices are more dependent upon their local area markets, deriving two-thirds of their business locally compared with 56 per cent for their Scottish counterparts. However, Irish offices achieved a much greater degree of export penetration — 16 per cent of sales than the Scottish ones (4 per cent), due to the size of the country which limits the scope for expansion based upon domestic demand. Third, the median number of offices in competition with the Scottish offices (25) is almost double the number identified by their Irish counterparts (14); the major difference is that the Scottish offices face far more competition from outside the region than do Irish ones. Irish offices, however, are much more likely to encounter foreign competition, most of which arises from London. Fourth, Irish salaries are higher, although variations in pay rates at middle management and graduate levels are consistently less than for senior staff. Fifth, charge out rates at senior level are 16 per cent higher in Scotland but Irish rates are greater at middle management and junior levels.

The analysis has shown that there is a competent regional capability in business services in both Ireland and Scotland satisfying the bulk of local demand, except the high price/quality blue chip market segments. Indeed the differences between the business service sectors in Scotland and the South East of England in terms of competitiveness, value-added, exporting, degree of specialisation, nature of clients and so on are greater than the differences between Scotland and Ireland. The question, therefore, is whether the business service sector contributes substantially to the regional export base i.e. by selling extra-regionally or by exporting thereby ensuring that there are negligible displacement effects from employment creation. The finding that Scottish businesses generate 41 per cent of their sales beyond the local area within a 40 mile radius and Irish ones 35 per cent underlines the great potential that exists for business service enterprises to contribute to regional and national economic growth. A number of firms in Ireland are at a critical phase in their development whereby they have reached a limit to the market share they can achieve in Ireland and must either remain static or grow on the basis of export sales.

In order for a Scottish business service office to successfully penetrate the South East market, or for an Irish one to export, they need to evolve through a number of development stages. First, it is desirable for the firm to identify and target a specific market niche or segment(s). Second, once the firm has started to produce services for a particular niche(s), it is important that, as an on-going process, it continuously seeks out ways to increase value-added thereby enhancing differentiation. Third, the organisation must demonstrate an ability to produce a high quality service for the selected segment and to signal it to the market. It is difficult for firms to become specialised niche suppliers because of the small size of both the Irish and Scottish markets. Fourth, the next logical step is to sell this service to local blue chip companies, a process which, if successfully implemented, will permit the firm to build a reputation and charge an appropriate price premium. At present many blue chip firms in both countries use London business service suppliers for key strategic service inputs. Targeting the local region's blue chip firms has several benefits. They provide a base of demand in extra-regional markets to help offset the costs of entry. Being sophisticated buyers, the blue chip firms provide an excellent simulation of the exacting demand specifications of extra-regional and overseas clients. In addition, by capturing this market segment local firms will be import substituting. Fifth, having become firmly established as a regular supplier with repeat orders to local blue chip companies, the business service firm is then capable of entering extra-regional or export markets. Initial entry to the latter may be facilitated by trying to capitalise on their specialist knowledge of the Irish market for foreign firms.

A crucial stage in this evolutionary process arises when the business service firm has successfully broken into the blue chip market in the region but is still dependent for a large proportion of its business on the demand from SMEs which require a wider range of service offerings, lower prices and less exacting quality standards. This arises from a demand side difference in both Ireland and Scotland , namely the reluctance of most client companies to differentiate business service suppliers on the basis of quality and, therefore, there is greater emphasis upon price competition. Hence the weighting of the criteria upon which business service companies must compete on both the Irish and Scottish markets with price viewed as more important (except for the blue chip company sector) is different from London where perceived quality is rated more highly. Therefore, neither the Scottish nor the Irish markets are a perfect simulation of the South East of England or export markets. As a corollary, when the majority of jobs are won largely on the basis of price in a less sophisticated market, it is much more difficult for the same personnel to compete for other jobs primarily upon the quality criterion.

Top quality Scottish and Irish business service organisations are faced with a major dilemma. In order to succeed locally, they need to be a generalist providing a range of services; while to penetrate extra-regional and export markets it is important to be a specialist. Most Irish and Scottish companies argued that they would need an office in London, or to network with other organisations in order to be able to compete since their regions would be perceived as "far away and culturally distinct", and not a "serious competitor" in business services. The converse does not hold; some London firms compete effectively in Ireland and Scotland on their reputation without an office in the region. The negative image and perceived remoteness of Scotland and Ireland is compounded by the fact that most business service organisations do not produce tangible outputs and, therefore, it is impossible to demonstrate to potential clients the quality of service they can deliver ex ante, unlike a manufacturer who can provide samples or produce trial batches. Hence, reputation is a major source of competitive advantage (O'Farrell et al., 1992b).

The ability to generate competitive advantage is, perhaps surprisingly, a spatially localised phenomenon influenced by: nature of the demand side; quality of local supply infrastructure; level and intensity of locally based competition; local institutions and policies. Active local competition, demanding sophisticated and discriminating local customers and pressures to use resources efficiently and enhance quality are crucial in enhancing competitive advantage. One of the most powerful conclusions of this work is the association between vigorous local rivalry and the creation and maintenance of competitive advantage enabling firms to sell extra-regionally and internationally. Successful firms arise from strong competition in their regional and national market. In the absence of powerful local rivals, firms deploy factors less efficiently. The presence of local competitors also works to educate local buyers making them more sophisticated and demanding. This is the case in London and the spatial concentration of competitors there magnifies these benefits. Also, if demand is somewhat less sophisticated, as in Scotland and Ireland, then there is less incentive for local suppliers to improve their competencies and competitive advantages which may lead to the regional business service system, including sub-contract suppliers, becoming insular and inward-looking. The problem is exacerbated if most of the firms are sheltered from international competition. If the general thrust of these arguments is accepted, it suggests that government intervention should focus upon: (a) the educational system to ensure the supply of highly educated graduates; (b) improving the telecommunications infrastructure; (c) a rigorous application of competition policy to eliminate any unnecessary regulations; (d) a strong anti-trust policy especially in the area of horizontal mergers and collusive behaviour; (e) positive encouragement of entrepreneurship in business services via the tax system since deregulation will not succeed without active local competition; (f) using government procurement as a means to improve the quality of supply in the regions by acting as a sophisticated buyer, as Scottish Enterprise have done in Scotland, by setting stringent specifications and quality constraints.

Acknowledgement

This research was supported by an ESRC grant (R 00023 1891), Scottish Enterprise and Shannon Development. The author acknowledges the contribution of Mrs L.A.R. Moffat who helped to analyse the data.

REFERENCES

Bannon, M.J., Moore, K. and O'Keefe, A. (1989): "The Growth and Importance of Producer Services in National Development", Working Paper No.3, University College Dublin: Service Industries Research Centre.

Baumol, W.J. (1990): "Entrepreneurship: Productive, Unproductive, and Destructive", *Journal of Political Economy*, 98(5): 893-921.

Blade, D. (1987): "Goods and Services in OECD Economies", Paris: OECD.

Buckley, P.J., Pass, C.L. and Prescott, K. (1990): "Measures of International Competitiveness: Empirical findings from British Manufacturing Companies", *Journal of Marketing Management*, 6(1): 1-13.

Hitchens, D.M., O'Farrell, P.N. and Conway, C. (1992): "The Competitiveness of Business Services in the Two Parts of Ireland, Wales and South East England", Belfast: The Queens University of Belfast.

Keeble, D., Bryson J. and Wood P. (1991): "Small Firms, Business Services Growth and Regional Development in the United Kingdom: Some Empirical Findings", *Regional Studies,* 25: 439-457.

Marshall, J.N. (1961): *Principles of Economics*, 9th edition, London: Macmillan.

Marshall, J.N. (1982): "Linkages between Manufacturing Industry and Business Services", *Environment and Planning A*, 14: 1523-1540.

Marshall, J.N. (1988): *Services and Uneven Development*, Oxford: Oxford University Press.

Marshall, J.N., Damesick. P. and Wood, P. (1987): "Understanding the location and role of producer services in the United Kingdom", *Environment and Planning A*, 19, pp. 575-93.

Martinelli, F. (1991): "A Demand-orientated Approach to Understanding Producer Services" in Daniels, P.W. and Moulaert, F. (eds.) *The Changing Geography of Advanced Producer Services*, London: Belhaven Press: 15-29.

Moulaert, F. and Daniels, P.W. (1991): "Advanced Producer Services: Beyond the Micro-economics of Production" in Moulaert, F. and Daniels, P.W. (eds.) *The Changing Geography of Advanced Producer Services*, London: Belhaven Press.

O'Farrell, P.N. (1986): *Entrepreneurs and Industrial Change*, Dublin: IMI.

O'Farrell, P.N. and Hitchens, D.M. (1988): "Interfirm Comparisons in Industrial Research: The Utility of a Matched Pairs Design", *Tijdschrift voor Economische en Sociale Geografie*, 79(1): 63-69.

O'Farrell, P.N. and Hitchens, D.M. (1990a): "Producer Services and Regional Development: A Review of Some Major Conceptual, Policy and Research Issues", *Environment and Planning A,* 22: 1141-1154.

O'Farrell, P.N. and Hitchens, D.M. (1990b): "Producer Services and Regional Development: Key Conceptual Issues of Taxonomy and Quality Measurement", *Regional Studies*, 24(2): 163-171.

O'Farrell, P.N., Hitchens, D.M. and Moffat, L.A.R. (1992a): "The Competitiveness of Business Service Firms: A Matched Comparison between Scotland and the South East of England", *Regional Studies*, 26(6): 519-533.

O'Farrell, P.N., Hitchens, D.M. and Moffat, L.A.R. (1992b): "Does Strategy Matter? An Analysis of the Relationship between Generic Strategy and Performance in Business Services", *Business Strategy Review*, 3: 71-87.

O'Farrell, P.N. (1994): "The Role of Services in the Economy", in Hare, P.G. and Simpson, L. (eds.) *British Economic Policy*, London: Heinemann: 165-188.

O'Farrell, P.N., Hitchens, D.M. and Moffat, L.A.R. (1995): "The Performance of Business Service Companies in Peripheral Economies: a comparison between Scotland and Ireland", *Tijdschrift voor Economische en Sociale Geografie* (forthcoming).

O'Farrell, P.N. and Moffat, L.A.R. (1991): "An Interaction Model of the Production and Consumption of Business Services", *British Journal of Management*, 2: 205-221.

Porter, M.E. (1990): *The Competitive Advantage of Nations*, New York: Free Press.

Quinn, J.B. and Gagnon, C.E. (1986): "Will Services Follow Manufacturing into Decline?", *Harvard Business Review*, 86(6): 95-106.

Riddle, D.I. (1986): *Service Led Growth: The Role of the Service Sector in World Development*, Middlesex: Penguin.

Smith, A. (1976[1970]): *The Wealth of Nations*, Skinner, A. (ed.) Harmondsworth, Middlesex: Penguin.

Wood, P.A., Bryson, J. and Keeble, D. (1993): "Regional Patterns of Small Firm Development in Business Services: Evidence from the United Kingdom", *Environment and Planning A*, 25(5): 677-700.

9

ENTERPRISE FORMATION AND SMALL FIRM GROWTH IN THE TWO ECONOMIES OF IRELAND

Mark Hart and Eric Hanvey

INTRODUCTION

The ability to generate sufficient numbers of successful indigenously owned small firms is seen by many commentators as one of the key characteristics of a successful industrial economy. It has been argued that the significance of new and small firms rests in their ability to play an important role in technological change by introducing new products and ideas; that their flexibility enables them to benefit from the fragmentation of mass markets and the proliferation of niche markets; and that they are an important source of new jobs. As a direct result of these claims, the last 15 years in particular have witnessed a dramatic shift in industrial development policy in most developed economies towards the small firm sector.

In the two economies in Ireland there has, in the past, been a different emphasis placed on the role of indigenous enterprise in an overall industrial strategy. Throughout the 1970s and 1980s the Republic of Ireland relied heavily upon the ability to attract foreign multi-national companies. In Northern Ireland, the strategy, as a result of the difficulties in attracting foreign direct investment against a backdrop of political instability, has been very different. Most industrial policy expenditure in Northern Ireland has been directed towards existing companies, the vast majority of which are indigenously owned.

In the 1990s there has been a growing realisation in the Republic of Ireland that a greater policy focus on the indigenous manufacturing sector is warranted in an attempt to generate further economic growth. This has come about for two main reasons. First, as Gudgin et al. (1995) argue there has been a "plateau effect" among the externally-controlled sector in the Republic of Ireland, whereby there has been no further rise in the number of multi-national manufacturing companies or in their aggregate employment.[1] Second, there has been growing concern that the policy focus on the externally-owned sector has been detrimental to the performance of the indigenous manufacturing sector in particular, and the economy overall (Foley and Griffith, 1992; Barry and Hannan, 1995). This has operated through a combination of the "crowding-out" of indigenous employment by multi-national investment and the possible effect of barriers to entry for indigenous firms in export markets (O'Malley, 1989).

The aims of this chapter are two-fold. First, to highlight the growing importance of the small firm sector (section 2) and to document recent trends in new firm formation rates in Northern Ireland and the Republic of Ireland (section 3). Second, given the widely stated claim that the small firm sector is an important source of jobs, to investigate the contribution of new and small firms to the job generation process in the manufacturing sector in the two economies of Ireland over the period 1973-90 (section 4). The chapter concludes with a critical discussion of the potential role of small indigenous manufacturing firms in the economic development of Ireland.

THE SMALL FIRM SECTOR IN IRELAND

The total number of businesses, and hence mainly small businesses, has grown substantially in both Northern Ireland and the Republic of Ireland over recent years. Using VAT registration data the number of registered businesses in the Republic expanded by 82 per cent over the period 1979-93, which was a significantly greater increase than in Northern Ireland (27 per cent) or Great Britain (22 per cent). The higher rate of increase in the Republic can, in part, be associated with the different timing of the economic cycles between the Republic and

---

[1] Once the stock of multi-national companies becomes large, even a small annual closure rate leads to the need for a substantial number of new replacement companies to avoid a decline in numbers of firms and employment (Gudgin et al, 1995).

the UK. Nevertheless, the longer term trend has been one of much faster growth in the numbers of small businesses in the Republic than in either Northern Ireland or Great Britain.

With respect to the production (largely manufacturing) sector Northern Ireland experienced a more rapid rise than in Great Britain over the period 1979-93: 65 per cent compared to 18 per cent (Gudgin et al., 1995). No sectoral VAT data was available for the Republic for this period, but using data from the IDA Database, the increases in Northern Ireland and Great Britain were both greater than in the Republic, where the total stock of manufacturing plants has fallen substantially since 1987.

As a result of these changes the manufacturing sector in Northern Ireland is now more dependent on small firms than that of the Republic or of Great Britain (Table 9.1). This is a significant reversal since 1979 when the Republic had twice as many businesses relative to employment, than Northern Ireland. As well as the increase in the number of small businesses in Northern Ireland, this trend has been assisted by both the decline in the numbers of small indigenous firms in the Republic's manufacturing sector since 1987, and in addition the collapse of the externally-controlled sector in Northern Ireland in the 1973-86 period (Gudgin et al., 1989; Hart, 1993).

TABLE 9.1: EMPLOYMENT IN SMALL (< 50 EMPLOYEES) MANUFACTURING FIRMS (% OF TOTAL EMPLOYMENT IN MANUFACTURING)

	Republic of Ireland	*Northern Ireland*
1973	21.0	13.9
1986	28.5	25.5
1990	27.5	29.5
1993	25.5	28.6

Sources: NIERC Industrial Database, IDA Industrial Database.

Furthermore, as Gudgin et al. (1995) show, the fall in employment in the indigenous small firm sector is even longer established in the Republic: peak employment was reached in 1981, and by 1993 the number of jobs in indigenous small firms had fallen by 18 per cent below this peak. This point will be examined in greater detail later in the chapter.

TRENDS IN NEW FIRM FORMATION

Since 1987 the rate of business formation (using VAT registration data), across all industrial sectors, was lower in Northern Ireland compared with either the Republic or with Great Britain (Table 9.2). In part, the higher rate in the Republic reflects a higher rate of growth in the economy as a whole, and as noted above, in the stock of businesses. This higher rate was achieved despite its large farm sector, but a comparison with Great Britain is again affected by the sharp difference in economic conditions over the last seven years. In 1993 alone, when neither economy was in recession, the formation rate in the Republic was similar to that in most of Great Britain outside the South East. The exclusion of farms from the data seems certain to bring the Republic's formation rate up to at least the average for 1993 (Table 9.3)

TABLE 9.2: ANNUAL AVERAGE NUMBER OF NEW COMPANIES, 1980-93 (PER THOUSAND PEOPLE OF WORKING AGE)

	1980-86	1987-93
Republic Of Ireland	N/A	6.7
Northern Ireland	3.7	4.0
Great Britain	5.0	6.1

Sources: VAT Statistics — UK Department of Employment, ROI Office of the Chief Inspector of Taxes.

Note: Figures for the Republic of Ireland are an average for the years 1987, 1989, 1990, 1991 and 1993.

Within the UK formation rates (based on VAT registrations) have risen over the last decade and a half. Unfortunately, comparable data is not available prior to 1987 to establish a temporal trend for the Republic. A great deal of research has been conducted into examining the reasons for the changes in formation rates over time in the UK (see for example Keeble, Walker and Robson, 1993). The results indicate that a range of demand and supply variables were associated with annual changes in the rate of formation: levels of GDP, unemployment and vacancies, personal sector wealth, income tax rates and inflation.

TABLE 9.3: REGISTRATIONS FOR VAT IN 1993 (PERCENTAGE OF STOCK AT START OF YEAR)

Region	Registrations
South East	14.0
East Anglia	10.3
South West	10.5
West Midlands	11.4
East Midlands	11.1
Yorkshire & Humberside	11.3
North West	12.2
North	10.4
Wales	8.8
Scotland	10.8
Northern Ireland	7.5
United Kingdom	11.9
Republic of Ireland	10.7

Sources: VAT Statistics — UK Department of Employment, ROI Office of the Chief Inspector of Taxes.

The formation of new firms in the manufacturing sector is particularly important for economic growth due to their potential in export markets. Fortunately, it is possible to undertake a comparative investigation of the temporal trends in new firm formation between Northern Ireland and the Republic set within a broader UK regional context. Instead of the VAT statistics, data on locally-owned new firms was obtained from the NIERC and IDA industrial databases. However, in the case of the planning regions of Great Britain the VAT remains the only available source. For the period 1980-90 data was obtained for the *gross* number of new firms created and the *net* number, defined as the number of new firm survivors in 1990 (Table 9.4).

The level of gross formation in the Republic of Ireland, at 18.5 new firms per 1,000 employees, is significantly lower than that for the whole of the UK during the 1980s (28.2)[2]. This contrasts with the comparison made above for new VAT registrations in all sectors since 1987. Further, it demonstrates that the high formation rates, relative

---

[2] The net formation rate (a measure of the number of surviving new firms in the period) was 11.5 new firms per 1,000 employees.

to the UK and other countries, observed by O'Farrell and Crouchley (1984), for the manufacturing sector over the period 1973-81 have not been maintained in the 1980s. The gross formation rate of 22.2 new firms per 1,000 employees in Northern Ireland is also below the UK average but higher than in the Republic in the 1980s. Northern Ireland is ranked sixth out of the 11 UK regions and has performed better than some other peripheral regions. There is a clear north-south divide in the level of gross formation rates within the UK with the highest rates being recorded in the South East, South West and East Anglia respectively. The Republic of Ireland is clearly aligned with those regions recording the lowest gross formation rates, namely Scotland (17.1) and the North (15.3).

TABLE 9.4: FORMATION RATES IN MANUFACTURING, 1980-90: UK REGIONS AND THE REPUBLIC OF IRELAND (NUMBER OF COMPANIES FORMED, 1980-90 PER 1,000 EMPLOYEES IN MANUFACTURING IN 1980)

Region	Gross Formation Rate	Change in Stock
South East	42.3	4.9
South West	38.8	10.6
East Anglia	36.1	11.2
West Midlands	17.8	4.8
East Midlands	27.2	7.4
North West	20.7	3.0
Wales	25.3	8.1
Yorks & Humb.	21.3	3.9
Northern Ireland	22.2	7.5
Scotland	17.1	3.7
North	15.3	4.3
UK Average	28.2	5.3
Republic of Ireland	18.5	1.4

Sources: VAT Statistics — UK Department of Employment; IDA Industrial Database, Dublin.

Table 9.4 also presents comparative data on the change in stock of indigenous firms in the 1980s. The increase in the stock in the Republic was only 1.4 firms per 1,000 employees, which compares very unfavourably with the UK average (5.3) and below that of any UK region. On this measure, Northern Ireland is one of the better performing UK regions being similar to that for the moderately rural regions in the UK (Wales and the East Midlands), although well below that of East Anglia and the South West. Both Wales and the East Midlands are similar to Northern Ireland in their degree of ruralness. The role of an active small firm agency in Northern Ireland (LEDU — the Local Enterprise Development Unit), which seeks to strengthen the competitive position of new and small firms, could be a significant factor in Northern Ireland's UK ranking. Clearly, these observed differences between the two economies of Ireland warrant further investigation along the lines of that presented by Keeble, Walker and Robson (1993) for the UK as a whole.

There is evidence to suggest that the performance of the indigenous sector in the Republic of Ireland since the late 1980s has been an important influence on its comparative performance. For example, as reported in the "Task Force on Small Business" (Government of Ireland, 1994), between 1988 and 1992 there was a sharp fall in the number of indigenous manufacturing start-ups. Furthermore, between 1990 and 1993, the stock of indigenously-owned manufacturing businesses in the Republic has declined by 8 per cent (Gudgin et al, 1995). In Northern Ireland there was a comparable rise of 5 per cent over the same period. Clearly, these observed differences between the two economies of Ireland warrant further investigation along the lines of that presented by Keeble, Walker and Robson (1993) for the UK as a whole.

However, for the Republic of Ireland there have been attempts to identify the determinants of spatial variations in new firm formation across the 26 counties (O'Farrell and Crouchley, 1984; Hart and Gudgin, 1994). In summary, the results of these analyses demonstrated that it was possible to statistically account for some 70 per cent of the variation across counties through the influence of a small number of variables which reflect supply and demand influences. The incubator hypothesis, which suggests that new firm founders are drawn from existing small businesses, was confirmed for Irish counties. High formation rates were associated with counties possessing a larger stock of small firms. In addition, rural counties had higher formation rates, as did counties with higher proportions of the population in managerial and professional occupations.

Rising local demand was associated with high formation, but unlike many comparable studies in the UK, in-migration was not. In other words, counties losing more people through emigration had higher rates of firm formation. The Irish case, however, is somewhat different to that in Britain due to the fact that emigration does not necessarily imply population decline, and certainly does not indicate residential unattractiveness. There was evidence that counties with higher proportions of individuals achieving access to higher education had lower formation rates. The explanation here is that alternative careers to entrepreneurship become more attractive where academic standards are high.

JOB GENERATION AND NEW AND SMALL FIRMS

Having provided an indication of the key trends in new firm formation in Ireland the analysis and discussion in the remainder of the chapter will focus on the contribution of surviving new firms and existing small firms to employment change in the manufacturing sector. As Storey and Johnson (1990) have argued, the growing importance of small firms in terms of employment may be due to a combination of factors ranging from higher formation rates of small firms, the decline of large firms to the growth performance of surviving small firms. To unravel the relative importance of these factors it is necessary to undertake a components of change analysis which disaggregates net employment change into gross job gains and losses. These gains and losses can be examined further in terms of size, sector, ownership and region.

The analysis reported in this section adopts such a components of change approach for the two economies of Ireland for the period 1986-1990, although brief reference to earlier work covering the 1973-86 period will be made (Gudgin et al., 1989). The analysis is dependent upon the availability of data on individual manufacturing plants in each area. For the Republic of Ireland the data was obtained from the IDA industrial database, while for Northern Ireland a specially created database held at the NIERC was used.

Due to the variable length of the two periods and the very different economic circumstances they represent it is not the intention to draw direct comparisons between the two economies for each of the time periods reported here. Rather, the aim is to show for each time period the relative importance of new and small indigenous firms to the overall process of employment change. An understanding of an economies position on the business cycle is crucial to any form of comparative analysis and we return to this issue later in the section.

The methodology adopted for the analysis permits the comparison of three mutually exclusive and complete components of change in manufacturing employment. These are:

- Growth and decline of established indigenous firms (large and small) and externally-owned plants

- Inward moving companies and branch plants

- Formation of new indigenous companies.

The analysis presented will focus primarily on the contribution of surviving new firms and existing small firms to manufacturing employment change.

Components of Change, 1973-86

It is clear from Table 9.5 that the Republic performed better in every component of the job generation equation in the 1973-86 period. In both of the Irish economies the established companies, both indigenous and external, suffered a severe contraction. However, Northern Ireland fared worst in comparative terms with the loss of 52.1 per cent of its manufacturing employment in firms established in 1973, compared to an employment loss of 41.4 per cent for established firms in the Republic. The Republic also had a higher rate of new firm formation in the 1973-86 period, with an increase in employment in new firms of 13.3 per cent compared to 9.8 per cent in Northern Ireland.

By far the most significant difference was the level of new inward investment into the Republic which was five times greater than that for Northern Ireland. It was this dramatic difference which helped to maintain the level of manufacturing employment at 1973 levels in the Republic despite the poor performance of the indigenous sector. Thus, the Republic suffered a relatively minor drop in total manufacturing employment of 8.9 per cent over the 1973-86 period. This is in contrast to the majority of the western industrialised nations were service sector employment was growing at the expense of the manufacturing sector throughout this period. But even against this background the manufacturing employment loss in Northern Ireland can only be seen as disastrous with the disappearance of 38.4 per cent of total manufacturing employment during the 1973-86 period.

TABLE 9.5: COMPONENTS OF CHANGE IN MANUFACTURING EMPLOYMENT, 1973-86

Region	Northern Ireland	Republic of Ireland
A. Companies Established in 1973	(Thousands)	
Pre-1973 Inward Moves	-35,700 (-68.8)**	N/A
Other Externally-owned	-20,100 (-49.9)**	-28,600 (-41.9)**
Indigenously-owned*	-35,500 (-42.7)**	63,900 (-41.4)**
Net Change	-90,800 (-52.1)	92,500 (19.4)
B. Inward Moving Firms and Branch Plants	6,900 (4.0)	43,100 (19.4)
C. New Indigenous Firms	17,000 (9.8)	29,600 (13.3)
Total Change	-66,900 (-38.4)	-19,800 (8.9)

Source: NIERC Industrial Database, IDA Industrial Database.

* Includes Harland & Wolff and Short Bros.

** Percentage of Base Year Employment in that Category.

Components of Change, 1986-90

In Table 9.6 we can see that the overall situation has changed considerably from the pattern for the 1973-86 period. Manufacturing employment in Northern Ireland has grown faster than in the Republic during this more recent period. Although, the increase for Northern Ireland in total manufacturing employment was not large at 2.4 per cent over this four year period, the presence of any growth is noteworthy given the massive manufacturing employment losses of the 1973-86 period. The Republic has also experienced an increase in manufacturing employment, but this increase at only 0.6 per cent was less than that for Northern Ireland and when viewed against the Republic's significantly better performance in the 1973-86 period has to be seen as disappointing. What is all the more striking is that this reversal was entirely due to a dramatic improvement in the performance of the established indigenous sector in Northern Ireland.

TABLE 9.6: COMPONENTS OF CHANGE IN MANUFACTURING
EMPLOYMENT, 1986-90

Region	Northern Ireland	Republic of Ireland
A. Companies Established in 1986		
Pre-1986 Inward Moves	-2,520 (-7.4)**	N/A
Other Externally-owned	-1,046 (-10.6)**	-545 (-0.7)**
Indigenously-ownedD*	973 (1.5)**	-15,160 (-12.9)**
Net Change	-2,593 (-2.4)	-15,705 (-7.9)
B. New Inward Moving Firms and Branch Plants	1,247 (1.2)	4,513 (2.3)
C. New Indigenous Firms	3,984 (3.7)	12,411 (6.3)
Total Change	2,638 (2.4)	1,219 (0.6)

Source: NIERC Industrial Database, IDA Industrial Database.

* Includes Harland & Wolff and Short Bros.
** Percentage of base year employment in that category.

In the 1973-86 period the established indigenous sectors in both economies experienced substantial job losses. In the Republic this trend has continued in the 1986-90 period, but in Northern Ireland this sector had shown a modest but significant increase of 973 jobs. The employment generated by indigenous new firm formation continues to make a greater contribution to job creation in the Republic, than it does in Northern Ireland. The externally controlled firms (both established and new) have also continued to perform better in the Republic, although the relative increase in employment in new inward investment is now only twice that of Northern Ireland at 2.3 per cent and 1.2 per cent respectively.

It is interesting to note this dichotomy, with the established indigenous sector performing well in Northern Ireland relative to the Republic, whilst in the Republic it is the established external sector which is performing best in comparative terms. This is clearly illustrated in Table 9.7 which gives an indication of the extent of these differences. The relative importance of the individual components of change to the overall employment differences between the two economies can be measured using a simple standardisation technique. In Table 9.7 a standardised employment change is calculated for Northern Ireland by estimating the employment change which would have occurred if each individual component in Northern Ireland had grown or declined at the rate experienced in the Republic of Ireland. The hypothetical "standardised" change can be subtracted from the actual change to measure the contribution of each component to the overall employment change.

The largest single difference is in the established indigenous sector where Northern Ireland would have lost 8,268 jobs rather than gaining 973 if this sector had grown at the Republic rate. This difference accounts for Northern Ireland's better overall performance and in doing so cancels out the superior performance of the Republic in all of the other components.

TABLE 9.7: THE RELATIVE IMPORTANCE OF THE COMPONENTS OF INDUSTRIAL CHANGE, 1986-90: NORTHERN IRELAND AND THE REPUBLIC OF IRELAND

	Actual Change in Employment	Standardised Change	Actual Less Standardised Change	
A. Companies Established in 1986				
Externally-owned	-3,566	-295	-3,270	-163.6
Internally-owned	973	-8,268	9,241	462.2
B. New Inward Moving Firms And Branch Plants	1,247	2,453	-1,206	-60.3
C. New Indigenous Firms	3,984	6,748	-2,764	-138.2
Total Change	2,638	638	1,999	100.0

Source: NIERC Industrial Database, IDA Industrial Database.

An examination of the evidence regarding the job creation performance of the small firm manufacturing sector in the Republic of Ireland and Northern Ireland over the period 1973-86 highlighted the inability of surviving small firms to grow fast enough to compensate for job losses through the closure and contraction of other small firms (Gudgin et al, 1989). In an attempt to explain this poor performance of the small indigenous manufacturing sector in Ireland, considerable reliance was placed upon the matched-plant comparative analyses of Hitchens and O'Farrell (1987; 1988a; 1988b).

The results of their research pointed to a lack of competitiveness among Irish small firms — North and South -compared to their counterparts in other parts of the British Isles. In particular, they argued that the relatively poor performance of small Northern Irish firms was a consequence of uncompetitive prices, poor quality, and a lack of freshness in design. All of these weaknesses stemmed from an over-reliance upon the relatively sheltered markets in Northern Ireland (Hitchens and O'Farrell, 1987 p 552).

Established Small Firms

A continuation of the job generation analysis in Ireland for the period 1986-90 has revealed some interesting changes in the employment dynamics of small firms in Ireland. In the case of Northern Ireland it would appear that either the deficiencies identified by Hitchens and O'Farrell were less serious than they seemed, or that they were over-come/offset very quickly after the studies were conducted. Closure rates were lower and the growth rates of survivors were now faster than in the other comparator areas in the study, and especially the Republic of Ireland (Hart, 1993; Hanvey and Hart, 1994; Hart and Hanvey, 1995). There was a 11.5 per cent net increase in employment in small firms in Northern Ireland between 1986-90 compared to a net decrease of 9.4 per cent in their southern counterparts (Table 9.8). Furthermore, this net growth of the small firm sector in Northern Ireland was, unlike the case of the Republic of Ireland, sufficient to offset the employment decline of large indigenous firms.

TABLE 9.8: EMPLOYMENT CHANGE WITHIN INDIGENOUS ESTABLISHED FIRMS, 1986-90

Region	Northern Ireland	Republic of Ireland
(Percentage of Base Year Employment in Categories)		
Small Firms (<50 Emp)	11.5	-9.4
Large Firms	-5.1	-15.9
All Firms	1.5	-12.9

Source: NIERC Industrial Database, IDA Industrial Database.

In order to understand the processes lying behind these differences, Table 9.9 disaggregates the net employment change in small firms into closures and the performance of survivors. Surviving small firms in Northern Ireland grew by 28.5 per cent (6330 jobs) compared to a growth rate of 16 per cent (6778 jobs) in the Republic of Ireland. Jobs lost through the closure of small firms was lower in Northern Ireland (-13.3 per cent) than in the Republic of Ireland (-21.9 per cent). There-fore, the better performance of the Northern Ireland small firms is the result of the twin mechanisms of faster growth and higher sur-vival rates.

TABLE 9.9: MODE OF EMPLOYMENT CHANGE, 1986-90: SMALL INDIGENOUS FIRMS

Region	Northern Ireland		Republic of Ireland	
		%		%
All Established	2,931	11.5	-5,100	-9.4
Survivors	6,330	28.5	6,778	16.0
Closures	-3,399	-13.3	-11,878	-21.9

Source: NIERC Industrial Database, IDA Industrial Database.

As a result of the expansion of surviving small indigenous firms be-tween 1986-90, coupled with the 4,000 jobs in surviving new indige-nous firms over the same period, the small firm sector created 10,500 jobs in Northern Ireland. It is interesting to note that this compares very favourably with the creation of 1,200 jobs in the same period through the process of new inward investment to Northern Ireland (Hanvey and Hart, 1994). In 1991 small firms accounted for just over one-quarter (28 per cent) of total manufacturing employment, which represented a significant change from the early 1970s when their share of manufacturing employment was only around 10 per cent. The ability of the established small firm sector to regenerate itself is of vital importance when we come to consider the role of the new in-digenous firm. If the established small firms are able to maintain or increase their employment, then any jobs created through the process of new firm formation are truly net additional to the economy overall. We return to the issue of new firm formation later in this section.

The superior performance of the small firms in Northern Ireland may be due to a better industrial mix. This issue is addressed in Table 9.10 where Leicestershire sectoral growth rates[3] are applied to the base employment for each sector in Northern Ireland and the Republic to obtain an expected employment change. It is clear from the expected changes that if the small firm sectors in the two economies of Ireland had performed like their counterparts in Leicestershire then the Republic would have performed slightly better than Northern Ireland, suggesting that it has a marginally better sectoral mix. However the outcome, as has already been shown, is very much the opposite with strong employment growth for small firms in Northern Ireland and large job losses in the Republic. This analysis would indicate that there are no great differences between the sectoral structure of small firms in Northern Ireland and those in the Republic which would explain the difference in their performance. Northern Ireland's advantage in its established indigenous firms is due almost entirely to the performance of the small firm sector.

TABLE 9.10: ACTUAL AND EXPECTED EMPLOYMENT CHANGE, 1986-90: SMALL INDIGENOUS COMPANIES

	Emp. in 1986	Emp. Change		Expected Emp. Change		Actual Less Expected	
Northern Ireland	25,598	2931	11.5	-262	-1.0	3,193	12.4
Republic of Ireland	54,116	-5100	-9.4	-162	-0.3	4,937	9.1
Leicestershire	31,760	-625	-2.0	-625	-1.9	0	0.0

Source: NIERC Industrial Database, IDA Industrial Database.

How can we explain the dramatic improvement in the fortunes of the small firm sector in Northern Ireland and its sharp divergence from the performance of the small firm sector in the Republic of Ireland?

---

[3] The choice of Leicestershire in this calculation derives from the fact that the research team at NIERC have consistently used the region as a comparator on the grounds that its industrial sector has displayed above average growth rates in most of the post-war period.

Furthermore, how can we reconcile the evidence on the significant growth of small firms in Northern Ireland between 1986 and 1990 with the Hitchens and O'Farrell conclusion regarding their weak competitive position?

First, it must be acknowledged that the resurgence of the small firm sector in Northern Ireland could have commenced before 1986 but was not identified by the previous study which covered the relatively turbulent years between 1973 and 1986 without any intervening sub-periods.

Second, the widespread and perhaps convenient use of the Hitchens and O'Farrell work to "explain" the poor performance of the small firm sector in Northern Ireland was perhaps overstated. Much of their research was undertaken during the early part of the 1986-90 period, when as outlined above, the *full population* of small firms in Northern Ireland were performing relatively well in terms of growth of survivors and the overall cohort survival rate. Thus, we would argue that it is rather erroneous to generalise their results to be indicative of the small firm sector as a whole. The importance of continually monitoring the individual components of employment change, using databases containing *populations* of firms, cannot be overstated.

Third, the modest growth in manufacturing GDP in Northern Ireland towards the end of the 1986-90 period may have, in part, contributed to the improved performance of the small firm sector. Furthermore, whilst not fully benefiting from the effects of the economic boom in the UK since 1986, Northern Ireland did not experience the rapid economic downturn towards the end of 1989 and throughout 1990.

Fourth, the role of public policy is a key factor in understanding any aspect of the Northern Ireland economy. An intensive regime of grant assistance has been provided by LEDU, the Northern Ireland small business agency, with an average budget of £20 million each year (at 1991 prices) during the late 1980s to encourage job creation in small firms. Recent comparative research at the NIERC has established that LEDU has had an active role in stimulating fast growth, improving survival rates and encouraging higher rates of start-up in the small firm sector in Northern Ireland (Hart et al, 1993). LEDU-assisted firms outperformed average companies in all the comparator areas used in the analysis (i.e. Wearside, Leicestershire and the Republic of Ireland) in addition to non-assisted small firms in Northern Ireland. Further evidence has shown that the proportion of output exported by LEDU-assisted firms has been growing (Hanvey et al, 1994). Therefore, subsidised investment may be seen as offsetting the general competitive weaknesses in the Northern Ireland small firms identified by Hitchens and O'Farrell.

Why then has the availability of public sector finance for industrial development in the Republic of Ireland not had the same effects? Part of the explanation must lie with the nature and focus of that policy with its emphasis upon the attraction and development of a large externally-controlled sector at the expense of the *existing* indigenous sector. In the period 1986-90 existing externally-controlled firms in the Republic of Ireland performed considerably better than their counterparts in Northern Ireland while the level of new inward investment was much higher (Hanvey and Hart, 1994). By way of contrast, the existing indigenous sector (both large and small firms) in the Republic of Ireland declined dramatically compared to Northern Ireland.

Recent research on the indigenous manufacturing sector in Ireland has shed some light on this dichotomy. Foley and Griffith (1992, p. 385) argue that:

> most of the "good" features of manufacturing in Ireland are due to the foreign-owned firms. In 1987, they provided 61 per cent of net export earnings .....; 88 per cent of manufactured exports going to the mainland EC markets (i.e. excluding the UK) were from foreign-owned firms. By contrast, the indigenous or Irish-owned enterprises export less than one-third of output and account for one-quarter of manufactured exports . . .

Despite repeated calls for an industrial development policy aimed at creating an internationally competitive indigenous sector the emphasis would appear to be still firmly focused on the role of foreign direct investment as a vehicle for industrial growth (O'Malley, 1991; Culliton, 1992). With the publication of the Task Force on Small Business in March 1994, coupled with the recent re-organisation of the IDA to create Forbairt, whose sole responsibility will be to develop indigenous industry, there is a clear expectation that small firms will feature more strongly in future industrial development strategies (Government of Ireland, 1994).

New Indigenous Firms

As noted from the 1986-90 components of change analysis, Northern Ireland's only advantage lies with the indigenous established firms, because the Republic has a higher rate of job creation in new indigenous firms. We can examine this more closely in Table 9.11 which looks at the rate of new firm formation for the two economies. There are two figures given, the first is based on manufacturing employment, and the second on manufacturing employment plus 12 per cent of non-manufacturing employment. These formation rate calculations are based on the premise that there is a propensity for those who start new manufacturing firms to have been previously employed in the manufacturing sector. In other words the size of the manufacturing sector reflects the pool of potential entrepreneurs. It can clearly be seen that regardless of the denominator the Republic has a higher new firm formation rate, although the difference is not as great as the raw job creation figures might suggest.[4]

TABLE 9.11: NET FORMATION RATES FOR NEW FIRMS, 1986-90

	Number of Firms	Formation Rates	
		(A)	(B)
Northern Ireland	554	5.1	3.6
Republic of Ireland	1267	6.4	4.4

Source: NIERC Industrial Database, IDA Industrial Database.

(A) Manufacturing employment in 1986.
(B) Manufacturing employment plus 12 per cent of non-manufacturing in 1986.

---

[4] The data on new firm formation presented in Table 9.11 refer to *surviving* new firms and therefore, the findings for the 1986-90 period can be viewed as consistent with the general pattern observed earlier for "net" formation rates in the manufacturing sector over the longer 1980-90 period (see Table 9.4): that is, that the Republic has higher formation rates compared to those in Northern Ireland.

The explanation for this can be seen in Table 9.12 where we see that not only does the Republic have a higher rate of new firm formation than Northern Ireland, but that the average size of firms at start-up is also greater. The combination of these two effects has created 12,411 new jobs in the Republic, and this job creation has helped to offset the high level of closures in the indigenous firm sector. These two phenomenon, high formation rates and high closure rates would suggest a more volatile environment for indigenous small firms in the Republic. There are two scenarios which might explain this situation. Firstly, that a virtuous cycle was taking place within the restructuring of the small firm sector, as established firms closed in older declining industries, and new firms opened in new high-tech, high productivity sectors. Secondly, that the closures were simply replaced by new firms in the same sectors, perhaps with small productivity gains.

TABLE 9.12: EMPLOYMENT IN 1990 IN NEW FIRMS FORMED, 1986-90

	Number of Firms	Average Employment	Total	Employment % of Base Year Manufacturing
Northern Ireland	554	7.2	3,984	3.7
Republic of Ireland	1,267	9.8	12,411	6.3

Source: NIERC Industrial Database, IDA Industrial Database.

In Table 9.13 we address this issue by examining the sectors in which the new firms have been formed. The evidence from this table is not conclusive because we are unable to disaggregate the engineering sector. The general picture is one of high formation in the traditional sectors such as Footwear and Clothing, and Food and Drink. However, the high formation rate in Other Manufacturing might suggest that a degree of virtuous restructuring was taking place. The conclusions then are mixed, with continuing high formation rates in the traditional sectors, accompanied by a high level of formation in Other Manufacturing. There is some uncertainty about what is happening in the Engineering sector. What we can say, however, is that regardless of the exact nature of this restructuring it has been not insignificant for the indigenous manufacturing sector.

The sectoral balance of new firm formation in Northern Ireland shows a very large increase in the Timber and Furniture sector, clearly not one of the dynamic new sectors because of its local market focus with the attendant problems of low export potential and high displacement effects. In fact, the overall picture for Northern Ireland is one of high new firm formation in the traditional small firm sectors, such as Mechanical Engineering and Food and Drink

TABLE 9.13: NET FORMATION OF NEW FIRMS, 1986-90 BY SECTOR

Sector	Northern Ireland		Republic of Ireland	
	No.	%	No.	%
Mineral Products	32	5.8	59	4.7
Chemicals	8	1.4	52	4.1
Mechanical Engineering	89	16.1	N/A	N/A
Electrical Engineering	40	7.2	382	30.2
Other Engineering	60	10.8	N/A	N/A
Food and Drink	62	11.2	174	13.7
Textiles	15	2.7	80	6.3
Clothing and Footwear	25	4.5	143	11.3
Timber and Furniture	157	28.3	96	7.6
Printing, Paper	34	6.1	56	4.4
Other Manufacturing	32	5.8	225	17.8
Total	554	100.0	1267	100.0

Source: NIERC Industrial Database, IDA Industrial Database.

The established indigenous firms are clearly those that provide Northern Ireland with it's advantage in job creation during the 1986-90 period. The small firm sector was responsible for 10,762 gross job creations in the 1986-90 period. The larger firms make some contribution by not shedding as many jobs as their counterparts in the Republic. The majority of the jobs lost in the indigenous sector in the Republic were due to a high closure rate, a corollary of which was a high new firm formation rate. However, this was not sufficient to negate the poor performance of the established indigenous sector.

CONCLUSIONS

One of the most important conclusions to draw from the components of change analysis is that in Northern Ireland the indigenous small firms have been the most successful job creators in the manufacturing sector. In the Republic it is the externally-controlled large firm survivors and the new firm start-ups whether indigenous or external that have been the job creators during this period. How does one explain these contrasts between the two economies? Some simplistic explanations may be advanced. For example, the performance of the indigenous small firm sector in Northern Ireland can be explained by the high levels of public expenditure, supported by the £3 billion subvention from the UK exchequer, and the public service sector income that this generates. For the Republic it could be argued that it is the low rate of corporation tax, at 10 per cent, which is so attractive to externally controlled firms who use the Republic as an export base into the EU. Neither of these explanations is fully satisfactory, although both contain an element of truth.

Some recent evidence (Hanvey, Scott and Hart, 1994) indicates that the proportion of output exported by Northern Ireland small firms, assisted by LEDU, has been growing. The impact of LEDU assistance to small firms has also been estimated by the NIERC (1993) at approximately 1,000 net job creation per annum during this period, allowing for both dead-weight and displacement effects. This would suggest that not all of the growth in small firm employment is based on increased domestic market demand, fuelled by government expenditure, although clearly government assistance to the small firm sector is a component of this. In the Republic it could also be argued that the performance of the external sector reflects the skill with which the IDA has selected foreign investment projects, and that at least part of the restructuring in the indigenous sector is the result of linkages into the local economy by, and spin-offs from, the high-tech mobile investments that have set-up in the Republic.

These issues pose several questions for each economy. Firstly, for how much longer can the Republic continue to attract multinational investments at this rate? Secondly, what effect will the global restructuring that is currently taking place in the computer industry have on those firms already situated in the Republic? We have already seen the closure of the high profile Digital plant in Galway. The Republic's dependence on the externally controlled sector has also raised some important issues about their impact on the National Accounts. The recent large increases in GDP in the Republic, and its large trade surplus, have mainly been fuelled by rising output and exports in the externally controlled sector, and questions have been asked with regard to the substance of these increases. It has been suggested (Murphy, 1994) that these large increases in GDP are heavily influenced by transfer pricing practices within MNC who clearly see the 10 per cent corporation tax as a major incentive to declare profits properly accruing to plants outside the Republic in the Republic. This process artificially inflates GDP and output per employee in those industries dominated by MNCs. The way in which these MNCs repatriate their profits also causes problems for the national accounts. The beneficial tax rate in the Republic means that they do not wish to repatriate directly thereby incurring corporation or company tax at the rate prevailing in their country of origin, for this reason profits are repatriated in the form of loan to the parent company. These loans are not reported in the National Accounts. This means that the values of GNP for the Republic economy are also inflated, this clearly has serious implications for any ratios which use either of these measures as an indication of the financial soundness of the economy. Thirdly, and perhaps more importantly, what will be the long term impact of the indigenous sector's persistent decline?

For Northern Ireland the question has to be whether or not the indigenous sector, and local small firms in particular, can continue to create employment at the rate they have during this period? Essentially, was this growth the result of increasing entrepreneurship and self sustaining growth through increasing sales to export markets, or was it simply a reflection of the high levels of government expenditure and the recession proofing that this provides? Although it is unlikely, regardless of the outcome of the current "peace process" that the subvention from the UK exchequer will disappear overnight, it is very possible that it will gradually wither away. If this is the case then the question is the extent to which the indigenous manufacturing sector is supported or hindered by the high levels of government expenditure, and public sector employment, in the province? The continuing poor performance in both attracting and maintaining jobs in externally controlled companies is also an issue for Northern Ireland. However, the presence of MNEs in any economy is always something of a double edged sword, with the lack of local control and the absence of any significant attachment to the local economy making them a fickle source of employment which can be particularly volatile in recessionary periods. We have also seen in the case of the Republic that they can create a somewhat phantom economy.

Without doubt Northern Ireland has been transformed into an economy with an above average dependence on small firms. The benefits that this affords to the local economy are varied. A greater degree of diversification in the industrial structure, controlled by owner-managers with a commitment to the local economy offers a cushion against the impact of the closure and contraction of multinational investment. Nevertheless, the reliance upon indigenous growth strategies to regenerate local and regional lagging economies is fraught with difficulties for three main reasons.

First, the link between changes in employment and unemployment can be extremely weak at the regional level. This is particularly so in a small region such as Northern Ireland where job creation can be more instrumental in reducing migration and increasing participation rates than in reducing unemployment. Furthermore, the rate of job creation during a period when the national economy was experiencing a boom was not sufficient to make any significant in-roads into the region's chronic unemployment problem. Regional policies aimed at small firms are, therefore, unlikely, in the short run at least, to have any significant impact on the convergence of unemployment rates.

Second, the quality of the jobs created in small firms may be markedly different from those created elsewhere in the economy. They may, for example, be less well paid, less stable and offer considerably less protection for basic workers rights than larger firms. Too often the debate on the economic impact of small firms concentrates on the quantity of jobs at the expense of a consideration of the types of jobs being created. At first glance it may look encouraging in Northern Ireland to talk about 4,000 jobs in new start-ups and nearly 6,500 job creations in expansions (1986-90), but the important question is the quality of that employment (skill levels, gender, wage rates, hours worked etc.). In addition, there will be job losses associated with these job gains through the mechanism of displacement, which as noted above, is a very real problem in Northern Ireland, especially among the very small (less than 5 employees) firms.

Finally, it must be acknowledged that small firms are not as independent as many observers would have us believe. They operate within broader economic frameworks that involve consideration by researchers and policy-makers of the roles and strategies of large firms (indigenous and foreign). An understanding of the relationships and networks that exist between large and small firms is essential in order to comment accurately on the economic impact of new and small firms.

To translate the evidence presented above of the poor comparative performance of the Republic of Ireland in terms of new firm formation and the change in stock of indigenous firms into a call for greater policy emphasis on Irish start-ups would be overly simplistic. Therefore, small firm policy in Ireland which seeks to encourage entrepreneurship through the twin mechanisms of company start-up and subsequent growth is only *one*, albeit important, dimension of an overall industrial development strategy for regional economic development.

Such a conclusion takes us full circle to a consideration of the most appropriate forms of policy response to the problems of lagging peripheral economies. The policy implications suggest that the effectiveness of government assistance to small manufacturing firms may have waned in recent years in the Republic of Ireland, while it has been strengthened and reformed in Northern Ireland — thus, leading to the divergence in the employment performance of established small firms. However, much more research is needed before definitive statements can be made about the effectiveness of policy.

REFERENCES

Barry, F. and Hannan, A. (1995): "Multinationals and Indigenous Employment: An "Irish Disease?", Paper presented at the Irish Economics Association Annual Conference, May.

Culliton (1992): "A Time for Change: Industrial Policy for the 1990s", Report of the Industrial Policy Review Group, Dublin: The Stationary Office.

Foley, A. and Griffith, B. (1992): "Indigenous Manufacturing Enterprises in a Peripheral Economy and the Single Market: The Case of the Republic of Ireland", *Regional Studies,* 26(4): 375-386

Government of Ireland (1994): "Task Force on Small Business", Dublin: The Stationary Office.

Gudgin, G., Hart, M., Fagg, J., D'Arcy, E. and Keegan, R. (1989): "Job Generation in Manufacturing Industry 1973-86", NIERC, Belfast.

Gudgin, G., Scott, R., Hanvey, E. and Hart, M. (1995): "The Role of Small Firms in Employment Growth in Ireland North and South", Paper presented at the joint ESRI/NIERC conference on The Two Economies of Ireland, March 1995, Dublin.

Hanvey, E., Scott, R. and Hart, M. (1995): "The Performance of Northern Ireland Assisted Firms", NIERC Working Paper.

Hanvey, E. and Hart, M. (1995): "The Impact of LEDU Assistance on Small Firm Performance in Northern Ireland", Paper presented at the RSA European Conference on "Regional Futures", 6th-9th May 1995, Gothenburg, Sweden.

Hart, M. (1993): "The Labour Market Impact of New and Small Firms: Some Evidence from the 1980s" in Teague, P. (Ed.) *The Northern Ireland Economy*, London: Wishart

Hart, M., Scott, R., Keegan, R and Gudgin, G. (1993): "Job Creation in Small Firms", NIERC.

Hart, M. and Gudgin, G. (1994): "Spatial Variations in New Firm Formation in the Republic of Ireland, 1980-90", *Regional Studies*, 28(4): 367-380.

Hart, M. and Hanvey, E. (1995): "Job Generation and New and Small Firms: Some Evidence from the Late 1980s", *Small Business Economics*, 7(2), April: 97-109.

Hitchens, D.M. and O'Farrell, P.N. (1987): "The Comparative Performance of Small Manufacturing Companies in Northern Ireland and South East England", *Regional Studies*, 21(6): 547-553.

Hitchens, D.M. and O'Farrell, P.N. (1988a): "The Comparative Performance of Small Manufacturing Companies in South Wales and Northern Ireland: An Analysis of Matched Pairs", *Omega*, 116(5): 429-438.

Hitchens, D.M. and O'Farrell, P.N. (1988b): "The Comparative Performance of Small Manufacturing Companies in the Mid-West of Ireland and Northern Ireland", *Economic and Social Review*, 19(3): 177-198.

Hitchens, D.M. and Birnie, E. (1991): "The New Industrial Strategy in Northern Ireland: Will it Work?", *Irish Banking Review*, Winter: 13-22.

Keeble, D., Walker, S. and Robson, M. (1993): "New Firm Formation and Small Business Growth in the UK: Spatial and Temporal Variations and Determinants", Department of Employment Research Series No. 15.

Murphy, A.E. (1994): "The Irish Economy — Celtic Tiger or Tortoise", MMI Stockbrokers.

Murshed, M. et al (1993): "Growth and Development in the Two Economies of Ireland", NIERC and ESRI.

O'Farrell, P.N. and Crouchley, R. (1984): "An Industrial Spatial Analysis of New Firm Formation in Ireland", *Regional Studies*, 18: 221-236.

O'Malley, E. (1989): *Industry and Economic Development: The Challenge for the Latecomer*, Dublin: Gill and MacMillan.

O'Malley, E. (1991): Foreword, in Foley, A. and McAleese, D. (Eds.) *Overseas Industry in Ireland*, Dublin: Gill and Macmillan.

Storey, D.J. and Johnson, S. (1987): *Job Generation and Labour Market Change* London: Macmillan.

Storey, D.J. and Johnson, S. (1990): "A Review of Small Business Data Bases in the UK", *Small Business Economics* 2(4): 279-299.

10

LEGAL FACTORS AFFECTING ENTERPRISE: OWNERSHIP AND THE S-FIRM

Patrick McNutt

INTRODUCTION

In an enterprise culture that is pervasive across Irish firms, workers are legally entitled to a package of statutory incentives which may include bonuses, paid leave, sick leave, pension rights, redundancy awards, health benefits and overtime rates *inter alia*. This package is generally negotiated on their behalf by elected trade union officials. The incentives are supplementary to the basic wage. The productivity of the workers is monitored by management and any disagreement between management and workers on productivity, on pay or on elements of an agreed incentive package, inevitably translates into industrial action. Such a scenario is not atypical of the Irish worker-management relationship as witnessed by the Waterford Glass, Irish Steel, TEAM Aer Lingus disputes in 1993/94 and the more recent Dunnes Stores dispute.

Changes in the international political economy, in particular the increased internationalisation of business coupled with deregulation may undermine the promotion of full utilisation of labour resources. Economies like Ireland, for example, are increasingly characterised by firms engaged in batch production and niche marketing while in practice we observe a move towards smaller production sites, short production runs and a growing division of the workforce into a skills hierarchy. These observations on the corporate economy and on the nature of the enterprise may suggest a need to re-orient our understanding of ownership and entrepreneurship which have been so frequently ignored in the theory of the firm. In particular, there is the need for an approach which stresses the importance of *idiosyncratic* elements of production within the enterprise.

A different enterprise culture which may contribute to a greater realisation of productive enterprise is now on the horizon. It is best characterised by firms offering flexible working hours, minimal fringe benefits, retraining opportunities, subsidised child care while encouraging tele-working, outsourcing, sub-contracting; it is an enterprise culture interspersed with contract workers, contingent workers[1] and "portfolio workers", an enterprise culture within which it is predicted[2] that "the supply of enterprise seems destined to outstrip the demand". We refer to such firms as *s-firms* and the workers are defined as *stakeholders* in the firm, they are part of the firm, managing themselves, monitoring quality and productivity. This is in contrast to the neoclassical model, Arrow (1994, p. 7), wherein

> workers are *not part* of the firm. They are inputs purchased on the market, like raw materials or capital goods. Yet they (or some of them) carry the information base . . . . *they are neither owners* nor slaves. There is therefore *a dilemma in defining the firm* as a locus of productive knowledge [emphasis added].

Ownership and Property Rights

Earlier debates on privatisation (Prentice and Holland, 1993), revolved around the issue of "people's shares", *Volksaktiem*, and about empowerment of workers. In this chapter we focus on the empowerment of workers, and proceed to identify the hallmarks of an s-firm by introducing the Trojan horse of ownership within the s-firm. Since there is no concept of absolute ownership in law, ownership is characterised by a set of rights, for example, property rights in the use of resources by the s-firm and by different stakeholders in the s-firm. The emphasis is on providing incentives and in increasing the scale of

---

[1] Contingent workers do not have security of tenure, rather they have security of employment in the s-firm. It follows that workers in the s-firm have a greater incentive to improve work-effort to remain in employment.

[2] The concept of "portfolio worker" in Handy's (1989) *The Age of Unreason* is akin to workers in the s-firm, see *The Economist* "Career Opportunities", 8 July 1995.

profit opportunities within the s-firm rather than in insulating the worker against risks and contingencies. The s-firm is not a worker's co-operative; within a worker's co-operative ownership is *acquired* outright by the workers, whereas within the s-firm, property rights short of ownership, *accrue* to the stakeholders.

What are s-firms? If the s-firm is not a co-operative, do workers have ownership in the firm? This chapter will attempt to answer these questions. Reconciling the attributes of the s-firm with those of a more traditional neoclassical firm is a pre-requisite for an economic evaluation of profit opportunities within a modern firm. The essential point is reconciling Arrow's dilemma in defining the firm is that worker-stakeholders have property rights short of ownership, in the s-firm. The entrepreneurial skills of the workers and the s-firm are *co-special assets*; in other words, the skills, reminiscent of Becker's firm-specific human capital, complement the asset value of the s-firm. More importantly, the skills are highly specific to the s-firm in which the worker operates. In this case, the workers are at a disadvantage and any breakdown in bargaining between the workers and the owner will lead to large costs on both sides (Milgrom and Roberts, 1992). However, unless bargaining costs are prohibitive, the Coase theorem dictates that the workers and the owner will agree on some value-maximising agreement. Efficiency is not affected in this case, but the *redistribution* of the value will be skewed in favour of the owner.

This is the real social cost of *hold-up* as workers — receiving less of the value of the firm and consequently less property rights in the firm — have no incentive to improve productivity or work-effort. As argued later in section two, management failure to assign property rights across workers will reduce the amount of productive enterprise, the ϕ-factor. But where are these property rights located and in what sense are they characteristic of the s-firm? The *property right to choose how much to produce* is a reward for enterprise. The production output may be owned by the s-firm but the firm specific human capital is embodied in the worker-stakeholders. Management must realise *á la* Arrow (1994) that "embedded in workers, managers and technical personnel is an important part of the market's valuation of the capital of a firm, though not property in the usual sense".[3]

It is this realisation that behoves both workers and management to re-evaluate the worker-management relationship. In addition, workers realise independently of management that an *assurance* of collective work-effort within the s-firm (induced by an increased probability of unemployment in the s-firm's product-market coupled with less job security in general) increases the amount of productive enterprise. We suggest that changes in the Irish corporate environment is facilitating an s-firm enterprise culture. With increasing unemployment and a growing labour force, modern firms are less compelled than hithertofore to offer job security. Against this background the workers *per se* have to consider themselves as stakeholders in the firm, having property rights short of ownership in the firm, in order to create a pro-worker enterprise culture and avoid the exploitation of workers.

Economic analyses of ownership concentrates on "the possession of residual decision rights and the allocation of residual returns" (Milgrom and Roberts, 1992, p. 289). In this chapter the concept of firm ownership is broadened in order to re-examine worker-ownership, vitiating the more traditional approach to worker-ownership *vis-à-vis* co-operatives. Ownership is broadened by anchoring ownership to an intra-firm assignment of property rights (analogous to the possession of residual rights) and by releasing the legal concept of ownership from the statutory incorporation of the firm *vis-à-vis* shareholders. Our worker-stakeholder firm, the *s-firm*, is presented as an alternative to the traditional approach to the theory of the firm. The s-firm is recognisable as a proper subset of Eichner's (1985) "megacorp" which operates not one but several s-firms in each of the industries to which it belongs with each s-firm embodying (in the form of a fixed set of technical coefficients) the least-cost technology and a menu of property rights and enforceable contracts.

---

[3] Entrepreneurism suggests that senior managers do not have a monopoly on ideas in the firm and that knowledge is the firm's most valuable asset. Management are expected to exploit the superior depth of employees' talent by linking them up, see *The Economist* "The Changing Nature of Leadership", 10 June 1995.

THE DOMAIN OF PROFIT OPPORTUNITIES

Within the traditional theory of the firm, emphasis is placed on what we shall call the proprietory firm, the *p-firm*; the paradigmal example is the textbook neoclassical firm. Management's goal within such firms is long-run profit maximisation and workers are often regarded as expendable costs. In the neoclassical model, for example, the p-firm is capable of operating only a single plant with a management team limited to one or two owner-entrepreneurs. Managerial discretion is limited however as profit opportunities are diminished by conflicts within the firm, conflicts which emanate from principal-agent type problems so characteristic of the management-worker relationship. Consequently both management and worker's objectives in the p-firm begin to undermine the role of profit opportunities in ensuring the economic performance of the firm.

The p-firm is subject to decreasing returns when it expands output beyond the minimum efficient scale plant. Management make one decision continuously over time on how much to produce. Investment occurs *infrequently* in the Neoclassical p-firm but when it does occur the firm can be expected to rely on bank financing because of the firm's inability to generate funds internally. The decision on the amount of employment is *left to the firm* (Blanchard and Fischer, 1989). With such hallmarks the environment of a p-firm is *not conducive* to realising profit opportunities as the legitimacy of worker's rights within the firm is relegated to short term objectives. In the p-firm, management "is more nearly the essential definition of the firm" (Arrow, 1994, p. 7). Furthermore, the most successful companies rely on a process of entrepreneurism which can be better accommodated within the framework of the s-firm.

Competitiveness increasingly depends on how work is organised and on the work- effort within the firm (Kogut, 1993). We therefore attempt to articulate intra-firm distributional concerns which may impinge on the level of profit opportunities available to the worker-stakeholders in the s-firm. The notion of the s-firm with its jointness characteristic and attendant rent-dissipation (incomplete contracting) offers a basis for ownership. In particular, by applying this concept of ownership across workers in the firm, the labour input is *commodified* and terms like "worker", and "employee" are replaced by the term "worker-stakeholder" or stakeholder. The supply of enter-prise is the source of ownership. Management's role, therefore, is to assign the property rights within the firm without invalidating the work-effort. Their role affects enterprise and output.

Change of Ownership

The s-firm is an organisation of pairwise individuals; the atmosphere within the firm is co-operative rather than adversarial. As pairwise individuals the stakeholders realise that their respective contributions to the work-effort are not necessarily mutually exclusive. In other words, any dispute within the firm can be resolved by compromise and negotiation. In particular, any dispute over the use of real resources within the firm can be so resolved. One thinks of ownership from the perspective of shareholders or workers' co-operatives, where ownership translates into shares or an intangible stake in the firm. As alluded to earlier, ownership is about property rights and the nature of the s-firm allows worker-stakeholders to have a property right short of ownership in the firm, contingent on an enforceable contract (see below) between the worker-stakeholder and the s-firm.

The legal nature of the s-firm, for the purposes of this chapter, is principally about the assignment of those property rights and the elimination of quasi-rents. For example, an inequitable assignment of rights and the existence of quasi-rents generate conflict within the p-firm and undermine the level of productive profit opportunities available to that firm. In other words, rights and quasi-rents circumscribe the conduct of enterprise and the intra-firm (stakeholder) conflict retards the scale of profit opportunities. The nature of the s-firm, however, is such that it represents the embodiment of property rights across the various stakeholders in the firm. The firm uses the real resources of society in order to produce; the rights to the use of the resources are privately held by each worker-stakeholder.

Each stakeholder has a property right, φh, in the use of real resources by the firm. For the worker-stakeholder, the property right is invested in their respective work- effort; instead of taking the p-firm view that higher wages are paid to encourage increased work-effort, higher wages are considered as a means to *assure* increased work-effort when the work-effort cannot be observed before a productive opportunity is realised but only experienced in the course of employment (Nelson, 1970; Holler, 1987). Labour is assumed to be an *experi-*

ence good for the s-firm and the work-effort is not exogenously enforced. The work-effort solution proposed by McNutt (1995), implies
that a work-effort better than a minimum is self-enforcing and subject to an enforceable contract.

Consequently the level of enterprise activity depends on φh, the
worker-stakeholder's share in the s-firm. The property right short of
ownership assigned to a worker-stakeholder, for example, translates
into his or her right to choose how much to produce. This is denied
the worker in the p-firm. Therefore the s-firm incorporates a twin set
of realistic microeconomic elements, enforceable contracts and property rights, and is located in an economy of heterogenous s-firms en-
meshed in a web of intricate stakeholder conflicts. The stakeholders
engage in a contracting system of co-ordination and information
sharing as a solution to the stakeholder conflict. The idea is not without precedent in history with the guild system in early industrial
Europe and the kinship networks in Tokugawa Japan.

Commodification

Primarily, the s-firm acts as an allocating mechanism for the transfer
of property rights and economic rents across the contracting stakeholders. It is inevitable that conflict will arise in the assignment of
property rights. For example, the worker-stakeholders may disagree
with management on work practices or productivity awards. For each
stakeholder there is an expectation of greater *employment* security. As
an organisation dependent on stakeholder harmony, the s-firm management is disciplined by each stakeholder's right to convert their
respective expectations into a near-contractual obligation, backed by
law. This could manifest itself in the demand for health and safety
regulations or in the implementation of unfair dismissals legislation
inter alia.

However, the corporate environment has dramatically changed.
The epoch of organised capitalism or Fordism based on mass production and semi-skilled labour and an interventionist government, has
been replaced by a new period of disorganised capitalism. In this new
post-Fordist era, Pierson (1994) comments that:

> These new circumstances will not see the wholesale withdrawal of
> the state from intervention in the organisation and reproduction of

labour power. Indeed the role of the state and the movement in and out of paid work may be enhanced.

In what Offe (1984) calls "administrative recommodification", the role of government in promoting fuller utilisation or commodification of capital and labour will emerge indirectly through corporate tax concessions, training programmes and subsidised industrial loans *inter alia*. The Irish government could have inadvertently adopted this strategy of administrative recommodification — in practice, however, it promotes a process of decommodification, that is, it undermines the circumstances for a fuller utilisation of labour resources. This is reflected in the continually high price of Irish labour through PRSI payments, in the continual welfare trap between employed and unemployed welfare entitlements, in the toleration of profit repatriation by foreign companies and in the inability of government to create productive employment.

The Technology Set of the S-Firm

We define the technology of the s-firm whose netputs are denoted by vector z as $f(z) \leq 0$, and if X-inefficiency is present $f(z) < 0$. Assume that X-inefficiency depends on the change of ownership of the firm. The change of ownership can come about in either of two ways (a) a re-alignment of property rights within the s-firm or in the transition from p-firm to s-firm and (b) a change in the corporate environment in which the s-firm operates. The change may have been precipitated by privatisation, mergers or acquisitions.

A first intuitive approach would assume that changing the ownership shifts the production function represented by the production possibility frontier $f(z) + F(H) = 0$ with the inefficiency function $F(H) \geq 0$, decreasing in H if the change of ownership within the s-firm or from the p-firm to the s-firm leads to more profit opportunities. If every worker-stakeholder, h, has a share, φh, in the s-firm, then $H = \Sigma$ $h\varphi h$ is an ownership parameter where $H = 1$ represents the p-firm, H = 0 represents a public (state-owned or a worker's co-operative) firm and $0 < H < 1$ represents the s-firm. The (property right) "gain" to each worker-stakeholder in the s-firm is contingent on individual compliance to an increased work-effort as monitored by the ϕ-factor, that is, an increased commodification of the labour input.

By assuming an additive structure of the production function, Bos (1987), changes in the extent of ownership will also influence the variable costs of production. In other words, productive profit opportunities arise because the production possibility frontier is moved in such a way that *given* worker-stakeholder inputs produce *more* output (that is, Q* > Q1) as illustrated by shaded area in Figure 10.1. This will impact on the measure of productivity within the firm as the marginal productivities will depend on H. The management team have the responsibility for ensuring compliance in order to realise the profit opportunities as they arise. Failure to assign property rights across worker-stakeholders will be reflected in the amount of productive enterprise, the φ-factor.

FIGURE 10.1: EFFECTIVE HOURS WORKED

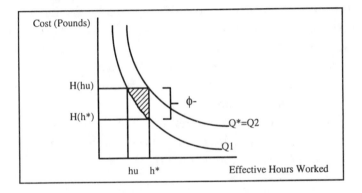

Productive Demand for Enterprise

In the s-firm, co-ordination failure is unlikely to occur if an enforceable contract exists between management and the worker-stakeholders. With workers as stakeholders, management have a different set of problems with which to contend. The worker-stakeholder is not short-sighted in the sense of sacrificing wages for higher profits, rather, the worker may discount the present value of a management decision in order to assess the benefit to the worker-stakeholder group in the firm. Elsewhere we have made the argument that the output level at which traditional productivity (average productivity gL) is measured, assumes full capacity utilisation of real resources (denoted by Q^*).

Full capacity utilisation requires of each worker-stakeholder a level of maximum work- effort and mandates the smooth and uninterrupted progress of work. Apart from mechanical failures, there is every incentive for a worker to shirk, that is, to supply a less than maximum work-effort, unless there is some assurance in the firm that all worker-stakeholders are not shirking. Alternatively, the incidence of absenteeism will ensure that output is not at the full capacity utilisation level. Worker-stakeholders have an interest in consolidating productivity levels and ensuring that the Q^* level is reached within the s-firm. A more traditional p-firm average product measure gL is denoted by Q_1/L_1 and neoclassical theory dictates that gL increases to Q_2/L_2, if $Q_2 > Q_1$ and $L_2 > L_1$ or Q_1/L_1 increasing until diminishing returns sets in. In the s-firm the intuition is rather different: an increased utilisation output level, Q^*, reached by the no-shirking L_1 worker-stakeholders may record an average productivity measure, Q_1/L_1 increasing to Q^*/L_1 with (i) $Q^* = Q_1 + \phi$ and (ii) $Q_1 < Q^* \leq Q_2$ with L_1 constant. The ϕ-factor reflects *the workers ability to choose the amount they work or produce*, an ability denied workers in the p-firm in a Keynesian economy.

A p-firm approach would attribute all of the slowdown in European productivity growth after 1979 to the real wage and cyclical effects. Gordon (1987) once commented that:

> The counterpart of rising unemployment is, of course, slow or negative growth in *labour hours*. Obviously some part of the European unemployment problem results from output falling below trend. . . . [b]ut it also possible to look at the implications for labour hours of the underlying trends in output and productivity [emphasis added].

In the interim, consider Figure 10.1 where *effective hours* worked is measured on the horizontal axis and H(h), average variable cost (the reciprocal of average productivity) is measured on the vertical axis. The reciprocal H(h) is negatively correlated with effective hours worked. The measured difference [H(hu) — H(h*)] is a proxy measure of the opportunity cost to the s-firm at the production level Q1 of failure to assign property rights across the workers. For example, the standard contract is (say) a 40 hour week at h*, but with shirking and conflict *inter alia* the effective number of hours worked is only hu < h*, the average variable cost increases to H(hu). Consequently (with average productivity falling) *the real cost of hiring workers* at h* increases to H(hu) with Q1 production. Since each worker-stakeholder has a share, φh, which translates into a property right, the value of that right is now reduced (for example, employment may no longer be secure within the s-firm). It is only with increased work-effort that the effective hours are increased to the contracted number of hours H(h*).

The φ-factor

With improved work-effort and capacity utilisation, Q1 increases to Q* in Figure 10.1 by the φ-factor. In other words, the increase in labour productivity, gL, can be equivalent to an increased utilisation or commodification of the labour units in the s-firm. It is important to note in this context that greater work-effort is the same as greater efficiency.[4] The computation of average product is not with respect to *changes in the numbers employed*, denoted by the increase from L_1 to L_2 but rather with respect to a higher Q* output level being reached which is *greater than the actual measured capacity output*, denoted by Q1. For a given number of worker-stakeholders, the average productivity can increase, with no change in output *per se* but with an increase in the utilisation of the productive resources. By investing ownership in the workers whose hidden-action most affects the value of the resources of the firm, a hold-up problem is avoided and the average productivity for all worker-stakeholders can increase with a complementary increase in the utilisation of the productive resources and a positive change in output *per se* to Q* = Q2 > Q1.

---

[4] It has been reported (see *Financial Times*, 14 November 1994, p. 19) that some modern firms casually talk about moving its output towards (say) 130 per cent of rated capacity. It is hard to capture this increased capacity in the official statistics. A belief structure that increased work hours are required for job security is beginning to emerge; increased work hours, however, do not create greater efficiency or productivity for the s-firm unless there is an increased in effective hours. This requires an assignment of rights and an assurance across workers that there are no free riders on effort.

Within the s-firm there is no reason for the wage to be equal to the marginal product of labour. As in a Barro-Hall world, wage-rigidity is irrelevant for employment determination in the s-firm world. What is important for employment creation is an increase in capacity utilisation to Q^* due to reduced shirking and greater work- effort from worker-stakeholders and the ability of management in high-wage firms to screen and obtain a higher quality labour force. The improved work-effort arises from an enforceable contract between management and the workers. For output to be produced at the Q^* level, management has to ensure that the interests of the worker-stakeholders, interests which may range from an improvement in working conditions to the level of real wages to the level of profit opportunities, are satisfied.

In this context the decision on the amount of employment is contingent on the behaviour of the worker-stakeholders. The approach subscribes to the new-Keynesian view that nominal rigidities do not originate in the labour market. Within the s-firm, hiring and firing is less common than in the more traditional p-firm. Management create synergies across the worker-stakeholders which enables each stakeholder acquire their respective property right. In other words, property rights within the s-firm are more clearly defined as the firm-specific resources become more valuable. In the s-firm, zero transactions costs arise as the costs of negotiating, policing and enforcing contracts are zero.

Enforceable Contracts

Conflicts across worker-stakeholders and management which may impact on the growth of the s-firm are possible, and the conflicts ought to be resolved. The problem may arise due to the hierarchical structure in modern firms which requires of each worker or manager a supply of work-effort and entrepreneurial talent respectively. While each individual stakeholder is contracted to the firm there is no such contract, implicit or otherwise, between the stakeholders. Consequently some managers and workers may be unwilling to supply their respective skills. Within a given organisation the competitive hierarchical structures may even militate against the sharing of entrepreneurial skills. It is the nature of the s-firm that every effort is made to ameliorate any adversarial fallout from the hierarchical structure.

This can be achieved by enforceable contracts within the s-firm, in other words by coerced transfers of property rights in return for compensation, that is by *coerced compensated contracts* (McNutt, 1995).

In the enforceable contract the passive party is obliged to render a personal service, that is, obliged to do something and get a financial reward in return or a public good within the firm (an assurance that all other workers are *not* shirking) or a share in the capital value of the firm. Enforceable contracts in the s-firm coincide with increasing monitoring and manipulation of the payoffs to both workers and management so that monitoring becomes a dominant strategy and compliance becomes the only best reply. Each worker-stakeholder realises that other stakeholders can adopt positions which conflict with their own. Indeed any worker-stakeholder has the capacity to respond in such a way as to disadvantage the other stakeholders in this game of shirking-monitoring, thus retarding profit opportunities within the s-firm. The intuition behind the outcome in McNutt (1995) is that the worker-stakeholders realise the diseconomies (for example, loss of employment or closure of the s-firm) in supplying anything *less* than maximum effort.

In each specific case where stakeholders shirk, there is an element of conflict which has to be resolved. Indeed a co-operative solution in which neither stakeholder opts to supply the work-effort, is not uncharacteristic of some peer structures in the p-firm. The time and effort into the resolution of the dispute translates into high opportunity costs for the s-firm and thus high costs for the worker-stakeholders. In other words, for a representative worker-stakeholder, the opportunity cost of co-ordinating failure is positive — the opportunity cost argument has a parallel in Leibenstein's X-inefficiency where the real resources of the firm are channelled into unproductive areas of activity which may adversely affect the long term viability of the firm.

THE CORPORATE LANDSCAPE

In the competitive environment in which the s-firm operates there is an increased probability of unemployment, therefore the real resources of the s-firm are valuable to all the worker-stakeholders. In the modern corporate environment the structure of property rights between stakeholders and across worker-stakeholders in the representative firm has changed — the irrelevance of the p-firm is captured rather well by DeAlessi (1983), quoting Alchian: "[d]ifferent systems of property rights present decision makers with different structures of incentives, resulting in different alignment of resources".

Unless different incentive structures are put in place in the modern firm to reflect the different ownership structures, worker-stakeholders will continue to realise quasi-rents, thus retarding productive opportunities as they arise within the p-firm. The level of enterprise activity will depend on the assignment of worker-stakeholder rights. In a climate of job losses, stakeholder conflicts will arise, impinging negatively upon the realisation of productive enterprise in the firm. However, if the worker-stakeholder's property right in the s-firm can be compensated, increased work-effort may buffer the workers within the firm against layoffs. Albeit, across the landscape of Irish corporate business *ownership is changing*. There appears to be an increasing lack of sensitivity to unemployment, the emergence of an anti-trades union lobby and little retraining of the workforce, factors which affect both the supply and demand for enterprise. The issue of ownership raises the question: in whose interests should the firm be run? In this chapter, the answer is in the interest of the workers.

The Irish Commercial Law Environment

Companies incorporated by an Act of Oireachtas are candidates for privatisation while the private sector is in the crest of a mergers and acquisitions boom:

> 1994 so far has seen Smurfit in a deal worth £683m, CRH piling up acquisitions worth £44m in the US, Fitzwilton buying out its partner's stake in Wellworth for £43m and Green purchasing Na Mara for £42m. Last year the total value of the 83 acquisitions made amounted to £455m. This year's figure could be three times as high (*Business and Finance*, 1 September 1994).

A contributory factor, apart from the economic and financial indicators, is the drive towards competitiveness and efficiency. Surprisingly there is popular acquiescence in the erosion of the labour base and in a diminution in labour rights that is increasingly coupled with gaining competitiveness. The economic benefits of privatisation, it is true, include the substitution of the ownership of shares for non-negotiable assets such as the citizen's shareholding in a public sector enterprise.

The new ownership structure, however, can only improve the role of labour and management once the old structure of property rights has been changed and quasi-rents eliminated. One must remember that the X-inefficiencies in the public sector enterprise may have contributed to its rather unsatisfactory performance as measured by increasing indebtedness.

Traditional p-firm ownership continues to underpin Irish company law in the Berle-Means tradition of separation between owner-shareholders and management. In Irish company law, for example, there are different types of companies which may be *incorporated* by registration under the Companies Acts 1963-1990. Companies limited by shares which represents the majority of companies where liability to creditors is limited to paying the full amount payable on their shares. Public companies are defined by the Companies (Amendment) Act 1983, are limited by shares, they are public and comply with the requirement as to registration, in particular, that the share capital is to be not less than an authorised minimum. Any company that is not a public company is a private company. A small number of public companies are quoted on the stock exchange. The name of a public company must end with the words "public limited company", plc. In a more s-firm culture, labour rights would be protected, that is, *contracted-in* company law analogous to the labour rights *contracted-in* the production technology of the s-firm.

Fair Behaviour

The modern enterprise which has emerged in Ireland in this century has paralleled the developments in financial markets, management techniques and corporate law. One particular area of the law which increasingly impinges on enterprise is commercial law. In the commercial world in which the enterprise operates, the business activities are under the scrutiny of both company law guidelines and competition law precedents. From the point of view of management of a modern enterprise, the laws and regulations governing business activity could be divided into two spheres of impact, *vis-à-vis* a demand side impact and a supply side impact.

The danger in such an approach, however, is to relegate competition policy to having a demand side impact only on the firm's behaviour. By default, every other piece of legislation would inevitably impact on the supply side of the enterprise. Regulations on work practices and product safety guidelines, for example, would enter the production function while conditions of sale both on the quantity and price of the service or product would remain governed by competition policy. What remains at issue in competition policy is the interpretation of *fair behaviour*; albeit, what is perceived to be fair may just simply reflect *acceptable* business practices. In Ireland pre-1991, the behaviour of both public and private monopoly firms was beyond the remit of restrictive practices legislation.

Connected Person

In the case of plc's, any person who acquires an interest in 5 per cent or more of the issued shares having unrestricted voting rights, must inform the Company of the acquisition of that interest. Failure to comply with the notification obligations is an offence and will mean that no right of interest relating to the shares concerned may be enforced by action or legal proceedings. Furthermore a plc is entitled to carry out investigations into the *true ownership* of interests in its shares. The holders of 10 per cent or more of the paid-up voting share capital of the Company may, having given reasonable grounds, require the Company to carry out such an investigation. This mitigates any serious principal-agent co-ordination problem arising within the firm.

A holder of voting shares in a listed plc must give notice to the Stock Exchange when the holders interests increases or decreases through a series of thresholds of the Company's issued shares having unrestricted voting rights. The Stock Exchange must then publish this information. Part V of the 1990 Companies Act contains the statutory provisions against insider dealing. The Act makes it unlawful to deal in securities:

> a person who is or has been in the previous six months "connected" with a Company is in possession of information that is not generally available but which if it were, would be likely materially to affect the price of the securities.

The term "connected person" is of crucial importance and is defined as:

a *natural person* who is an officer of or shareholder in the Company or related Company or has a professional, business or *other relationship with the Company* or related Company or is an officer of a substantial (5 per cent of nominal share capital) shareholder in the Company or a related Company [emphasis added].

Within the Companies Act, a connected person, "a natural person who ... has ... (an)*other relationship with the Company*" would be analogous to the stakeholder; a connected person is important in law and in defining ownership within the s-firm.

New Rules of the Game

However, business enterprises in general are affected by a range of public policies and in many instances the policies are *captured* by the successful lobbying of the business sector. Firms and industries across the world differ greatly by age and product group, they differ by size and style of ownership, $0 \leq H \leq 1$: consequently there is *no homogenous business environment*. Traditionally there remains intact, in most countries, including Ireland, a group of natural monopolies in the provision of public utilities, which differ from the private shareholder company, paradigmal of the private sector and so easily identified in antibusiness lobbies. The new rules of competition are contained in Section 4 of the 1991 Irish Competition Act which prohibits anti-competitive agreements and arrangements and Section 5 which prohibits the abuse of a dominant position. In the absence of any general proscription on anti-competitive behaviour in Ireland pre-1991, monopoly firms continued unencumbered by restrictive practices law. By 1992 it could be reported, in the *Annual Report* of the Competition Authority that "No monopoly was ever referred for investigation by the Commission and, accordingly, no order was made in respect of any monopoly" (p. 3).

The 1991 Act augurs well for the future of Irish competition policy in general. The premise underpinning competition legislation is the attempt to curtail monopoly power under the subterfuge of protecting the consumer. Lawyers have argued that Part IV of the 1991 Act construes the word "monopoly" as being a reference to an abuse of a dominant position for the purposes of the Act. Section 16 amends Section 5 of the 1978 Act by providing for the notification to the Minister of a proposed merger or take-over, while Sections 6-9 of the 1978

Act are also amended so as to provide for investigation on subsequent reporting by the Competition Authority of any notified merger or take-over. The principle is inscribed in the preamble to the 1991 Irish Competition Act:

> An Act to prohibit, by analogy with Articles 85 and 86 of the Treaty establishing the European Economic Community, and in the interests of the common good, the prevention, restriction or distortion of competition and the abuse of dominant positions in trade in the State, to establish a Competition Authority (p. 3).

The Act also established a new independent body, the Competition Authority to replace the Fair Trade Commission. The rules apply to "all agreements between *undertakings*, decisions by association of undertakings and *concerted practices* (emphasis added)". The term undertaking is nowhere defined in the EC Treaty (of Rome 1957). However, the EC Court of Justice and the EC Commission have used it to cover any entity engaged in economic or commercial activities; it is the proverbial firm or enterprise introduced in microeconomics texts; throughout the literature the words "firm", "enterprise" and "undertaking" are used interchangeably, while the emphasis here is on the nature of the s-firm.

Take-overs and acquisitions are about shareholder ownership; there is a high cost of defending against the transfer of ownership of a company. Mergers, however, are planned in advance as ownership is relinquished for a price nominated in earnings per share. Competition policy focuses on mergers *per se* which enable competitor firms to share the market and to improve their post-merger dominant position. In such a situation there is a need to monitor the activities of the merged firm particularly its pricing policy and cost rationalisation policies which tend to translate into layoffs or plant closures, thus violating labour rights. The decision to apply Section 4(1) to mergers in Ireland affords the Authority the luxury of "policing" modern business rationalisation plans which *may* include mergers and acquisitions with the covert intent of lessening competition.

WORKER-STAKEHOLDER AFFILIATION

The corporate governance literature distinguishes between the enterprise-orientated approach and the company-orientated approach. The enterprise-orientated approach, with its clearest expression in Germany and the Netherlands, differs from the company-orientated approach with respect to ownership and power structures within the enterprise. In the Anglo-Saxon company-orientated model, for example, the securities market and more effectively the institutional investors, monitor the p-firm with the maximisation of shareholders wealth as the primary short-term objective. This has arisen because of the wide share distribution across p-firms and the constant risk of take-over and bankruptcy. Within the enterprise-orientated approach, the monitoring by shareholders is rather different, geared towards development and to the long term success of the business, not to the short-term profits.

Legal Basis of Ownership

In these enterprises, entrepreneurial ownership, family ownership and closely held control is more characteristic with control transferred by private negotiations. The economics of the s-firm belongs to an enterprise-orientated approach. In any discussion of the firm emphasis is unduly placed on the organisational structure; either unidimensional as in the case of the small firm where the owner is the manager or multidimensional as witnessed by the layers of bureaucracy in a large modern corporation. Inevitably conflicts of interest will emerge between principals (the owners) and agents (the management team), but what are the implications of the separation between ownership and control for the realisation of profit opportunities within the s-firm? Our reply to this question would contend that issue of ownership in an ownership-control dichotomy is of secondary importance to the issue of ownership which assigns property rights within the s-firm.

The neoclassical profit maximisation p-firm model diminishes the importance of the long standing debate in the theory of the firm literature concerning the separation between ownership and control. The body of evidence in the international literature disputes the relevance of the separation doctrine in assessing the performance of the firm. Larner (1966) concluded his study:

> On the basis of the evidence presently available, I conclude that, although control is separated from ownership in most of America's

largest corporations, the effects on the profit orientation of firms and on stockholders welfare have been minor (p. 66).

In a later article, DeAlessi (1973) was rather more forthright in his criticism of the proponents of the doctrine when he commented:

> The empirical evidence so far does not provide a definitive test of the hypothesis that different degrees of dispersion imply different outcomes to the firm's decision process.

Privatisation programmes in the 1980s, with their wider share-ownership and the creation of a market for corporate control on the stock exchange, have not increased accountability or reduced bureaucracy. Ownership impacts on a set of property rights. These property rights may vary between different capitalist countries but it is imperative that they do not differ across stakeholders within each country. Public limited companies or firms are generally considered to belong to the private sector. Government, however, could still own some of the shares. Although privatisation can be interpreted as a reduction in the role of government in the economy it is still quite possible that privatisation may be a ruse for government involvement in the economy, principally as a stakeholder in a privatised firm. Inefficient legal provisions, for example, and failure to determine the hierarchy within the privatised p-firm may precipitate an imperfect allocation of property rights. This would paradoxically relegate the behaviour of the privatised firm to that reminiscent of the firm when it was state-managed or government controlled.

Who Are the Owners?

The transnational corporation, TNC, has changed the legal and political dimensions of the business environment; Stopford and Strange (1991, p209) refer to a "new triangular diplomacy":

> The dominant structural changes in the world of today and tomorrow are likely to be global, perhaps regional *but not national or local*. These changes directly affect national options and the feasible forms of adjustment within states. They have heightened the importance of the new dimensions of diplomacy — the bargaining between governments and firms, especially multinationals and bargaining among firms (emphasis added).

This may augur badly for the corporate landscape in Ireland, a landscape that increasingly relies on foreign-owned firms for employment growth and export potential in a declining manufacturing sector. Their impact has an important bearing on public policies towards big business in Ireland. They affect the local economy through jobs and sub-contracts, while also affecting the quality and pace of life in rural communities. From an ownership perspective, the majority of manufacturing firms in the Irish economy are foreign-owned firms who either proffer piece-rate incentive contracts or encourage outside procurement, both of which introduce systems of management which are anathema to the types adopted by more traditional p-firms. Furthermore, there is a re-emergence of mergers and acquisitions both in Ireland and across the world, due in part to a realisation that mergers improve productivity and benefit shareholders. From an economic perspective there is some foreign supply in domestic Irish oligopolistic markets which may discipline firms.

The APSS Scheme

The idea of owning part of the company you work for is generally associated with small family businesses or with the more recent "share options" available to senior management of large TNCs. The introduction of the *Approved Profit Sharing Scheme* (APSS) by the Irish government in 1982 represented an attempt to introduce incentives into firm ownership by allowing employees to acquire shares up to an agreed amount and to sell them tax free after five years. The tax free shares must be provided under an APSS as recognised by the Irish Revenue Commissioners. A decision in the 1995 Budget to increase the value of shares to £10,000 from a previous low of £2,000 is a welcome addition although the scheme may only be relevant to quoted companies or companies which plan to be quoted, otherwise the workers have shares with no equivalent market value attached. It would be imperative for the success of the scheme to recognise the APSS as a performance related scheme allowing the worker-stakeholder to acquire more shares when certain targets are actually met.

Furthermore, labour rights would be protected within the s-firm, that is, rights are *contracted-in* the organisation and into the production technology of the firm. A contributory factor in analysing ownership, apart from the economic and financial indicators, is the drive towards competitiveness and efficiency. Surprisingly there is acquiescence in the erosion of the labour base and a diminution in labour rights that are increasingly coupled with gaining competitiveness. The economic benefits of privatisation, it is true, include the substitution of the ownership of shares for non-negotiable assets such as the citizen's shareholding in a public sector enterprise. The new ownership structure, however, can only improve the role of labour and management once the old structure of property rights has been changed and quasi-rents eliminated. One must remember that the X-inefficiencies in the public sector enterprise may have contributed to its rather unsatisfactory performance as measured by increasing indebtedness. Recall from section two earlier that each worker-stakeholder has a share, φh, which translates into a property right. It is that property right which is captured by the *effective* hours per worker-stakeholder.

In conventional models of the p-firm the labour supply remains non-descript. The debate on explaining macroeconomic performance swings in favour of the relative flatness of the supply function and the existence of real rigidities in the market. But there remain some intriguing dimensions on real world firm data which do not fit squarely with the underlying theories. In particular we note the discrepancy across measures of labour productivity and *the paradox of employment setting*, that is, while unions are prepared to negotiate wages the decision on the amount of employment is left to the p-firm. This is not the case in the s-firm. One is reminded (Eichner, 1985, p95) of the importance of employment creation:

> The *amount of employment being generated* is the single most significant factor in determining the rate at which new skills and competencies are being added by the labour force, and thus the single most significant factor in determining the society's long-run potential growth rate. The rate at which employment opportunities are being generated is certainly *more critical* to the skill acquisition process than all the sums spent on education and other forms of training (emphasis added).

Here we challenge the conventional approach to the demand for and supply of labour which assumes that they are independent. Labour in the s-firm world is subdivided into (a) demand for and supply of entrepreneurs and (b) access to jobs. The latter is well documented in the literature from the segmented labour market thesis of Ginzberg (1976) and his team at Columbia University to the labour queue theory of Thurow (1976) to the screening hypothesis in human capital theory. In the traditional firm it is the absence of co-ordination and information which eventually triggers the dispute and the inability of both management and workers to co-ordinate becomes the touchstone for further disputes. We develop this elsewhere in McNutt (1995).

Rent-seeking and X-inefficiency

An important concern for management is whether or not the allocation of property rights can reduce rent-seeking and X-inefficiencies in the s-firm. McNutt (1995) introduces an enforceable contract as a possible mechanism for resolving the dispute. The contract is a rights allocation mechanism, a general self-interested process for ensuring the transfer of rights and the transfer of rents across the different worker-stakeholders in the s-firm. Within the domain of neo-institutional economics, (Eggertsson, 1990), for example, it is the rules of the game that determine the extent of the negative contribution of the amount of real resources devoted to the dispute. The rules of the game within the s-firm requires enforceable contracts between stakeholders in the first instance.

A theory of property rights as applied to the s-firm requires a complete theory of the firm. In the absence of a clear definition of what the firm is, except a coalition of competing stakeholders, one may have to incorporate a rent-seeking dimension into the theory of property rights. The s-firm organisation as a coalition of competing stakeholders contributes to the dissipation of quasi-rents. Rent-seeking behaviour is a necessary information activity in an otherwise disaggregated s-firm organisation. However, the rent-seeking literature does not explicitly mention property rights, although *undesirable* rent-seeking may be interpreted as an abridgement of someone's property rights in an *unwilling transfer*. Sisk (1985) identifies the unwilling uncompensated transfers as the essence of the undesirable Tullock-Posner-Krueger rent-seeking. Quasi-rents are positive when property rights are unassigned within the s-firm. Posner (1974) had earlier advanced the idea that property rights will be more clearly defined as the resources become more valuable. Worker-stakeholders will be prepared to enter into near formal contracting arrangements with the s-firm in return for a property right share, φh (of the value of the firm); the share may manifest itself in job security during periods of high unemployment in the industry, better working conditions or in the ability to choose the amount of work effort.

CONCLUDING COMMENTS

While the economic analyses of ownership within organisations concentrates on residual rights, a legal basis of ownership across workers within the firm is not fully explored in the literature. Unresolved ownership issues — popularised in the literature as co-ordination failures — may retard the scale of profit opportunities within any enterprise. The economic characteristics of the traditional p-firm, where ownership revolves around private shareholders may not be conducive to exploiting profit opportunities. In this chapter a new approach for evaluating ownership within the firm is presented with emphasis placed on the worker-stakeholder firm, the *s-firm*. The level of enterprise activity depends on the assignment of the worker-stakeholders' property right in the s-firm, which translates into the right *to choose how much to produce*, a reward for enterprise which is denied workers in the Keynesian world of enterprise activity.

As an organisation dependent on worker-stakeholder harmony, the s-firm is disciplined by each stakeholder's right to convert their respective expectations into a near-contractual obligation. Thus economic performance across firms depends upon *commodified* labour and *enforceable contracts*, thus ensuring a supply of worker-stakeholders whose best reply strategy is no-shirking. The contract between worker and the s-firm is analogous to a rights allocation mechanism, a general self-interested process for ensuring the willing transfer of rights and the transfer of rents across the different worker-stakeholders in the s-firm for reward. It is therefore incumbent upon management to adapt productive opportunities within the s-firm by assuring maximum work-effort across worker-stakeholders and mobilising ownership in order to realise the productivity-enhancing activities of the s-firm.

Productive enterprise in any developed economy is about ownership and about worker ownership in particular. In an attempt to release the concept of worker ownership from a worker co-operatives bias, the s-firm is introduced which interprets the worker-stakeholders as having a transferable (property) right in the firm. In other words, the property right short of ownership translates into a reward for enterprise, the right to choose *how much* to produce. The *enforceable contract* is analogous to a rights allocation mechanism for ensuring the willing transfer of rights (and the transfer of rents) across different worker-stakeholders in the s-firm, for reward. Worker-stakeholders in the s-firm realise the economic disadvantages of supplying anything *less* than maximum work-effort. It behoves management to mobilise worker ownership in order to realise the productive opportunities of the s-firm.

REFERENCES

Arrow, K. (1994): *Information and the Organization of Industry,* Milan: Lectio Magistalis, Catholic University of Milan.

Blanchard, O.J. and Fischer, S. (1989): *Lectures on Macroeconomics,* Cambridge, MA: MIT Press.

Bos, D. (1987): "Privatisation of Public Enterprises", *European Economic Review,* 31: 352-360.

DeAlessi, C. (1983): "Property Rights, Transactions Costs and X-Inefficiency: An Essay in Economic Theory", *American Economic Review,* 73: 64-81.

Eggertsson, T. (1990): *Economic Behaviour and Institutions,* Cambridge, MA: Cambridge University Press.

Eichner, A.S. (1985): *Toward a New Economics,* Basingstoke: Macmillan.

Ginzberg, E. (1976): *The Human Economy,* New York: McGraw Hill .

Gordon, R. (1987): "Productivity, Wages and Prices Inside and Outside of Manufacturing in the US, Japan and Europe", *European Economic Review,* 31: 685-733.

Holler, M. (1987): "Labour Quality Strategies", *Aarhus University Memo ,* No. 1987-24.

Kogut, B. (1993): *Country Competitiveness: Technology and the Organisation of Work,* Oxford: Oxford University Press.

Larner, R.J. (1966): "Ownership and Control in the 300 Largest Non-Financial Corporations 1929-1963", *American Economic Review*, 56, September: 13-37.

Leibenstein, H. (1966): "Allocative Efficiency and X-Efficiency", *American Economic Review*, 56: 392-415.

McNutt, P. (1992): *Competition Policy and the 1991 Irish Competition Act*, Centre in Economics and Law, CIEL, University of Ulster at Jordanstown.

McNutt, P. (1995): "Legal Factors Affecting Enterprise: Ownership and the s-Firm", CIEL Working Paper WP 05/95, University of Ulster at Jordanstown.

Milgrom, P. and Roberts, J. (1992): *Economics, Organisation and Management*, London: Prentice Hall.

Nelson, P. (1970): "Information and Consumer Behaviour", *Journal of Political Economy*, 78: 311-329.

Offe, C. (1984): *Contradictions of the Welfare State*, London: Hutchinson.

Pierson, C. (1994): *Beyond the Welfare State*, Cambridge, UK: Polity Press.

Posner, R. (1975): "The Social Costs of Monopoly and Regulation", *Journal of Political Economy*, 83: 807-827.

Prentice, D.D. and Holland, P.R.J. (1993): *Contemporary Issues in Corporate Governance*, Oxford: Clarendon Press

Sisk, D. (1985): "Rent-seeking, Non-Compensated Transfers and Laws of Succession: A Property Rights View", *Public Choice*, 46: 95-102.

Stopford, J.M. and Strange, S. (1991): *Rival States, Rival Firms*, Cambridge: Cambridge University Press.

Thurow, L.C. (1975): *Generating Inequality*, New York: Basic Books.

11

EDUCATION, TRAINING AND THE GROWTH OF THE OWNER-MANAGED FIRM: RECENT EVIDENCE IN THE IRISH CONTEXT

Jim Walsh

INTRODUCTION

The Small Firm: A Policy Priority for Ireland

The development of a strong, internationally-focused indigenous small firm sector has become an increasingly important priority of industrial policy in Ireland, as in other industrialised and industrialising countries (Hendry, et al., 1995; Industrial Policy Review Group, 1992; Birley and Westhead, 1990). Such a policy priority has a particular importance in Ireland. The strategy of developing the indigenous firm sector through greater integration with the foreign-owned sector has provided the foundation of Irish industrial policy since the 1960s (O'Malley, 1989). Notwithstanding the limited success of this strategy, particularly where medium- and large-sized indigenous firms are concerned, small indigenous firms do account for significant shares of employment and output in Ireland (See Table 11.1). As a result of (a) a partially successful prior strategy, (b) a resilient, if smaller, indigenous firm sector than previously planned for, and (c) high growth of the overall labour force, the growth of the indigenous small firm — especially in employment terms — has recently been re-emphasised (Department of Industry and Commerce, 1990, p. 77; Industrial Policy Review Group, 1992, pp. 22-23). Specific objectives of the national small firm development programme in the 1990s include employment growth and wealth creation in the economy nationally (Department of Industry and Commerce, 1990).

This renewed emphasis on the indigenous firm sector occurred at a time when the critical importance of the effectiveness of management training in international and Irish organisations continued to mount throughout the late 1980s and early 1990s (Hilb, 1992; Holden and Livian, 1992). For example, the Galvin Committee (1988), who were asked by the government to report on the state of management training in Ireland, found that over one-fifth of the top 1000 Irish companies ranked by turnover could not quantify their investment in management training — a result neither of the vast amounts of Irish pounds being spent nor of poor memory, but of no interest or attention being paid by these firms to management training whatsoever!

More recently, the Industrial Policy Review Group was equally scathing in its conclusions:

> Management training has received inadequate attention in many Irish firms....Not only should the (State) agencies support and encourage management training, but adequacy in this area should be a prerequisite for the provisions of other services and aids (Industrial Policy Review Group, 1992, p. 55).

In this context of renewed emphasis on the importance of indigenous small firm growth, therefore, this chapter attempted to empirically assess the relationship between management training in the owner-managed firm and the employment performance of the enterprise. Let us now turn to a consideration of the contribution of the indigenous, small-firm sector to the Irish economy.

The Small Firm in Ireland

In Ireland, the government uses 50 employees and fixed assets of not more than £0.8 million as the conjoint measure to distinguish small firms from medium and large-sized firms, engaged in manufacturing (Department of Industry and Commerce, 1990 p. 76). This differs from the OECD use of 100 employees as the upper limit to define the small firm. Such disparity makes it difficult to compare the small firm sector in Ireland with that in other economies. However, even if the figures cannot be compared directly with those of other countries, because of the different definitions, some comparisons are useful to put the Irish experience in a wider context. Table 11.1 shows the share of manufacturing employment in manufacturing industry in Ireland in 1990.

TABLE 11.1: INDUSTRY OWNERSHIP, SIZE, EMPLOYMENT AND EMPLOYMENT SHARES: MANUFACTURING INDUSTRY, IRELAND, 1990

Industry Ownership and Size	Numbers Employed	Per cent Share
Indigenous		
Small Industry (<50 People)	60,000	28
Medium-Large (>50 People)	68,000	31
Foreign-owned		
All Sizes	90,000	41
Totals	218,000	100

Source: Department of Industry and Commerce, *Review of Industrial Performance,* 1990, pp. 51, 70, 80.

In 1990, there were approximately 6,500 firms, with a majority Irish ownership, classified as small in the indigenous industrial sector. These employed some 60,000 people. They accounted for about 80 per cent of all industrial establishments, 28 per cent of total manufacturing employment and 15 per cent of all industrial output (Department of Industry and Commerce, 1990, p. 76). Medium and large firms in the indigenous industrial sector in Ireland are defined as being comprised of majority-owned Irish firms with employment of more than 50 people. In 1990, these firms accounted for just over 30 per cent of the manufacturing workforce, 68,000 jobs, and some 20 per cent of manufactured exports (Department of Industry and Commerce, 1990, p. 50). The international trend of most net job-creation being accounted for by small firms has also been reflected in Ireland in the period 1983-89. Indigenous small industrial (i.e. manufacturing) firms provided a net gain of 9,234 jobs during the period. This compares with a net loss of 31,881 jobs in indigenous medium and large-sized industrial firms. The foreign-owned industrial sector (all-sized firms), while suffering an overall net loss of 521 jobs during the same time period, had a net gain of 7,328 jobs during 1988 and 1989.

The relatively poor employment performance of indigenous medium and large firms, coupled with the mixed performance of foreign-owned firms, has served to increase the Government's dependence on the indigenous small firm as a key element in its approach to economic development. The Government has assessed the role of the small firm sector as being as follows:

> The significance of the small industry sector to Ireland's economic development lies mainly in its contribution to balanced regional and rural development but it also has a role to play in: building a seedbed of industrial enterprises from which larger internationally trading enterprises can develop; fostering an industrial tradition in an economy that is, by European standards, still heavily dependent on agriculture as a source of employment; and developing an industrial infrastructure that can link with, and provide services for, larger industrial enterprises (Department of Industry and Commerce, 1990 pp. 76-77).

The Indigenous and Foreign-owned Sectors

Recent studies have suggested, however, that substantial differences exist between the dynamism and productivity of foreign-owned multinational subsidiaries and the low growth or decline of much indigenous industry in Ireland (Industrial Policy Review Group, 1992). Such differences would make the development of a strong indigenous firm sector more difficult. A number of comparisons bear out this distinction between the indigenous firm sector and the foreign-owned sector of the Irish economy. The profitability of Irish-owned industry, as measured by profit before tax as a percentage of sales, was 3.9 per cent in 1989, compared with 23.9 per cent for foreign-owned firms (Department of Industry and Commerce, 1990). Total direct employment in all manufacturing industry in Ireland was 218,000 in 1990. Of this total, approximately 59 per cent were employed in indigenous firms. However, the traditional component (e.g. textiles, footwear, food) of the indigenous manufacturing sector has been in decline, shedding 37,000 jobs over the period 1980-86 (Department of Industry and Commerce, 1990). The employment growth record of indigenous Irish industry overall has, however, been historically weak. Since 1973, only 1 per cent of new enterprises in Ireland have grown to employ more than 50 people and most new ventures established in Ireland do not grow beyond 30 employees (Department of Industry and Commerce, 1990, p. 81). These figures suggest that the national priority of growing indigenous firms, particularly indigenous firms which grow to a size employing more than 50 employees, is faced with significant obstacles.

More recently the employment performance of indigenous industry has shown improvement. There has been net employment creation in small indigenous firms and a considerable reduction in job loss in the indigenous medium/large firm sector. The small indigenous firm sector showed increases in net employment from 481 jobs in 1983 to 3,687 jobs in 1989. During the same time period, job losses in the indigenous medium/large firm sector decreased from 8,014 to 1,525. This net gain of 2,161 jobs (3,687 − 1,525) in indigenous firms in 1989 compares with a net employment increase of 4,487 in the foreign-owned sector in the same year (Review of Industrial Performance, 1990, p. 80).

HOW DO SMALL FIRMS GROW?

From a review of the literature in management, it would appear that research on small firm growth has been concentrated in three primary areas:

1. **External environmental issues**: These include issues such as the effects of price imperfections in wages, taxes, the product/market structure, access to technology and the location of the firm (Woo and Cooper, 1981; McGee, 1989; Hughes, 1989; Rothwell and Beesley, 1989; Loveman and Sengenberger, 1990);

2. **Internal structural dynamics of the firm**: These involve issues such as the firm's management structure, control and reporting situation (Cyert and March, 1963; Filley and Aldag, 1978; Scase and Goffee, 1980; Sandberg and Hofer, 1987; Bosworth and Jacobs, 1989);

3. **Characteristics of the owner/manager**: The characteristics examined include age, socio-economic background, sex, education, prior work history, personality traits (Kets de Vries, 1977; Brockhaus, 1982; Begley and Boyd, 1986; O'Farrell and Hitchins, 1989; Lorrain and Dussault, 1988; Hebert and Link, 1988; Chell, et al., 1991).

Much of the research within these areas has concentrated on the start-up phase of the firm and on single characteristics of either the firm founder or of the small firm itself (Davidsson, 1989; Stanworth and Gray, 1991). Further, the majority of this research has been conducted in isolation from measures of enterprise growth or decline (Barber et al., 1989; Chell et al., 1991). More recent research attention devoted to the small enterprise has begun to reflect concern with the narrow focus of the traditional areas of research interest. Increasingly, management research attention is being directed to factors influencing the *established* small firm. Thus, the emphasis has begun to shift from analysis of the process of small business *start-up* to concentration on the process of small firm *growth* (Birley, 1987; Woo, Dunkelberg and Cooper, 1988; Davidsson, 1989; Birley and Westhead, 1990; Gibb, 1991).

Recent studies indicate that internal managerial issues are the most significant obstacles to growth in the small firm (McGee, 1989). Maintaining growth (a) often strains the internal marketing and innovative resources of the firm and (b) is largely dependent upon the continuous development of product and cost advantages (Barber, et al., 1989). Further, most small firms grow by moving from operating in relatively narrow market niches to serving a larger number of market segments. This requires a broadening of the internal skill and knowledge bases of the enterprise in order to match the demands of a changing environment (Stasch and Ward, 1985).

McGee (1989) has argued that this process of continual realignment with the two primary environments of the firm (external and internal) puts particular pressure on the firm in its early growth stages. In particular, the early growth of the enterprise may reflect the general growth of the firm's market, rather than any specific advantages of the firm. This may mask longer-term strategic weaknesses. McGee (1989) further contends that those firms which overcome these problems at the initial stages of growth will display better strategic resource allocation decisions. They will have overcome what he considers to be the most fundamental potential barrier to small firm growth, namely, the internal management of the firm. Central to this growth orientation in the small firm is the owner/manager (O'Farrell and Hitchins, 1989; Davidsson, 1989; Gibb and Davies, 1990). The owner/manager has been deemed to be a *critical* provider of the internal management in the small firm, even though not all small firms are run by owner/managers (Boswell, 1973; Child, *et al.*, 1975; Deeks, 1976; Carland et al., 1984; O'Farrell and Hitchins, 1989).

In summary, the indigenous small firm sector of the economy has been assigned a critical internationally-oriented role by the Irish government in terms of the implementation of its national economic development strategy. A critical element in determining the ability of the Irish small firm to begin to fulfil this role, and thereby continue its recent strong employment generation performance, is the small firm owner/manager. As yet, however, management research which has examined the role of the owner/manager *in relation to the growth of the small firm* has not yielded satisfactory results.

This is the case, notwithstanding the significant body of research which has followed Adam Smith in examining the issue of the "anxious vigilance" required of the managers of other people's money. The issue of the separation of ownership and control in "quasi-public" and professionally managed corporations has been extensively researched, especially given the rise of the latter during the twentieth century (Berle and Means, 1932; Coase, 1937; Baumol, 1959; Alchien and Demesetz, 1972; Jensen and Meckling, 1976; Green and Berry, 1991). This research has focused on the ownership-control debate almost exclusively in larger firms, however, where the manager's role as an agent of the owner is a common feature of the large, diversified organisation. In small firms ownership and control are more likely to be vested in the same individual, i.e. the owner/manager, and where this occurs, the issue of an agent operating on the owner's behalf does not arise (Stanworth and Curran, 1977; Birley, 1989). This has led to the contention that many of the findings of research pertaining to large firms, as in the case of agency theory, may not be entirely relevant to the *small* firm (Birley, 1989; Mintzberg, 1989).

THE OWNER/MANAGER AND THE SMALL FIRM

The research which has focused on the owner/manager's role as a critical determinant of small firm performance has been concentrated largely in two areas. First, attention has been devoted to the identification of the psychological and personality characteristics of the owner/manager as firm *founder* and *initiator*. This focus has led to the formulation of many typologies of the innovative nature of the owner/manager, and the examination of various related attributes.

These include attributes such as independence, affiliation and risk-taking in samples of owner/managers (McClelland, 1961; Liles, 1974; Hornaday, 1982; Gartner, 1983; Stephenson, 1983; Sexton and Bowman, 1986; Brockhaus and Horwitz, 1986; Woo, Dunkelberg and Cooper, 1988). The questions being addressed in much of this research are:

1. Who is likely to found a business venture?

2. What attributes do these potential owner/managers have in common?

3. Can innovative owner/managers be identified in advance so as to better concentrate resources towards those most likely to establish and grow a business?

The answers to all of these questions have been deemed to be largely inconclusive (Davidsson, 1989; Gibb, 1991). A second major stream in small firm research has focused on the owner/manager's behaviour *following* the establishment of the firm. This research has been directed at the type of behaviour which is prevalent in existing firms, but has not tested its effect on firm performance i.e. profitability, employment growth (Hornaday and Aboud, 1971; Kets De Vries, 1977; Doutriaux, 1987; McClelland, 1987; Egge, 1987; Begley and Boyd, 1987; Davidsson, 1989; Lafuente and Salas, 1989). The direction of this research converges on the following set of questions:

1. What behaviour is manifested by the owner/managers of the small firm?

2. What objectives do owner managers tend to have — do they pursue profit, or self expression, or independence?

3. How can owner/managers be characterised in terms of their managerial motives and abilities?

In this case the answers are no more precise than those provided by the research identified above (Sexton and Bowman, 1986; Stanworth and Gray, 1991; Gibb, 1991).

The research which has emphasised the characteristics of potential owner/managers, and that which has focused on the behaviour of owner/managers in existing firms, has not yet resulted in a coherent body of results in the management research field. In particular, little research on the owner/manager aspect of small firms has been undertaken which investigates its role in *growing the established firm* (Davidsson, 1989). Instead, most attention to the owner/manager has been directed at (a) the role played in new venture creation and (b) towards the determination of dominant characteristics of the individual likely to become an owner/manager. Both of these research directions have developed largely without reference to the performance of the firm (Stanworth and Gray, 1991; Chell et al., 1991).

The lack of research linking the owner/manager to small firm performance and employment generation coupled with the importance and urgency of the employment issue in Ireland provides the scope for this chapter. A number of issues present themselves in this regard. Among these can be included questions such as what it is about SME owner/managers which facilitate the growth of their enterprises? What elements of owner-management, hitherto not measured in the context of being of importance to firm growth, can be usefully assessed in an empirical study? Finally, what is the role of management training — both of the owner/manager and of other managers in the firm, in the growth process? These are the critical questions addressed in this chapter. Before we consider the answers, however, let us consider how these questions were addressed in the context of this particular chapter.

METHODOLOGY

In March 1992, 500 firms were chosen at random from IDA (Industrial Development Authority), private directory and magazine listings. Every fourth firm was selected from the listings until 500 firms had been chosen. These firms were then cross-checked to establish both that they displayed indigenous ownership and were firms primarily engaged in either manufacturing or services. A survey questionnaire was mailed to 500 firms selected as described above. A follow-up reminder/thank-you postcard was mailed one week later. The total number of returns received was 173. Of this total, 40 replies were mis-classified. These included firms which were no longer indigenously owned. Twenty replies were also received which were either incompletely filled out or were completed by someone other than the owner/manager. All 60 of these mis-classified or incompletely filled out returns were eliminated from the sample. This resulted in 113 usable returns, yielding a response rate of 22.6 per cent. However, since the mis-classified returns do not represent firms of interest for this research it could be argued that they should be eliminated from the sample pool. If this was done it would reduce the sample base from 500 to 440 and yield a response rate of 25.7 per cent (113/440).

The chapter used the employment numbers as reported by firms, as a surrogate for firm growth performance. This method was chosen for a number of reasons. First, such information is more readily available in aggregate form from published records than are other firm details such as turnover or profit (IDA, 1990; Census of Industrial Production, 1992). Second, it has been held for some time that, particularly for small firms, data pertaining to financial turnover and profit are both difficult to establish and are seldom completely reliable (Birley and Westhead, 1990). Third, international studies of small firm performance have used employment as a measure of that performance. This makes possible valid comparison of Ireland's small firm population with that of other nations, once this measure is used on an Irish population of small manufacturing firms (O'Farrell and Hitchins, 1988b; Birley and Westhead, 1990).

The chapter assessed the characteristics of the owner/manager on three dimensions, hitherto relatively unexplored in the management research literature pertaining to small firm growth. Milne and Thompson (1982), and Gibb and Scott (1985) argue that the owner/manager's ability *to learn from* and *adapt to* the internal and external contexts of the firm are critical determinants of whether the small firm grows. Their thesis is that this ability — coupled with an implicit *orientation towards growth* by the owner/manager (Stanworth and Curran, 1976; Sexton and Bowman, 1986) — will provide a significant rationale for firm growth, or the lack of it. Prior to this chapter, however, no research has been conducted which sought to tie these owner/manager characteristics to firm growth performance. In terms of education and training, the chapter assessed the total amount of in-company training received by owners and non-owning managers in the firm, along with the highest formal (i.e. full-time attendance) educational qualification obtained by the responding owner/managers. These five variables — the three owner/manager characteristics outlined above, the educational background of the owner/manager and the amount of training received both by owner/managers and non-owning managers in the firm, were then correlated with firm employment using appropriate statistical tests. The results of these analyses are shown below.

RESULTS

Dependent Variables

Two dependent variables were used in the chapter as surrogate measures of firm performance. These were total employment and employment growth. Employment growth is reported in two categories — percentage growth in employment, and absolute growth in the number of persons employed. The tables which report the results show the dependent variables using abbreviations. These abbreviations are as follows: Total employment is represented by the designation EESNOW. It is the total number of employees in the firm at the time the survey was conducted (March, 1993). Employment growth is represented by the designation EGR. It is measured both in percentage terms and in absolute terms over two time periods; over the last six years and over the last three years. The designations for each of the employment growth measures are as follows: (a) EGR%–6 represents the percentage growth in employment in the firm during the last six years. (b) EGR%–3 represents the percentage growth in employment in the firm during the last three years. (c) EGRAB–6 represents the absolute growth in the number of persons employed in the firm during the last six years. (d) EGRAB–3 represents the absolute growth in the number of persons employed in the firm during the last three years.

Respondent Profile

Forty-five percent of the survey respondents were founders of their firms. The next largest group of respondents (34 per cent) had no family relationship to the firm. This group represented other managers and business partners of the firm owner who reported some ownership in the firm. Sons and daughters of the founder represented 13 per cent of the respondents. Other non-founder family members made up the remaining 8 per cent of the respondents. These included grandchildren and one respondent classified as a spouse.

Males dominated the survey, representing almost 96 per cent of the respondents. The majority of the respondents (59 per cent) had ownership of up to 49 per cent of the firm. Nine percent reported owning 74 to 99 per cent of the firm. Nineteen percent said they owned 100 per cent of their firm. Respondent owner/managers ranged in age from 28 to 78 years old. The mean age for the sample was 48.9 years. Four percent of the responding owner/managers were in their 70s. Thirty-five percent of the respondents reported that secondary school was the highest level of education they had achieved, with 1 per cent indicating that they had received only a primary education. Thirty-one percent reported they had some college education or a professional diploma. Nineteen percent of the respondents had earned bachelor's degrees, and 13 per cent had post-graduate qualifications. The MBA was the most frequent post-graduate qualification reported, held by 6 per cent of those responding. Three percent of the responding owner/managers had PhDs. These figures indicate that 64 per cent of the respondents had received either some college or further education past secondary school.

Firm Profile

Twenty-seven percent of the firms responding came from the Dublin City and County region. Of the other firms, 18 per cent were located in Cork City, 17 per cent were based in the East of the country, 13 per cent in the South-West, 11 per cent in the Midlands; and 14 per cent were located in the Mid-West and West. Eighty-two percent of the firms responding were engaged in manufacturing and 18 per cent were engaged in services, primarily in distribution and general retailing. On average, 74 per cent of respondent firm sales came from non-local markets — i.e. from nationwide and overseas customers. Thirty-four percent of sales came from nationwide markets and 40 per cent from overseas markets. Firms responding generally had a wide mix of customers. This mix included retail, wholesale, individual and mail-order customers.

The average number of suppliers for the primary materials required by the firm in their business was 75. Firms responding had added new suppliers at an average rate of 5 per year over the past two years. Ninety-nine percent of the firms reported that their owner/managers and other managers had received some management training in the past two years. Owner/managers received an average of 6 days of management training over the past two years, compared to an average of 8 days for non-owning managers. On average, respondent firms employed 85 people. Employment in respondent firms showed small increases over the time periods measured in the chapter. On average, 80 employees worked in respondent firms three years ago, compared to 74 six years ago. The largest respondent firm had 420 employees, while the smallest firm which replied had just a single employee.

OWNER/MANAGER EDUCATION, TRAINING AND FIRM EMPLOYMENT PERFORMANCE

Highest Level of Education of Owner/Manager

Owner/managers surveyed were asked to indicate the highest level of education which they had achieved. The categories were as follows:

1. Primary

2. Secondary

3. Some college (third-level)

4. Bachelor's degree

5. Other

Tables 11.2-11.4 show the results of the Analysis of Variance tests examining the relationship between the level of education achieved by the owner/managers and the employment measures. The tables show that no significant association was found between the highest level of education achieved by the owner/manager and the measures of firm employment. The strongest association is between level of education and total employment, at 0.07.

TABLE 11.2: ANOVA OF HIGHEST LEVEL OF EDUCATION OF
OWNER/MANAGER AND TOTAL EMPLOYMENT

Variable	n	Mean	Standard Deviation	p-Value
Total Employment				0.07
Education Level				
Primary	6	40.67	38.61	
Secondary	34	73.35	69.87	
Some College	37	84.19	74.49	
Bachelor's Degree	22	124.09	103.99	
Other	15	74.00	46.96	

TABLE 11.3: ANOVA OF HIGHEST LEVEL OF EDUCATION OF
OWNER/MANAGER AND PERCENTAGE EMPLOYMENT GROWTH

Variable	n	Mean	Standard Deviation	p-Value
Percent Employment Growth (last six years)				0.35
Education Level				
Primary	6	-12.40	20.20	
Secondary	34	54.70	92.70	
Some College	36	40.70	91.30	
Bachelor's Degree	22	130.70	382.80	
Other	15	97.20	187.00	
Percent Employment Growth (last six years)				0.12
Education Level				
Primary	6	-16.90	34.51	
Secondary	34	10.38	39.31	
Some College	36	20.05	54.09	
Bachelor's Degree	22	44.93	97.34	
Other	15	12.07	31.17	

TABLE 11.4: ANOVA OF HIGHEST LEVEL OF EDUCATION OF
OWNER/MANAGER AND ABSOLUTE EMPLOYMENT GROWTH

Variable	n	Mean	Standard Deviation	p-value
Absolute Employment Growth (last six years)				0.96
Education Level				
Primary	6	-9.17	16.35	
Secondary	34	11.26	75.27	
Some College	36	14.41	61.39	
Bachelor's Degree	22	12.49	108.56	
Other	15	17.92	43.32	
Absolute Employment Growth (last six years)				0.80
Education Level				
Primary	6	-9.50	20.32	
Secondary	34	-3.35	60.16	
Some College	36	11.97	33.74	
Bachelor's Degree	22	6.27	91.15	
Other	15	2.67	33.92	

Owner/Manager Training

Responding owner/managers were also asked how much training they had undertaken in the past two years. Table 11.5 shows the results of the regression analysis performed on replies to this question and the employment performance measures. The table shows that no significant association was established between the number of days of management training undertaken by the owner/manager and the employment measures. Only total employment approaches significance, with a p-value of 0.06.

Non-owner Management Training

Firms were also asked to report the total number of days of management training undertaken by managers other than the owner/manager in the past two years. Table 11.6 shows the results of the regression analysis of Non-Owner Management Training and the employment measures. The table shows that a significant association exists between the number of days of management training undertaken by non-owner management in the past two years and total employment (p = .01). The coefficient of determination indicates that

8 per cent of total employment in the firm can be explained by the number of days of management training undertaken by non-owner management in the past two years. None of the other employment measures was significantly related to this variable.

TABLE 11.5: REGRESSION OF OWNER/MANAGER TRAINING AND EMPLOYMENT MEASURES

Variable	Mean	Standard Deviation	R-Sq (Adj)*	p-value
EESNOW	80.00	7.54	.02	0.06
EGR%–6	69.80	19.40	.00	0.64
EGR%–3	18.60	5.89	.00	0.84
ERGRAB–6	13.60	7.21	.00	0.54
ERGRAB–3	4.00	5.59	.00	0.91

* R-Sq (Adj)- R-squared (adjusted)

TABLE 11.6: REGRESSION OF NON-OWNER MANAGEMENT TRAINING AND EMPLOYMENT MEASURES

Variable	Mean	Standard Deviation	R-Sq (Adj)*	p-value
EESNOW	76.00	7.50	.08	0.01
EGR%–6	69.40	19.89	.00	0.75
EGR%–3	18.40	6.04	.00	0.79
ERGRAB–6	15.60	7.35	.00	0.21
ERGRAB–3	4.50	5.72	.00	0.74

*R-Sq (Adj) — R-Squared (Adjusted)

Total Training by Owner/Manager and Management

Finally, the number of total training days undertaken by both owner/manager and management over the past two years was combined. Table 11.7 shows the results of the regression analysis of this combined total with the measures of employment. The table shows that a significant relationship exists between the total number of days of management training undertaken by both owner/manager and management in the past two years and total employment. This association is at the 0.05 level. The r-squared indicates that 6 per cent of total employment in the firm can be explained by the total number of days of management training undertaken by both the owner/manager and management. This finding supports Birley and Westhead's chapter (1990) which found that firms where management had undergone some management training reported the highest rates of total employment. None of the other employment measures was significantly related to total training by owner/manager and management.

TABLE 11.7: REGRESSION OF TOTAL TRAINING BY OWNER/MANAGER AND MANAGEMENT AND EMPLOYMENT MEASURES

Variable	Mean	Standard Deviation	R-Sq (Adj)*	p-value
EESNOW	77.60	7.57	.06	0.05
EGR%-6	70.10	19.82	.00	0.68
EGR%-3	18.40	6.02	.00	0.79
ERGRAB-6	15.00	7.34	.00	0.31
ERGRAB-3	4.40	5.70	.00	0.78

*R-Sq (Adj) — R-Squared (Adjusted)

OWNER/MANAGER CHARACTERISTICS AND FIRM EMPLOYMENT PERFORMANCE

Owner/Manager Adaptation-Innovation and Employment Performance

In order to assess the owner/manager's degree of adaptation, the Kirton Adaptation-Innovation Inventory (KAI) was used. The KAI was designed to measure an individual's problem solving style, i.e., an individual's preferred way of approaching a decision and managing change (Kirton, 1989 pp. 8-9). The KAI theory contends that individuals differ in their problem-solving style in two ways. Individuals are differentiated by the inventory as Adapters, who will seek to "do things better", and Innovators, who will attempt to "do things differently". The KAI Inventory produces a continuum of scores ranging from 40-160. The higher an individual scores on the inventory, the more "innovative" the individual's problem solving style. Location on the continuum is, in itself, neither pejorative nor praiseworthy. The general population mean for the KAI in the United Kingdom is 95

(Kirton, 1989, p. 43). The KAI was used in the chapter in order to ascertain the problem solving style of the respondent owner/managers. The KAI was incorporated into this chapter in an attempt to assess whether a particular problem solving style — adaptive or innovative — is associated with employment performance. Table 11.8 shows the results of the regression analysis of the respondent's KAI score and the employment measures. The table shows no statistically significant association between KAI score and either total employment or employment growth was found.

TABLE 11.8: REGRESSION OF KIRTON ADAPTATION-INNOVATION INVENTORY SCORE AND EMPLOYMENT MEASURES

Variable	Mean	Standard Deviation	R-Sq (Adj)*	p-value
EESNOW	48.10	0.48	.00	0.46
EGR%-6	11.00	1.21	.00	0.66
EGR%-3	-27.80	0.36	.01	0.23
ERGRAB-6	-37.70	0.45	.00	0.30
ERGRAB-3	-7.80	0.35	.00	0.75

*R-Sq (Adj) — R-Squared (Adjusted)

Owner/Manager Learning Style and Employment Performance

The Learning Styles Questionnaire (LSQ) is used to describe the attitudes and behaviours which establish an individual's preferred way of learning (Honey and Mumford, 1992, pp. 1-2). Responses to the Learning Style Questionnaire are grouped into four categories which indicate the respondent's learning style preference. The four categories are: Activist, Reflector, Theorist and Pragmatist. Each of the four categories is comprised of a continuous scale which ranges from 0 to 20. The LSQ was used in the chapter to establish whether particular learning style preferences are associated with employment performance. Table 11.9 shows the results of the regression analysis of owner/manager total scores on each of the LSQ scales and the employment measures used in the chapter. As the table reveals, no statistically significant association between the scores on the LSQ and the employment performance of the firm was established. The results indicate that no particular learning style is related to either total employment levels or to the employment growth of the firm.

TABLE 11.9: REGRESSION OF LEARNING STYLE QUESTIONNAIRE SCORES AND EMPLOYMENT MEASURES

	P-Value	R-Sq. (Adj.)
Total Employment		
Learning Style Scores		
Activist	0.65	.00
Reflector	0.64	.00
Theorist	0.99	.00
Pragmatist	0.46	.00
Percent Employment Growth (last six years)		
Learning Style Scores		
Activist	0.51	.00
Reflector	0.58	.00
Theorist	0.18	.02
Pragmatist	0.59	.00
Percent Employment Growth (last three years)		
Learning Style Scores		
Activist	0.19	.02
Reflector	0.70	.00
Theorist	0.27	.00
Pragmatist	0.43	.00
Absolute Employment Growth (last six years)		
Learning Style Scores		
Activist	0.21	.02
Reflector	0.87	.00
Theorist	0.30	.00
Pragmatist	0.21	.02
Absolute Employment Growth (last three years)		
Learning Style Scores		
Activist	0.17	.03
Reflector	0.41	.00
Theorist	0.69	.00
Pragmatist	0.32	.00

Owner/Manager Growth Orientation and Employment Performance

The Jackson Personality Inventory/Personality Research Form-E (JPI/PRF-E) provides a measure of an individual's propensity towards growth (Sexton and Bowman, 1986 p. 40-44). Nine scales make up the measure. Five of these scales consist of 20 true-false questions. Four of these scales consist of 16 true-false questions. Respondents are scored on each of the nine scales with the possible range of scores going from 1-20 or 1-16, dependent on the scale. Two further 16-item scales which detect response errors are included in the instrument: an Infrequency scale which tests for random selection of answers and a Desirability scale which tests for the provision of answers considered by the respondent to be "socially correct". Test results where respondents score 3 or more incorrect answers on either these scales are to be discarded. Eleven of the responses in the current survey exceeded this index and were discarded. This left 102 usable JPI/PRF-E returns. The JPI/PRF-E test was used in the chapter to assess whether owner/manager scores on the JPI/PRF-E test were associated with employment performance. The results of the regression analyses of the scores on the JPI/PRF-E measure and total employment are shown in Table 11.10. The table shows no statistically significant association between the respondents' JPI/PRF-E scores and total employment.

TABLE 11.10: REGRESSION OF JPI/PRF-E TEST SCORE AND TOTAL EMPLOYMENT

JPI/PRF-E Scale	Mean	Standard Deviation	R-Sq (Adj)	p-value
Energy Level	3.80	2.57	.08	0.14
Risk Taking	1.43	2.58	.00	0.58
Social Adroitness	-0.14	2.57	.00	0.96
Autonomy	0.63	3.73	.00	0.86
Change	1.71	3.04	.00	0.57
Inter-personal Effect	-0.68	2.20	.00	0.76
Conformity	-1.30	3.59	.00	0.62
Harm Avoidance	1.99	2.70	.00	0.46
Succorance	3.47	3.09	.01	0.26

*R-Sq (Adj) — R-Squared (Adjusted)

DISCUSSION

The chapter found that the amount of management training undertaken by both owner/managers and non-owning managers in the respondents' firms was significantly associated with the total employment numbers reported by the respondent firms. This finding supports the work of Birley and Westhead (1990) and it is suggested that, rather than proceed further with large-scale empirical approaches such as those conducted by the present author and studies such as that of Birley and Westhead, research and analysis of the management training *process* in the small firm could now generate useful new insight into how management training can be most effectively delivered in this sector of the economy.

The current chapter has further established that investment in management training is occurring in the small firm sector in Ireland, a finding which confirms other recent, empirical work (Heraty and Morley, 1994). However, detailed examination of the nature of management training in the small firm sector, along with analysis of the relationship of training assimilation and intervention to firm efficiency and effectiveness, has not been undertaken. Also, a more fully developed understanding of the nature of the owner/manager's role in the identification, delivery and evaluation of small firm management development in Ireland has yet to be elaborated. Tait (1988), for instance, has argued that this role should be the focus of more study in the small firm research field.

Although training in the small firm in Ireland has not been the focus of extensive empirical work derived from either quantitative or qualitative methodologies (see Heraty and Morley, 1994 for a recent review of HRD in Ireland), studies have argued for more focused approaches to the problems of employee and manager development (Gunnigle and Flood, 1990 p. 156). The Industrial Policy Review Group (1992) echoed this call when, in a comprehensive assessment of the needs of future economic policy requirements, it identified education and training as "the critical element of policy" and called for an increased separation of vocationally-focused and academically-oriented education. Citing international experience from Germany, Britain and Japan, the group argued that any workforce skill development process should include active industry involvement:

The skills gap needs to be addressed both by industry and by the educational system. The most successful training and education systems, in terms of enhancing competitiveness, are those where companies play an active role in the development of programmes and curricula ... (Industrial Policy Review Group, 1992, p. 54).

In terms of the remaining three owner/manager characteristics assessed in this chapter, it is possible that a relationship exists between the three owner/manager characteristics and the employment measures, but that the instruments used in the chapter failed to measure this relationship. In the case of owner/manager learning, it may be that *what* a person learns is more important than *how* they learn. The Learning Styles Questionnaire measures preferred ways of learning (i.e. how they learn), and consequently may have failed to assess the learning issue which is key to successfully growing a business. With reference to owner/manager adaptation-innovation preference, the Kirton Adaptation-Innovation Inventory is a measure of cognitive style, not of cognitive ability (Kirton, 1989, p. 5). It may be, therefore, that a relationship exists between an owner/manager's adaptiveness and employment performance, but (as with the LSQ) the KAI was not capable of measuring the critical element (i.e. adaptive *ability* rather than adaptive *style*).

The third owner/manager characteristic, growth orientation, was assessed by the Jackson Personality Inventory-Personality Research Form-E (JPI/PRF-E). Sexton and Bowman (1986, p. 45) argue that the combination of the seven scales comprising the JPI/PRF-E represent measures of entrepreneurship. These scales, however, may not represent a definitive set of measures in this regard. For instance, the energy level scale on the JPI/PRF-E measures the degree to which an individual is "active and spirited, possesses reserves of strength . . . and does not tire easily" (Sexton and Bowman, 1986, p. 45). The instrument cannot, however, measure to what purpose that energy is directed. For example, an owner/manager with high energy could just as easily employ that energy to stabilise the business, rather than grow it.

The absence of any significant relationship could be the result of the time frame covered by the chapter. During this time, external environmental influences (e.g. the recession in Ireland during part of this time) unique to the Irish culture could have temporarily minimised the owner/manager's influence on firm performance. This is not likely, however, as the current chapter found that employment gains were reported by the responding firms. This issue must, therefore, remain speculative until a study of small firm growth employing a longer and/or different timespan than that used in the current chapter is undertaken.

In conclusion, therefore, this chapter has attempted to shed new light on the growth of small, owner-managed firms, using an Irish sample. In particular, it has shown that while growth is already being pursued by many Irish SMEs, the precise nature of the role of the owner/manager in determining the success of this process remains unclear. New light has, however, been shed on three owner/manager characteristics which have been identified in the management research literature as having critical influences on firm growth. Further evidence concerning education and training and their impact on firm employment performance has been gathered and assessed. The evidence cited in this chapter suggests that the influence of these particular characteristics on firm employment growth may not be as substantial or as amenable to large-scale empirical investigation as previously thought.

REFERENCES

Alchien, A.A. and Demsetz, H. (1972): "Production, Information Costs and Economic Organisation", *American Economic Review*, 62(5): 777-795.

Report of the Industrial Policy Review Group (1992): "A Time For Change: Industrial Policy for the 1990s", Dublin: The Stationery Office.

Barber, J., Metcalfe, J.S. and Porteous, M. (1989): *Barriers to Growth in Small Firms*, London: Routledge.

Baumol, W. (1959): *Business Behavior, Value and Growth*, New York: Macmillan.

Begley, T.M. and Boyd, D.P. (1987): "Psychological Characteristics Associated with Performance in Entrepreneurial Firms and Smaller Businesses", *Journal of Business Venturing*, 2: 79-93.

Berle, A. Jr., and Means, G.C. (1932): *The Modern Corporation and Private Property*, New York: Macmillan.

Birch, D.L. (1979): "The Job Generation Process", Final Report to Economic Development Administration, MIT Program on Neighborhood and Regional Change (mimeo), Cambridge: MA.

Birch, D.L. (1987): *Job Creation in America*, New York: Free Press.

Birley, S. (1986): "The Role of New Firms: Births, Deaths and Job Generation", *Strategic Management Journal*, 7(4), July/August: 361-376.

Birley, S. (1989): "Corporate Strategy and the Small Firm" in Asch, D. and Bowman, C. (eds.) *Readings in Strategic Management*, Houndsmills, Basingstoke: Macmillan.

Birley, S. and Westhead, P. (1990): "Growth and Performance Contrasts between 'Types' of Small Firms", *Strategic Management Journal*, 11(7): 535-557.

Blackburn, R.A., Curran, J. and Woods, A. (1991): *Exploring Enterprise Cultures: Small Service Enterprise Owners and their Views*, Small Business Unit, Kingston Polytechnic.

Boswell, J. (1973): *The Rise and Decline of Small Firms*, London: George Allen & Unwin.

Bosworth, D.L. and Jacobs, C. (1989): "Management Attitudes, Behaviour, and Abilities as Barriers to Growth", in Barber, J., Metcalfe, J.S., and Porteous, M., (eds.) *Barriers to Growth in Small Firms*, London: Routledge: 20-38.

Brockhaus, R.H. Snr. (1982): "The Psychology of the Entrepreneur" in Kent, C.A., Sexton, D.L., and Vesper, K.H., (eds.) *Encyclopedia of Entrepreneurship*, Englewood Cliffs, NJ: Prentice Hall: 39-71.

Carland, J.W., Hoy, F., Boulton, W.R. and Carland, J.A.C. (1984): "Differentiating Entrepreneurs from Small Business Owners: A Conceptualisation", *Academy of Management Review*, 9(2): 354-359.

"Census of Industrial Production, 1989", (1992): Dublin: The Stationery Office.

Chell, E., Haworth, J.M. and Brearley, S.A. (1991): *The Entrepreneurial Personality: Concepts, Cases and Categories*, London: Routledge.

Child, J., Francis, A., Kieser, A., Nyman, S. and Silberston, A. (1975): "The Growth of Firms as a Field of Research", University of Aston

Management Centre Working Paper Series No. 30 R, Birmingham: University of Aston.

Coase, R.H. (1937): "The Nature of the Firm", *Economica*, new series, 4: 386-405.

Cyert, R.M. and March, J.G. (1963): *A Behavioral Theory of the Firm*, Englewood Cliffs, NJ: Prentice Hall.

Davidsson, P. (1989): "Continued Entrepreneurship and Small Firm Growth", Ph.D. Dissertation, Stockholm: Stockholm School of Economics.

Deeks, J. (1976): *The Small Firm Owner Manager: Entrepreneurial Behaviour and Management Practice*, New York: Praeger.

Department of Industry and Commerce, (1990): "Review of Industrial Performance, 1990", Dublin: The Stationery Office.

Doutriaux, J. (1987): "Growth Pattern of Academic Entrepreneurial Firms", *Journal of Business Venturing*, 2: 285-297.

Egge, K.A. (1987): "Expectations Vs. Reality Among Founders of Recent Start-ups", in Churchill, N.C., Hornaday, J.A., Kirchoff, B.A., Kranser, O.J., and Vesper, C.H. (eds.), *Frontiers of Entrepreneurship Research*, Wellseley, MA: Babson College, Center for Entrepreneurial Studies: 322-336.

Filley, A.C. and Aldag, R.J. (1978): "Characteristics and Measurement of Personality", *Psychological Bulletin*, 83(5): 956-974.

Gartner, W.S. (1985): "An Empirical Model of Business Start-Up and Eight Entrepreneurial Archetypes", Unpublished Ph.D. Thesis, Univeristy of Michigan.

Gibb, A. (1991): "Entrepreneurship and Growth: What are the Key Factors for SME Growth?", Paper presented at the 21st European Small Business Seminar, Barcelona, 18-20 September.

Green, S., and Berry, D.F. (1991): *Cultural, Structural and Strategic Change in Management Buy Outs*, Houndsmills, Basingstoke: Macmillan.

Haveman, H.A. (1993): "Ghosts of Managers Past: Managerial Succession and Organizational Mortality", *Academy of Management Journal*, 36(4): 864-881.

Hebert, R.F. and Link, A.N. (1988): *The Entrepreneur — Mainstream Views and Radical Critiques*, 2nd edition, New York: Praeger.

Hendry, C., Arthur, M.B. and Jones, A.M. (1995): *Strategy Through People: Adaptation and Learning in the Small-Medium Enterprise*, London: Routledge.

Heraty, N. and Morley, M. (1994): "Human Resource Development in Ireland — Position, Practices and Power", *Administration*, 42(3), Autumn: 299-319.

Hilb, M. (1992): "The Challenges of Management Development in Western Europe in the 1990s", *International Journal of Human Resource Management*, 3(3): 575-584.

Holden, L. and Livian, Y. (1992): "Does Strategic Training Policy Exist? Evidence from Ten European Countries", *Personnel Review*, 21(1): 12-23.

Honey, P. and Mumford, A. (1992): *Manual of Learning Styles*; 3rd edition, Maidenhead: McGraw-Hill.

Hornaday, J.A. (1982): "Research About Living Entrepreneurs" in Kent, C.A., Sexton, D.L. and Vesper, K.H. (eds.) *Encylopedia of Entrepreneurship*, Englewood Cliffs, NJ: Prentice Hall.

Hughes, A. (1989): "Small Firms' Merger Activity and Competition Policy" in Barber, J., Metcalfe, J.S. and Porteous, M. (eds.) *Barriers to Growth in Small Firms*, London: Routledge: 128-172.

Jackson, D.N. (1974): *Personality Research Form Manual*, Goshen, NY: Research Psychologists Press.

Jackson, D.N. (1976): *Jackson Personality Inventory Manual*, Goshen, NY: Research Psychologists Press.

Jensen, M.C. and Meckling, W.H. (1976): "Theory of the Firm: Managerial Behavior, Agency Costs and Ownership Structure", *Journal of Financial Economics*; 3: 305-360.

Kets de Vries, M.F.R (1977): "The Entrepreneurial Personality: A Person at the Crossroads", *Journal of Management Studies*; 14: 34-57.

Kirton, M.J. (1989): "A Theory of Cognitive Style" in Kirton, M.J. (ed.) *Adaptors and Innovators: Styles of Creativity and Problem Solving*, London: Routledge: 1-36.

Lafuente, A. and Salas, V. (1989): "Types of Entrepreneurs and Firms: The Case of New Spanish Firms", *Strategic Management Journal*, 10(1), January/February: 17-30.

Lahti, A. (1989): "A Contingency Theory of Entrepreneurial Strategy for a Small Scale Company Operating From a Small and Open

Economy in Open European Competition", *Entrepreneurship & Regional Development*, 1: 221-236.

Liles, P.R. (1974): *New Business Ventures and the Entrepreneur*, Homewood, IL: Irwin.

Lorrain, J. and Dussault, L. (1988): "Relation between Psychological Characteristics, Administrative Behaviors and Success of Founder Entrepreneurs at the Start-up Stage", in Kirchoff, L.A., Long, W.A., McMullan, W.E., Vesper, K.H., Wetzel, W.E, Jnr., (eds.) *Frontiers of Entrepreneurship Research*, Wellseley, MA: Babson College, Center for Entrepreneurial Studies: 150-164.

McClelland, D.C. (1961): *"The Achieving Society"*, Princeton, NJ: Van Norstrand.

McClelland, D.C. (1987): "Characteristics of Successful Entrepreneurs", *Journal of Creative Behaviour*, 21(3): 219-233.

McGee, J. (1989): "Barriers to Growth: The Effects of Market Structure", in Barber, J., Metcalfe, J.S. and Porteous, M. (eds.) *Barriers to Growth in Small Firms*, London: Routledge: 173-195.

Milne, T. and Thompson, M. (1982): "The Infant Business Development Process", Management Studies Working Paper 2, London: University of Glasgow.

O'Farrell, P.N. and Hitchins, D.M. (1989): *"Small Firm Competitiveness and Performance"*, Dublin: Gill & Macmillan.

O'Malley, E. (1989*): Industry and Economic Development: The Challenge for the Latecomer*, Dublin: Gill and Macmillan.

Rothwell, R. and Beesley, M. (1989): "The Importance of Technology Transfer", in Barber, J., Metcalfe, J.S. and Porteous, M. (eds.) *Barriers to Growth in Small Firms*, London: Routledge: 87-104.

Sandberg, W.R. and Hofer, C.W. (1987): "Improving New Venture Performance: The Role of Strategy, Industry Structure and the Entrepreneur", *Journal of Business Venturing*, 2(1): 5-28.

Scase, R. and Goffee, R. (1980): *"The Real World of the Small Business Owner"*, Beckenham, Kent: Croom Helm,

Sengenberger, W., Loveman, G.W. and Piore, M.J. (eds.) (1990): *The Re-emergence of Small Enterprises: Industrial Restructuring in Industrialised Countries*, Geneva: International Labour Office — International Institute for Labour Studies.

Sexton, D. and Bowman, N. (1986): "Validation of a Personality Index: Comparative Entrepreneurial Analysis of Female Entrepreneurs, Managers, Entrepreneurship Students and Business Students", in Ronstadt, R., Hornaday, J., Peterson, R., and Vesper, K. (eds.) *Frontiers of Entrepreneurship Research*, Wellseley, MA: Babson College, Center for Entrepreneurial Studies, 40-51.

Stanworth, M.J.K. and Curran, J. (1976): "Growth and the Small Firm — An Alternative View", *Journal of Management Studies*, 13: 152-171.

Stanworth, J. and Gray, C. (1991): *Bolton 20 Years On: The Small Firm in the 1990s*, London: Paul Chapman.

Stevenson, H.H. (1983): *A Perspective on Entrepreneurship*, Cambridge, MA: Harvard Business School Press.

Tait, E. (1988): "Researching Small Business Owner/managers' Perceived Management Education Needs: An Integrated Framework", Paper presented to the Eleventh National Small Firms Policy and Research Conference, Cardiff, Wales.

Woo, C.Y. and Cooper, A. (1981): "Strategies of Effective Low Share Businesses", *Strategic Management Journal*, 2(3): 301-318.

Woo, C.Y., Dunkelberg, W.C. and Cooper, A.C. (1988): "Entrepreneurial Typologies: Definition and Implications", in Kirchoff, B.A., Long, W.A., McMullan, W.E. and Wetzel, W.E. Jr. (eds.) *Frontiers of Entrepreneurship Research*, Wellseley, MA: Babson College, Center for Entrepreneurial Studies: 165-176.

III

RENT-SEEKING AND IRISH ENTERPRISE

12

ENTREPRENEURSHIP OR RENT-SEEKING?

William Kingston

ABSTRACT

This chapter begins with a brief discussion of entrepreneurship, showing that this is an activity that can only exist when individuals are free to act within a framework of law and private property rights. The second section deals with the alternative, collectivism, in which the State is no longer content to establish the conditions within which entrepreneurs can act on their own initiative, but insists on intervening directly in economic affairs. This generates "rents" for those whom this intervention favours.

The consequences of collectivism are dealt with in the third section. Whether central planning and control is substantially complete (as in the former Soviet Union) or partial (as in "mixed" economies) only affects the extent of the waste of resources and consequently, the speed with which an *unviable* economy will develop. This is because entrepreneurs (who know how to handle productive investment) are replaced by "rent-seekers" who know "how to work the system" so as to adapt the State's power to their own interest.

The fourth section shows how Ireland has always been collectivist, both in inclination and practice. Unlike the former Soviet Bloc countries, it has so far escaped having to face up to the consequences through borrowing and the availability of EU transfers. But its bureaucrats and rent-seekers will be of little use when these funds run out. This is why there is such an absurd and dangerous incipient campaign for yet more "compensation" from Brussels in exchange for Ireland's joining in the EU common currency.

ENTREPRENEURSHIP

Creativity in Business

It was the great Austrian economist, Joseph Schumpeter, who baptised Adam Smith's "undertaker" as "entrepreneur", and the idea of the individual whose initiative is essential if factors of production are to be co-ordinated is central to his thinking. He saw entrepreneurship in terms of human creativity applied to economic ends:

> [W]henever the economy or an industry or some firms in an industry do something that is outside the range of existing practice, we may speak of *creative* response...a study of creative response in business becomes coterminous with a study of entrepreneurship (Schumpeter, 1947, p. 150).

In his mind, this creative response has three essential characteristics: It can only be understood *after* it has taken place, hardly ever before. It shapes the whole course of subsequent events and their long run outcome. And thirdly, it has much to do with the quality of available personnel, both absolute and relative, and thus with individual decisions, actions and patterns of behaviour.

Schumpeter did not stress the distinction between innovation and entrepreneurship, although each activity is best understood when related to the other. An entrepreneur can then be defined as an innovator acting in an area of life where the appropriate measure is money. Traders also operate in such areas, but what an entrepreneur does requires more creative input than trading. The special qualities of entrepreneurs have been identified in a range from "gap-filling" and "input-completing" capacities (Liebenstein, 1968) to exceptional skill in persuasion (McCloskey and Klamer, 1995).

The Role of Economic Institutions

Schumpeter's ideas about entrepreneurship were formed in the period before the first World war, in a liberal and individualistic world where business was typically done with little reference to "the State". In particular, the markets which entrepreneurs faced, did not arise as a rule from public purchasing or financing. There were exceptions, of course: firms in the arms trade, such as Armstrongs and Vickers in England, always had to sell to governments; and Bismarck's innovation of the first social welfare system in the world, shortly after the unification of Germany, provided valuable markets for that country's nascent health-care industry. Nevertheless, the paucity of such examples testifies to the extent to which the general pattern was one in which business men did not have to think of the government as a source of their revenues.

There are strong grounds, indeed, for believing that it is only in a context of free markets based on private property rights that entrepreneurship can exist at all. This is because a crucial distinguishing ability of an entrepreneur is to be able to act in situations where much theoretically desirable information is lacking. Keynes (1945) noted that what appears to be necessary for economic success is "exuberant inexperience". Part of this ability comes from possessing what Michael Polanyi identified as *tacit* knowledge, that is, knowledge that cannot be articulated, that exists only in use and can be attained only by experience of its use, and that is expressed in flair and intuition: "We always know more than we can say". The corollary, as the philosopher, John Gray, has put it, is that:

> individuals are most likely to be able to deploy their personal tacit knowledge when they are least constrained by collective decision-procedures in which this knowledge is diluted or lost. (This is, perhaps, especially true of that species of tacit knowledge which is expressed in entrepreneurial insight). In order to be able to make the best of their personal fund of tacit knowledge, individuals need a domain in which they may act solely on their own judgement (and, of course, at their own risk). Such a domain is provided by private property in productive assets (Gray, 1993, p. 74).

Property Rights

Western countries are as rich as they are, simply because they developed a system of property rights which directed human creative energy fruitfully into economic channels (North, 1981, Rosenberg & Birdzell, 1986). Also, the empirical correlation between entrepreneurial activity and institutional arrangements which give individuals autonomy to act freely within limits laid down by law is highly persuasive in economic history: "those economies grew fastest which were freest" (Landes, 1970, p. 19).

It is important to note that many different kinds of law can provide a fruitful environment for entrepreneurial activity, as long as the key element of private ownership is included. For example, most ownership of productive assets today is through shareholding in corporations. However, the twelfth century saw an astounding outburst of entrepreneurship throughout Europe on the basis of a quite different type of law. The Cistercian reform of the Benedictine Order grew to 500 abbeys within a single century, because these monks were the entrepreneurs and technologists of the age, innovating large-scale farming and metal-working, the use of water-power and widespread provision of financial services. All this was done on the basis of the absolute property rights of ancient Rome, which had been continued unbroken through the monastic tradition (Kingston, 1993, 1994a).

Markets, then, are not part of the structure of the universe, as libertarians tend to believe. They are man-made artefacts, the result of positive law, and they can be changed accordingly. But their essential condition is freedom of entry, and this in turn depends upon the existence of private property rights which confer the power of autonomous action on individual entrepreneurs.

COLLECTIVISM

However, since Schumpeter formulated his theories about entrepreneurship, they have been made progressively more irrelevant through the world-wide growth of collectivism, of which Robert Skidelsky has recently written with much perception:

> Collectivism — the belief that the state knows better than the market and can improve on the spontaneous tendencies of civil society, if necessary by suppressing them, has been the most egregious error of the twentieth century. Its extreme manifestations were Communism and Fascism, but it was also seen in the authoritarian state-led industrialisation policies of many developing countries, and large traces have been evident in the industrial and social policies of most developed economies. My contention is that this belief in the superior wisdom of the state breeds pathologies which deform, and at the limit destroy, the political economies based on it (Skidelsky, 1995, p. xiii).

Inadequate Property Rights

There are many reasons for the growth of collectivism during the present century. Amongst the most important has been the inadequacy of the contemporary property rights systems. As John Stuart Mill pointed out, "the laws of property have never yet conformed to the principles on which the justification of private property rests" (Mill, 1848). One of those principles is that private property "civilises" self-interest in economic activity by forcing it to serve the common good. It is only to the extent that they do this that rights are efficient (North, 1990, p. 92). How to get efficient property rights has always been a problem, and it is the supreme problem of political economy in the post-Communist era.

Certainly, the pattern of property rights which developed over the nineteenth century was anything but efficient in this sense, however much economic growth it underwrote. The vast new wealth generated by the industrial revolution was highly concentrated, due to a combination of absolute ownership, new laws conferring limited liability on investments, unrestricted inheritance and low taxation, all combined with legal restraint on worker association for the purpose of generating countervailing economic power. It is hardly surprising, therefore, that those who were outside the circles of privilege could be persuaded by collectivist thinkers that state control of economic life would be in their interest.

The First World War showed that nations could operate through central planning in actual practice and not just in theory, and this experience was brought to bear again in every country in responses, such as the "New Deal" in the US, to the Depression. World War II repeated the earlier extension of state involvement in the economies of all combatants, and after it came the age of Keynes and the "managed capitalism" of his disciples. The oil shocks of the 1970s provided further opportunities for extending the role of the State, because when the OPEC surpluses were recycled, they did not go back to the firms and individuals from whom they had been exacted, but were lent to governments.

Pressures on Politicians

Two of the most important factors which contributed to the belief that "the state knows better than the market", have been increasing pressures on politicians to be immediately responsive to a mass electorate and a fundamental change in the demography of public bureaucracies.

Nineteenth century politicians did not have to cope with universal suffrage, nor with the enormous costs of present-day election campaigns, and they did not depend upon politics for their living. Today's typical politician is a professional, for whom loss or gain of a seat or a majority is supremely important. Also, electorates and lobbyists have learned how vulnerable modern politicians are to pressures which have a bearing on either funding or votes.

These have combined to produce what is known as the political business cycle, for which the time horizon is the next election. The short-term interests of politicians therefore diverge from any longer-term interests of their electorates. A similar divergence of interest is evident in relation to information. Truth is in the interest of electorates; secrecy and the spread of "good news" is in the interest of politicians. It is intervention, of course, which illustrates most clearly that the interests of politicians do not coincide with the common good.

Civil Service Changes

Even if it is politicians who decide on interventionist policies, these have to be carried into effect by public bureaucracies. A radical demographic shift in the civil services of the most important States played a significant role in the growth of collectivism. This began before the 1914-18 War, but becomes very evident after it. The "old" civil services of Europe were typified by Schumpeter's description of the Prussian one as "supremely efficient, totally incorruptible, altogether independent of politics" (Schumpeter, 1939, p. 346). By their preference for law over intervention, they were responsible for much fruitful legislation. The culture shared by nineteenth- century civil servants and business men was conducive to entrepreneurship, because it placed the emphasis on limited government; law and property rights were the means by which individual creativity could have an economic outlet.

Modern Counterparts

In contrast, their modern counterparts believe that the state knows better than the market. To them, expansion of the state machine has positive merit, since it generates promotion opportunities and the prestige that accrues to those who wield power. Interventionist policies coincide with self-interest, all the more because they are so easily "sugared over with pretence of public spirit" (MacNeice, 1936).

In advising Ministers, the case for market forces operating within a framework of positive law will never be advanced with anything like the same energy as that for some form of intervention, since this will expand the bureaucracy. No "market" approach is possible without creativity and imagination in constantly re-shaping the legal structure. In turn, these depend upon subconscious energies and tacit knowledge that will be released only when an individual's own interest is at stake. When both "interest" and "demographic" factors are taken into account, it is not surprising that modern civil servants are as much in favour of intervention as their Victorian predecessors were against it.

RENT-SEEKING

The disease of collectivism damages countries in three main ways: by eliminating entrepreneurship; by increasing the role of the new bureaucracy; and, worst of all, by causing divergence between the interest of those who run a country and the common good.

Eliminating Entrepreneurship

There is no half-way house between running an economy through laws and running it by intervention. The "mixed economy" is very far from being a free and competitive one. Because intervention invariably limits competition, it cannot avoid imposing increased costs on the economy as a whole, and the only possible source of funds to pay these costs is the entrepreneurial sector. The more intervention, the more costs, and the less the economic environment is capable of sustaining entrepreneurship.

To the extent, then, that intervention or "Industrial Policy" is adopted, politicians and civil servants are effectively turning their backs on the development of legal frameworks within which individuals, acting in their own interest within competitive markets, are forced to serve the common good.

Such frameworks do not come into being spontaneously; they are difficult to shape, and they can only come out of a political culture which has a strong belief in the value of limited government. But they are the essential environment for entrepreneurship, and to the extent that there is failure to develop and maintain them, entrepreneurs are being expelled from the economic system. Their place will be taken by "rent-seekers". The situation is even worse than Baumol's (1990) claim that the wrong kind of rules can cause entrepreneurship to become unproductive or even destructive. In fact, collectivist rules actually *change the kind of person* who becomes involved in investment activity.

Public Choice Economics

The concept of "rent-seeking" was developed by the Public Choice or Virginia school of economists. There are several technical definitions of rent, but what they all add up to is "the financial results of restrictions on competition". Since it is impossible for governments to intervene in an economy without causing such restrictions, all intervention generates rents. This changes the way in which money is made. In a competitive world, financial gain results from satisfying the demands of consumers or their intermediate suppliers better than others do; in a world where state intervention replaces competitive markets, money is made instead through becoming the beneficiary of the rents which intervention generates.

This does not mean just learning about and responding to what the state is doing; very often, it is the rent-seeker who actively stimulates the Government to make a particular intervention. The result, in the language of Public Choice, is that "[t]he entire federal budget can be regarded as a gigantic rent up for grabs for those who can exercise the most political muscle". (Muller, 1989, p. 243).

Dominance by Rent-seekers

To the extent that intervention becomes important in an economy, replacement of entrepreneurs by rent-seekers is inevitable. Individuals who are able to deal successfully with investment in competitive business, are inhibited from acting where politicians and bureaucrats are concerned, because they think in such different ways. On the other hand, those who are good at handling the political and bureaucratic dimensions of rent-capture, by definition do not want to have to deal with the kind of competition in which entrepreneurship flourishes, nor are they able to handle it.

In this process, entrepreneurs who can contribute to genuine long-term wealth generation must be progressively driven out by others who are better able to capture State-generated rents from projects with low (indeed frequently negative) economic returns for the community as a whole. The idea of "crowding-out" of private investment by the demands of government projects is well- known, but the parallel "crowding-out" of an even scarcer resource, ability to identify and act on opportunities to generate real wealth, is at least as economically harmful.

When the state turns to a policy of intervention, entrepreneurs are also replaced by bureaucrats. These can be regarded as a special type of rent-seeker, because all but a tiny fraction of their own remuneration is rent, captured out of taxation. On its own, this would make them a powerful influence for intervention, and unfortunately it is reinforced by a fundamental antagonism between them and entrepreneurs. They cannot share the same tacit knowledge, they operate according to quite different reward/punishment systems, and their scope for the exercise of creativity, and their attitudeS to risk cannot be equated (Kingston, 1995). This antagonism also explains why the managements who benefit most from the various incentives which are the instruments of intervention are the ones in which the bureaucrats who administer the incentives see the best reflection of themselves and their values. There is affinity between rent-seekers, just as there is antipathy between rent-seekers and entrepreneurs.

Economic Consequences

All intervention consequently widens the area of poor decision-making, by increasing the importance of bureaucratic rather than innovatory firms in an economy, and by strengthening the bureau-cratic element in *all* managements. Wherever direct government inducements are important to a business, the balance of influence in its management between entrepreneurs and "organisation men" is tipped in favour of the latter. This is because they think like the bureaucrats who control the award of contracts or grants, and so have most rapport with them.

Intervention of course distorts the profit measure, channelling money towards projects which are politically rather than financially rewarding. Organised labour in the public sector is then able to ratchet up wage rates because of the Government's power to tax and borrow to pay them. Tax rates also increase because of the need to remunerate debt issued to pay for uneconomic projects and higher public sector salaries, as well as higher social security benefits granted in exchange for votes. Each of these factors reduces the attractiveness of entrepreneurial activity; in combination, they make it impossible. Having themselves produced the conditions where it is perfectly natural for those whose own money is at risk, to refuse to invest, the politicians and bureaucrats unite in the claim that the market has failed once again. Consequently, they are called upon to intervene. Another opportunity for rent-seekers arises, and the true productivity of the economy is forced down a further notch.

Political Nemesis

No matter how rich a country may be, there is a limit to this process. In fact, Dan Usher has shown with convincing logic that unless a significant proportion of incomes are independent of the state, even democracy itself cannot survive:

> Whatever we assume, it turns out that the attempt to assign incomes by voting gives rise to consequences so unacceptable that the voting mechanism itself would sooner or later be abandoned (1981, p. 16).

"Assigning incomes by voting" means an economy of intervention and rent-seeking. Since intervention specifically makes incomes (rents) dependent on the state, it is consequently undermining democracy, and the politicians who respond to pressures for intervention are actively involved in digging democracy's grave.

In contrast, the most successful way of assigning incomes other than by voting is through individual property rights, so that:

> somewhere between full public ownership of the means of production and extreme *laissez-faire* is a line that the liberal society cannot cross or a grey area within which politics becomes increasingly factious and unwieldy as the public sector expands, until eventually the liberal society dissolves into despotism (Usher, 1990, p. 469).

There is unfortunately no shortage of historical and even contemporary examples of States which confirm and illustrate Usher's arguments. Every despotism in Africa began with a one-man-one-vote system, left by the departing Imperial power. Democracy is in fact another of the benefits of efficient property rights, and depends upon them. Voting works as a counterbalance to property, giving weight to numbers simply as numbers, and the amount of its influence that any economy can stand and still be economically efficient, depends upon how much property *independent* of the State there is.

Living on Capital

The fear must be that rent-seeking is a form of living on cultural and well as economic capital, and that Western countries are surviving, when the Soviet Union collapsed, for no other reason than that their stocks of capital were so much greater. In some cases, however, capital may have been run down so much through adoption of intervention and rent-seeking that the process is now politically irreversible. In that case, they could face the prospect that:

> [D]emocratic societies, as they now operate, will self-destruct, perhaps slowly but nonetheless surely, unless the rules of the political game are changed (Brennan and Buchanan, 1989, p. 150).

Changing the rules of the political game can mean nothing else than abandoning intervention, clamping down on rent-seeking, and attempting to govern through laws which can underwrite competitive markets. However hard it may be for politicians and bureaucrats to accept, the reality is that to the extent that they espouse intervention, they are expelling entrepreneurs from the economic system and replacing them with unproductive rent-seekers.

Unfortunately, since it is one of the effects of collectivism to cause the self-interest of politicians to diverge from the common good, devising and enacting such laws hold little attraction for them. Efficient property rights deny them the ability to benefit their constituents and lobbyists directly. They equally deny power without responsibility to bureaucrats and remove the fulcrum which rent-seekers need to exert leverage. It is in these very denials, in fact, that their greatest value is to be found.

IRELAND: NO COUNTRY FOR ENTREPRENEURS

It would scarcely have been possible for an independent Ireland to escape belief that the state knows better than the market. Those who run a state which has come into being through revolution can hardly be other than credulous about what intervention can achieve in economic matters. Every revolution is an attack on an existing property-rights system, so it is inevitable that success will carry with it a predisposition to intervene, since the new state is the expression of the energy which displaced the former property-owners. In Ireland, too, the world-wide trend towards collectivism during this century, converged with a local tradition from well before independence, of looking towards government for economic initiatives.

The Cumann na nGael government vacillated between *status quo* and interventionist policies. On the one hand, they wanted to maintain free trade with Britain and parity of the currency with sterling, and they were prudent about public borrowing; on the other, they were influenced by the old Sinn Fein doctrines which had been articulated by Arthur Griffith, inspired by the teaching of the German economist, Friedrich List, on industrial development through protection for infant industries.

The beginnings of rent-seeking can be observed during this period, therefore, in numbers of applications for tariff and quota protection. For example, the successful lobbying for preferential excise terms by P.J. Carroll, the Dundalk tobacco firm, was so blatant a reduction of competition as to exclude their Belfast rival, Gallaher's, completely from the Free State market. It is also significant that at least part of the stimulus for setting up the first of the semi-state bodies, the Shannon Scheme/ESB, was to pre-empt a private enterprise hydro-electric scheme on the Liffey (Manning and McDowell, 1984, pp. 13-14, 28). One of the most striking examples of successful rent-seeking during this, or indeed any other period, was the Irish Hospitals' Sweepstakes, the specific legislation for which made it possible for a former Government Minister and his associates to amass very large fortunes(Dáil Éireann, 1930).

The Lemass Era

A drift towards collectivism became a flood with the coming to power of Fianna Fáil in 1932. Indeed, it is not an unreasonable interpretation of Lee (1989, p. 241) that if Sean Lemass had had his way, the Irish economy might have become every bit as centrally controlled as any in Eastern Europe.

Nothing illustrates the meaning of rent-seeking better than the lobbying to capture the advantages of the industrial protection then being offered by the Irish state. This was all the more in evidence because many of the protective arrangements were individually negotiated by Lemass, and indeed kept secret. (Daly, 1992, p. 110).

This industrialisation policy, of course, was not at all to the taste of de Valera, whose ideal was a rural society. It is highly plausible that he did not object because the other side of the coin of industrial protection was financial support for the political party he had founded. The accountants and lawyers who specialised as go-betweens (two firms in particular) also shared in the resulting rents (Daly, 1992, p. 179; cf. McCague, 1994).

These new businesses needed little if any entrepreneurship. All that mattered was the level of protection. The rent-seekers who benefited from Government intervention consequently did not have to worry about either their customers or competition. Innovation of any kind was certainly not on their agenda — many of their plants were equipped with second-hand machines to produce the *obsolete* designs of British products.

Parallel rent-seeking within the civil service can be illustrated from the careers of two Principal Officers in Lemass's Department. These were persistent advocates of a nitrogenous fertiliser industry, but invariably came up against Department of Finance evidence that this had no economic rationale whatever. Eventually, they obtained a promise from their Minister that if ever they could persuade other departments of the project's value, they would have jobs "high up" in the proposed firm. The plant was eventually set up for political, not economic reasons (in what was possibly the most unsuitable site in the entire country because a seat had been lost locally); the civil servants became Chairman and Managing Director; and another continuing financial burden was loaded on to Irish farmers and taxpayers (Synon, 1970, p. 66).

Failure of Protection

Because they had so little creativity in them, the protected industries signally failed even to try to become internationally competitive, and they did nothing to raise the standards of employee skills, of craft and of the value placed on workmanship. After abandonment of the protectionist experiment in the 1950s, the country made a real advance, primarily, it should be noted, as a result of a *legal* change. Zero-rating of tax on export profits transformed the value of holding property in the form of manufacturing assets in Ireland. The associated interventionist system of grants was far less important as an incentive to investment from abroad, and was ultimately self-defeating. This was because grants are no more than capitalised subsidies to compensate for disadvantages of locating here. Their existence enables politicians to avoid having to shoulder the unpopular task of legislating about whatever is holding back entrepreneurship. This neglect allows the disadvantages to remain in existence; indeed, in some cases they grow to such an extent that in the end no possible level of grant aid can compensate for them.

Lessons from the Hyster Case

How self-defeating this aspect of industrial policy is, is well illustrated by the case of Hyster. This US manufacturer of fork-lift trucks and similar equipment played off the South of Ireland against the North, so as to get an exceptional grant for setting up a plant in Blanchardstown (the amount was so large that it could not be revealed). When this plant did not prosper, they approached the Industrial Development Authority with a proposal for another large grant, this time to enable them make spare parts in the large Limerick factory which a Dutch firm, Ferenka, had abandoned. This was of course welcomed, but Hyster then called attention to a difficulty: the parts they intended to manufacture were for their competitors' machines, not their own. A recent High Court ruling, following a British precedent, had given spare parts protection through the copyright in the drawings from which they were made. Hyster could therefore expect to be sued on this basis by competitors if they went ahead with their plan.

The Industrial Development Authority naturally lobbied on their behalf, and the upshot was a dramatic and urgent intervention in the

Senate by the Minister for Industry and Commerce. At the time, an amendment to the Copyright Act, outlawing video nasties, was being discussed. The Minister insisted that a second amendment be added, overturning the Court judgement (which had related to fish boxes). The Government fell shortly afterwards, and the amendment lapsed with it. Hyster's Blanchardstown project collapsed and they left the country. Nonetheless, in due course the amendment came up again before a new Dáil and Senate, and "the proposed change in the law to facilitate the proposed Hyster factory in Limerick" (Dáil Debates, 1987) was solemnly passed.

The subordinate position of law to intervention as means of achieving industrial development, in the minds of both politicians and bureaucrats, is very evident from this case. It is confirmed by the sequel. The British response to the judicial precedent referred to, was to introduce a quite new kind of functional design protection in the Copyright, Patents and Designs Act, 1988. This is particularly well suited to protecting the incremental innovations of the types of business which are common in Ireland (and could be made even more valuable if it included registration arrangements with Internet-type dissemination). The authorities had an opportunity of copying this in the Patents Act of 1992, but opted instead for the now outdated German system of "petty patents".

External Borrowing

The scale and harmfulness of the rent-seeking associated with the "infant industry" type of intervention was unfortunately surpassed by what followed as a result of the two oil shocks in the 1970s. Recycling of the OPEC surpluses came at a particularly unfortunate time for Ireland, when an unsophisticated form of Keynesian economics dominated in both academic and civil service circles. As a result, the advice which politicians were receiving confirmed their natural inclination to borrow and spend. None of this borrowed money ever earned an adequate return (in fact, much of it went on greatly increased public sector pay) so the cost of servicing it will remain indefinitely as a brake on Irish competitiveness. This problem can only continue to worsen year by year, because the EU's "monetary union" guideline for debt/GDP ratio — itself a particularly misleading measure in Ireland's case (Murphy, 1994) — has replaced a balanced budget as the accepted objective of policy.

European Union Funding

Borrowing has been increased still more to meet the requirement of matching transfers from the EU, which have further widened the field for rent-seeking. Politicians are under strong pressures to spend these funds in highly visible ways on public sector projects, in their own constituencies as far as possible and virtually without regard for financial return. The scramble for such funds is particularly fierce, because only they provide "Political Discretionary Income", so much of the regular budget being committed in advance for national rather than constituency requirements (Kingston, 1994c).

What escapes observation in respect of most EU-funded projects, many of which would never have been undertaken on a fully rational assessment, is the link — through operation, maintenance and debt service costs — with high taxation. This feeds through into wage levels that inhibit long-term productive investment, and these cannot be compensated for by lowering the exchange rate because of the scale of the country's external debt. Similar damage from structural and cohesion funding in other poor EU countries helps to explain why economic convergence will remain an unfulfilled aspiration of the Treaty of Rome (Kingston, 1994b).

A Harmful Voting System

Granted that the state sector has grown strongly in every country throughout the present century, why has it been more damaging in Ireland than in any other OECD country (cf. Mjoset, 1991)? Why, in particular, has Ireland's economic record been so much worse than that of Finland, which is otherwise so similar (Kingston, 1994c)? Much of the answer may be discovered in the country's electoral system. This is very effective at enabling individuals to bring their preferences to bear on politicians, who are almost defenceless against the claims of sectional interests, because neither the Constitution nor the prevailing social culture constrain Government powers to tax and borrow.

Since so much property in Ireland has been obtained directly or indirectly (by rent-seeking) through politics, the country has a very low proportion of property that is independent of the state. At the same time it has a voting system (multi-seat proportional representation) which gives a heavier weighting to numbers than any other type in practical use. (The property/numbers balance is exactly opposite in Switzerland which, significantly, is the richest country. Its frequent use of referenda also acts as a restraint on collectivist tendencies).

Consequently, Ireland has a much more democratic structure of representative government than is compatible with economic efficiency. This diagnosis not alone explains the profligacy of its modern public finance, but even enabled it to be predicted (Kingston, 1976). It is also the root cause, not just of an inhospitable environment for entrepreneurship, but of a general incompatibility of State ownership and competent management which is illustrated by the unhappy record of almost every one of the semi-state bodies.

The argument that there is a connection between the property/ numbers balance, the electoral system and the strength of collectivism has received powerful reinforcement from the case of Italy. Faced with national bankruptcy, that country's electorate has voted overwhelmingly to change its voting system from proportional representation in an attempt to discipline its politicians.

Unfortunately, the imbalance between weight to independent property and weight to numbers is so great in Ireland that it could not be rectified just by moving to the "first-past-the-post" voting system used in Britain or even to one of the "list" systems. Some more drastic relative reduction of the weight to numbers, or a correspondingly severe restriction on the power of Governments to tax and borrow, would be needed. In a country which is now so conditioned to look to politicians for favours, and where there is also the nucleus of an alternative standing army, the reaction to either change could literally be explosive.

Victory of the Rent-seekers

Needless to say, so much "unearned" money in the hands of politicians, whether from external borrowing or EU transfers, has been the target of a host of rent-seekers. These have been rewarded, for example, by special tax breaks (the Temple Bar area) legislation benefiting specific individuals (the Financial Services Centre) purchase of assets with public money at inflated prices (Telecom, the Kilrush marina) or disposal of public assets without competitive tendering (CIE) monopoly grant of export credit insurance (beef firms) and, of course, ubiquitous land rezoning (construction companies). Apart from the inevitable waste of resources which has resulted, several public enquiries have unfortunately provided evidence of how thin is the line between rent-seeking and corruption of the civil service as well as politicians. These include Curran, 1990; Glacken, 1991, 1993; the Beef Tribunal, 1993 (cf. O'Toole, 1994); and Committee on Public Accounts, 1994.

Indeed, the victory of rent-seekers over entrepreneurs in Ireland must now be considered to be virtually complete. In 1983-90, indigenous Irish manufacturing firms were only able to earn a rate of profit of 0.2 per cent on their sales (O'Hearn, 1993, p. 79). In 1994, in spite of all the employment-related subventions from the state, such firms could only add a nett 202 jobs. In the same year, again in spite of massive subsidies, there were only 11 more jobs in *all* manufacturing industry, both foreign-owned and indigenous, than in 1985 (Forfas, 1995). It is widely accepted amongst business men that total costs are £2,000 per worker-year higher in the Republic than in Northern Ireland, largely because of taxation differences.

These are no conditions to encourage entrepreneurial activity, and they compare most unfavourably with the relentless success of rent-seeking, both as indicated above, and in public-sector pay. A distressing aspect of the resulting imbalance is the increasing proportion of the population which is excluded from autonomous economic activity and dependent upon the state.

Last Chance in the EU Saloon?

Because EU guidelines are preventing politicians from borrowing as much as they would like, the continuation of the privileged position of the country's rent-seekers is now very dependent on transfers from Brussels. These are due to be reduced substantially within a few years, so it might be thought possible to hope for at least a limited conversion then to saner policies. It is not too difficult to identify changes in Company, Trades Union and Intellectual Property law which could produce a business environment much more conducive to entrepreneurship (Kingston, 1994c).

Some, however, are hoping instead for a last-ditch effort by the Government to obtain another round of EU funding to postpone having to face reality for a few more years. This would take the form of payments to Ireland to compensate it for difficulties in joining in the common European currency. For a country to claim that it is strong enough to join, at the same time as asking for compensation for joining, might seem the height of absurdity. Unfortunately, it fits in with a suggestion by M. Chirac that those who do not adopt the common currency should pay those who do. The logic of this argument is that by not over-valuing their national currencies, the countries which do not join would have an advantage in selling their products.

In the Irish case, then, it is not quite beyond the bounds of possibility that those who provide the EU with money, mainly of course Germany, would be willing to pay what by their standards would be a small amount for the sake of maintaining a vassal state in the North Atlantic world.

In that event, Irish credulity about the superior wisdom of the state would be sustainable in the interest of the rent-seekers who benefit from it, for just a bit longer. Sooner or later, however, Skidelsky's contention that collectivism destroys political economies is no less likely to be proved right in Ireland than it has already been in the countries of Eastern Europe.

REFERENCES

Baumol, W.J. (1990): "Entrepreneurship: Productive, Unproductive and Destructive", *Journal of Political Economy*, 98(5): 893-921.

Brennan, G. and Buchanan, J.M. (1989): *The Reason of Rules*, Cambridge: Cambridge University Press.

Curran, M. (1990): "Report into Siucre Éireann etc.", Dublin: The Stationery Office.

Dáil Debates, 14 October 1987, Mr. Desmond O'Malley.

Dáil Éireann, Hospitals' Sweepstakes (Temporary Provisions) Act, 1930. 30 per cent (7 per cent for any individual) of all revenues were allowed for the promoters' expenses.

Dáil Éireann Committee on Public Accounts, 1994: Second Interim Report on the Report of the Comptroller and Auditor-General for

1991, Dublin: The Stationery Office (PN 0574). For rent-seeking, see in particular finding No. 11.

Daly, M.E. (1992): *Industrial Development and Irish National Identity*, Dublin: Gill and Macmillan.

Forfas Annual Report (1995): Dublin: The Stationery Office.

Glackin, J.A. (1991), (1993): Chestvale Properties and Hoddle Investments Ltd. Interim and Final Reports to the Minister for Industry and Commerce, Dublin: The Stationery Office.

Gray, J. (1993): *Beyond the New Right*, London: Routledge.

Keynes, J.M. (1945): "Memorandum to Cabinet, 18 March", *Collected Writings 24*, London: Macmillan: 261.

Kingston, W. (1976): "The Lemmings of Democracy", *Studies 65*: 297-309.

Kingston, W. (1993): "Property Rights and the Making of Christendom" *Studies 82*: 402-25.

Kingston, W. (1994a): "A Reflection in Ganagobie", *Crisis* (November), Washington, DC.

Kingston, W. (1994b): "Economic Convergence: an Aspiration Unfulfilled", in Urban, S. (ed.) *Europe's Economic Future*, Wiesbaden, Gabler Verlag: 53-75.

Kingston, W. (1994c): "Why Ireland Failed to Keep Up", *Studies 83:* 251-264.

Kingston, W. (1995): "Innovation or Bureaucracy"? *Creativity and Innovation Management,* 5(3), September.

Landes, D. (1970): *The Unbound Prometheus*, Cambridge: Cambridge University Press.

Lee, J. (1989): *Ireland, 1912-1985*, Cambridge: Cambridge University Press.

Liebenstein, H. (1966): AEA Papers and Proceedings: 75.

McCague, E. (1994): *Arthur Cox*, Dublin: Gill and Macmillan.

McCloskey, D. and Klamer, A. (1995): "One Quarter of GDP is Persuasion". AEA Papers and Proceedings, 85(2): 194.

MacNeice, L. (1936): "Eclogue from Iceland", in *Collected Poems, 1966*, London: Faber and Faber.

Manning, M. and McDowell, M. (1984): *Electricity Supply in Ireland*, Dublin: Gill and MacMillan.

Mill, J. S. (1848): *Principles of Political Economy Book II*, Chapter I.

Mjoset, L. (1992): *The Irish Economy in a Comparative Institutional Perspective*, Dublin: National Economic and Social Council.

Muller, D. (1989): *Public Choice 2*, Cambridge: Cambridge University Press.

Murphy, A. (1994): *The Irish Economy: Celtic Tiger or Tortoise?* Dublin: MMI Stockbrokers.

North, D. (1981): *Structure and Change in Economic History*, New York: W.W. Norton Co.

North, D. (1990): *Institutions, Institutional Change and Economic Performance*, Cambridge: Cambridge University Press.

O'Toole, F. (1994): *Meanwhile, Back at the Ranch*, London: Vintage.

O'Hearn, D. (1993): "Global Competition, Europe and Irish Peripherality", *Economic and Social Review*, January. Figures quoted are from the Industrial Development Authority.

Rosenberg, N. and Birdzell, L.E. (1986): *How the West Grew Rich*, London: Tauris.

Schumpeter, J.A. (1939): *Business Cycles*, London: McGraw Hill.

Schumpeter, J.A. (1947): "The Creative Response in Economic History". *Journal of Economic History*: 152.

Skidelsky, R. (1995): *The World After Communism*, London: Macmillan.

Synon, M. (1970): Unpublished M.B.A. Dissertation, Dublin: Trinity College. Her information comes from interviews with Sean Lemass.

Tribunal of Enquiry into the Beef Industry (1993): Dublin: The Stationery Office.

Usher, D. (1981): *The Economic Prerequisite to Democracy*, Oxford: Blackwell.

Usher, D. (1990): *The Welfare Economics of Markets, Voting and Predation*, Ann Arbor: University of Michigan Press.

13

RENT-SEEKING OPPORTUNITIES

Sean D. Barrett

Rent is an allocatively unnecessary payment not required to attract resources to a particular employment (Buchannan, 1980). Rent-seeking is directly unproductive profit-seeking (Bhagwati, 1980). Early estimates of rent-seeking in India and Turkey showed that it accounted for 7.3 per cent and 15 per cent of GNP respectively (Krueger, 1974). Sources of rent cited by Krueger, such as product and labour market interventions, taxi regulation, investment incentives for favoured sectors, large public investment programmes and railways, are also rent-seekers in Ireland. The EU has added significant rent-seeking because of the Common Agricultural Policy (CAP) and its large transfers of funds to the Irish government. The evidence for Ireland is that the resource misallocations due to rent-seeking are probably larger then the early estimates by Krueger. The problem was stressed in the Culliton Report:

> In the attempt to boost economic performance over the years, the proliferation of tax breaks and grant assistance has had some un-intended negative side-effects, on the structure of industry, on the level of Government borrowing and on the self-reliance of Irish entrepreneurs. In particular, the competitive edge of Irish industry has been distracted from serving the market and achieving high productivity, into maximising the grant or tax benefit. Tax avoidance and grant maximisation are the directly unproductive activities (or "rent-seeking" in the economists' jargon) par excellence. Tax reform and a reduced emphasis on industrial grants, especially for non-mobile investment, should help refocus entrepreneurial effort (Culliton, 1992, p. 22).

Culliton's recommendations sought to reduce rent-seeking in the Irish economy:

> A transparent tax system will reduce the rewards to some kinds of directly unproductive activities and divert more of our most able people into more productive activities. Indeed, we are so convinced of the ultimate folly of a procedure where every special interest or perceived difficulty is accommodated by ad hoc adjustments to the tax code, that we have refrained altogether, despite many submissions to us, from proposing any new sectional reliefs (Ibid., pp. 24).

On the subsidy side of rent-seeking, Culliton recommended fewer grants and grant distributing bodies.

Ireland as a nation also engages in rent-seeking through EU transfers. Culliton reported:

> ... a widely-held perception, in both the public and private sectors, that the Structural Funds represent in some way "free money from Brussels" the allocation of which requires to be less rigorously evaluated and accounted for than normal. The allocation of resources by Departments to the management of activities co-financed by the Structural Funds appears to be on the minimalist basis of ensuring that the draw-down of funds is at the fastest possible level without sufficient attention to ensuring the most effective use of the Funds (Ibid., p. 49).

In Ireland, the government's share in the economy is some 7 to 10 percentage points of GDP higher than other countries at our stage of development such as Spain, Greece and Portugal (Culliton, p. 37). A large public sector promotes rent-seeking since it increases both the size of the taxes to be sheltered from and the subsidies possible. A lobbyist industry will thrive in such a situation. Successful lobbying by pressure groups for sectoral tax concessions increases the complexity of the tax code. This in turn leads to the employment of more tax lawyers and accountants. Culliton noted a three-fold increase in the number of accountants between 1971 and 1986 and the doubling of the number of auctioneers and lawyers. By comparison, the number of engineers increased by 50 per cent in the same period (p. 22).

Irish agriculture is heavily based on subsidies from the CAP. Quotas control over 80 per cent of the output of Irish agriculture (NESC, 97, p. 42). The CAP has:

> distorted the production structure and efficiency structure of Irish agriculture and maintained output from other inherently less competitive Community countries (Ibid. p. 27).

High input prices inhibit the development of the food sector. Dismantling the CAP would force producers and processors away from intervention to a market-led strategy.

Irish industry received some £1.6 billion of grants from the end of 1980 to the end of 1990. The firms which received this assistance added 7,000 employees, a grant cost of £229,000 per job. On the other hand firms which received no grants added some 9,000 jobs. Since the purpose of the grants was to promote employment their efficiency must be questioned. The firms examined seemed to be either efficient at rent-seeking or net employment generation but not both (Culliton, pp. 63-5).

In the protectionist era of 1932-65 Irish industry was heavily engaged in rent-seeking. Ryan (1949) estimated that the average Irish tariff level in 1936 was 45 per cent and cites evidence that this was fifth highest of a sample of twenty countries examined. Irish industry grew accustomed to government intervention on its behalf. An example of successful rent-seeking was the securing of a 10 per cent tax rate for manufacturing. Since the tax rate on the employment-intensive services sector is 38 per cent this distorts incentives against employment. Some of the excluded services sectors have taken legal actions to be designated as manufacturing and firms have used transfer pricing to artificially locate transactions in Ireland in order to avoid higher corporate taxation elsewhere. This, in turn, overstates the GNP per head, thus reducing the size of important ratios in economic policy such as taxation, government borrowing and government debt in relation to GNP.

The construction sector in Ireland has successfully engaged in rent-seeking through the public capital programme. This unanalysed set of spending programmes is based on a general belief in public expenditure per se, a designation of capital as any item which does not fall down within a year, and a belief that a healthy construction industry is a barometer of a healthy economy. No rate of return calculations are undertaken and the diversion of resources into construction from the traded goods sector of the economy is treated as a benefit rather than a cost in public sector statements concerning the programme. In 1994 some 65 per cent of the total public capital programme of £2,379 million was spent on construction. The £1,544 million of public capital expenditure on construction was 39 per cent of total construction output of £3,944m in 1994 (Public Capital Programme; Construction Industry Review and Outlook 1994 and 1995). In addition, the construction sector enjoys considerable fiscal privilege. The 1993 Statistical Report of the Revenue Commissioners estimates that the cost of mortgage interest relief in 1991-92 was £181.4 million, and that relief for rent paid in private tenancies was £1.1 million. The report also estimates that urban renewal relief cost £17.8 million and that relief for provision of rented residential accommodation cost £3.8 million. The report did not quantify the cost of reliefs for "expenditure on significant buildings" and "expenditure on certain buildings in designated inner city areas". The cost of exemption from capital gains tax of receipts from the sale of principal private dwellings is not stated.

RENT-SEEKING CONSUMERS

Consumer groups have also been successful in rent-seeking in Ireland. Prior to 1995 there was excess demand for university places in Ireland at typical fees of £1,800. The student body came overwhelmingly from the upper income groups since successful performance at primary and secondary sectors was a requirement for entry. The private return on the investment was 15 per cent per annum (de Buitlear, 1994, p. 2). There was a grant system for low-income students but it had faults such as failure to take account of assets and abrupt withdrawal of grants once thresholds had been exceeded. No reforms of the grants system were undertaken but fees were abolished for all. The benefits of state expenditure on third-level education are now skewed in favour of the richer sections of society. Callan (1992) estimates that almost the same share of student support expenditure goes to the middle 20 per cent of the income distribution as goes to the bottom 40 per cent. The abolition of third-level fees diverted state resources from dealing with the excess demand problem. The financial independence of the universities was undermined by the abolition of fees in the same way as the autonomy of local authorities had been undermined by the abolition of domestic rates in 1977. Colleges were reduced to a rent-seeking relationship with the legislature by the government decision to forbid them to sell their services to the public.

In 1991 a case of rent-seeking by the richest consumers of health services was included in the PESP national agreement. The richest 15 per cent of the population (eligibility Category 111) was given the same health service entitlements as the Category 11 middle income group (Programme for Economic and Social Progress, p. 28). Previously, persons in Category 111 were required to bear their own hospital consultant costs and "the vast majority in Category 111 insure themselves with the Voluntary Health Insurance Board against this liability" (Commission on Health Funding, 1989, p. 108). Unlike the 1995 education example however, there was no ban imposed on either direct payments to health service providers or the purchase of commercial health insurance.

RENT AND EQUITY

Controversial claims of social justice are part of the stock in trade of the Irish rent-seeker. Thus, in education and health the above concessions were secured by groups far in excess of average incomes. While vague social arguments are used to promote state expenditure on railways, the richest income quintile accounts for half of expenditure on rail travel compared to 5 per cent for the poorest income quintile. Report Number 30 of the Review Body on Higher Remuneration in the Public Sector stated that:

> it would be a clear injustice to those whose remuneration is being reviewed if all other considerations of fairness and practicality were to be entirely outweighed by a single factor, the state of the public finances (Review Body on Higher Remuneration in the Public Sector, p. 6).

In fact, the higher civil service obtained far greater increases in pay than average. The cost was borne by a combination of tax increases (thereby widening the tax wedge and causing unemployment) and by borrowing which is a tax on future generations.

Claims that teaching was an especially stressful occupation fuelled a campaign for early retirements. Notwithstanding evidence from the UK Registrar General's data on occupational mortality that teachers have the lowest standardised mortality of all occupations reporting, the government conceded the claim a mere seven weeks after a teacher strike on 23 May 1995. Early retirement throughout the public service is a sizeable economic rent now available for public service trade unions. The fact that the epidemiological evidence for early retirement for teachers was so weak, but successful, seriously undermines the ability of the exchequer to resist this new form of public sector rent-seeking. The rapidly ageing population structure in Ireland indicates that later retirement and a move to funded pensions should have been the options chosen.

Baumol (1990) notes litigation as a growing area of rent-seeking in recent times. The size of court awards means that "it must become tempting for the entrepreneur to select his closest advisers from the lawyers rather than the engineers". Ireland has a reputation as a "slip and sue" country with a high level of liability litigation. The number of affidavits filed in the High Court increased almost five-fold between 1970 and 1992 from 5,096 to 24,525.

DEREGULATION AND RENT

In the transport sector, successful rent-seeking by the shareholders of railway companies secured the banning of the operation of independent bus services without licence in 1932 and the banning of road freight companies on a similar basis in 1933. Successful lobbying by the shareholders, management, and employees of the protected companies in 1950 secured nationalisation. Since the 1970s railways have typically secured more then half their revenues from governments through subsidies and only the smaller proportion from customers. There are about two mainline rail journeys undertaken per head of the population per year. The industry devotes considerable resources to rent-seeking and enjoys greater success there than in the marketplace.

The deregulation of road freight in 1988 abolished rent and returned to the free market economy a sector removed by legislation in 1933. In the protectionist rent-seeking era, a survey in 1964 found that only 17 per cent of Irish road freight moved in hired haulage vehicles. The purpose of restricting the output of road hauliers was to assist the railways. Firms instead used their "own account" vehicles to carry 83 per cent of road freight. The scarce road haulage licences acquired a licence value of £20,000. Since deregulation the hired haulage sector has expanded to two-thirds of the market. The cost of the rent-seeking of 1933 was borne over some 55 years by increasing the cost of road freight to Irish industry, restricting the hired haulage sector, conferring windfall gains on the holders of licences, and requiring Irish firms to acquire "own account" fleets which they do not now require in the deregulated market. These costs are additional to the annual operating and capital subsidies to the railways.

The failure to deregulate the taxi business in Dublin is reflected in the rise of the value of a taxi licence from £3,500 in 1980 to £80,000 in 1995. Successful rent-seeking by the licence holders contrasts with the policy pursued in the case of road haulage licences. Similarly, public house licensing confers a scarcity value on the licences, particularly in new suburban areas of increasing population. There was strong political opposition to modification of the law to allow restaurants to sell spirits and beers. In the same fashion, proposals to abolish the solicitors' monopoly of conveyancing were dropped because of opposition from solicitors.

A striking example of the abolition of rents was the deregulation of air transport between Ireland and Britain in 1986. Following the Chicago Conference in 1944, international aviation was regulated by bilateral agreements between governments. The agreements specified one airline per country, the agreement of both airlines and governments on fares to be charged and the division of the market between the two airlines. While no explicit subsidy was paid to the Irish state airline, Aer Lingus, immunity from new entrants and from price competition from its partner international airline allowed it to earn rents. Prior to 1986, proponents of greater contestability in European scheduled aviation pointed to the large disparity in air fares between deregulated systems such as California and the European charter airlines on the one hand, and European scheduled airlines on the other. The airlines responded by disputing the fares data, drawing attention to the high cost environment for aviation in Europe, such as employee protection and expensive airports.

The Anglo-Irish deregulation has had remarkable results with fare reductions of as much as 80 per cent in real terms and the three-fold increase in volumes. The 1985 unrestricted fare of £208 on Dublin-London was available for £69 in the summer of 1995. The 1995 projection of traffic on the route is 3 million passengers, compared to a static 980,000 over the years 1978-85. The largest monthly increase in 1987 (the first full year of deregulation) over 1985 was in August, at

91.7 per cent (Barrett, 1991, p. 12). The rent-seeking policies of the protected airlines involved the use of yield maximisation programmes to choke off demand at peak times by pushing passengers into higher fare categories. The Green Paper on Aviation Policy in 1994 listed as the benefits from airline deregulation an increase of 60 per cent in visitor numbers to Ireland in 1993 over 1987 with additional foreign tourism earnings of £560 million, additional employment in tourism of 25,000, and an increase of 50 per cent in foreign travel by business people "which has undoubtedly helped our merchandise export drive" (Green Paper on Aviation, p. 4).

Ireland's access transport policy in 1986 was based on cartels for both sea and air transport. The airlines protected were not remarkably profitable despite charging fares far above those now charged in the deregulated market. The rents enjoyed from protection from competition were distributed not to shareholders, the taxpayers, but were absorbed in high labour costs and low productivity. European scheduled air fares were consistently the highest in the world in the ICAO annual surveys. European airline productivity was typically a third below that in the United States, and Aer Lingus productivity was only 53 per cent of the average of eighteen European national airlines (Barrett, 1987, chapter 3). Irish airline wage costs were 45 per cent above those of non-rent earning airlines such as British Midland (Barrett, 1990). In common with other successful rent-seekers, Aer Lingus attained "regulatory capture" over the Department of Transport which became known as a "downtown office" of the airline. In retrospect it is difficult to see how the Aer Lingus arguments against competition were influential for so long in Ireland, though national airlines still influence public opinion in countries such as France, Italy, Spain, Portugal and Greece. Aer Lingus was influential in both political and media discussions of the undesirability of airline competition. It also identified itself with Irish nationalism, projecting itself as a badge of Irish nationality. An ironic claim was that the "national airline" promoted tourism to Ireland through marketing campaigns, presumably financed by the excessive fares charged.

In sea transport the result of rent-seeking was the transfer of business to the Northern Ireland sea routes to Britain. During the operation of the sea cartel, the Irish state shipping company (the B & I Line) was heavily loss-making. In 1995 both of the former cartel member shipping companies have been privatised and Irish Ferries, which bought the B & I Line on its privatisation, is a sought-after share. The loss of traffic to Northern Ireland ports has also reduced the ability of the dock sector and its employees to earn economic rent.

RENT-SEEKING IN FACTOR MARKETS

Rent-seeking in labour markets has traditionally involved trade unions and professions restricting new entrants. Craft trade unions and professions alike offered reasons of quality assurance and consumer protection for their restraint on new entrants. The additional earnings of the protected occupations in industry provided employers with an incentive to substitute capital for labour with a resulting reduction of the role of craft unions compared to general trade unions.

In areas such as printing Ireland is uncompetitive compared to imported newspapers following the changes in Fleet Street and Wapping. The ability of craft trade unions to earn rents is thus limited by the availability of imported substitutes.

In the case of the professions competing, imports are also in evidence. Northern Ireland dentists have begun to advertise in the Republic. Hip replacement patients from Cork were airlifted to Belfast for treatment in 1994. There is also a competitive market between opticians on both sides of the border. Apart from their traditional prestige, the professions enjoy a large return on investment in human capital. In this context a key point by Schultz (1961) is that the professions and trade unions who control entry to certain occupations keep investment in human capital below its optimum. In Ireland the number of qualified but unsuccessful applicants for the professions is high and the school leaving certificate points for entry are also high. Earnings are in excess of the level required to attract a sufficient number of entrants. Given that the market is controlled by labour market insiders and the government, it is unlikely in the medium term that the rents can be bid away by new entrants.

An important new source of rent-seeking by trade unions has been the growth of national wage bargaining. Since labour is represented by trade unions in these negotiations, labour market insiders can ignore outsiders such as the unemployed, migrants and school leavers. The level of unemployment has risen from 247,000 in 1987 to 276,000 in 1995 under these agreements, which have nonetheless been hailed as a success by trade union leaders. Ireland is among the worst countries in converting economic growth into employment growth. Johns (1993) shows that output growth in Ireland and the United States was equal between 1960 and 1990, at 3.2 per cent per annum, but that annual employment growth in the US, at 1.9 per cent, was 7.3 times the annual employment growth in Ireland of 0.26 per cent. The success of the US labour market in translating economic growth into employment growth is regularly criticised by Irish trade union leaders, who represent labour market insiders. Since unionisation rates are almost three times as great in the public sector than in the private sector it is not surprising that over the period 1987-94 public sector pay per head grew by 62 per cent, compared to 35 per cent in industry and the consumer price index rise of 22 per cent (Lee, 1994). This echoes the finding of the official Review Body on Higher Remuneration in the Public Sector which stated that:

> the 1991 Public Service Pay and Pensions Bill amounted to £3.4 billion and absorbed 54 per cent of voted non-capital expenditure. It has increased by 25 per cent since 1987 and if account is taken of the reduction in public service numbers over the period to 1991 the average increase has been 33 per cent. Aggregate inflation over the same period amounted to about 13 per cent (Review Body on Higher Remuneration in the Public Sector, Report no. 35, p. 15).

O'Riordan (1989), in an examination of twenty OECD countries, found that public pay in Ireland, at 14.6 per cent of GDP in 1985, was exceeded only by Sweden (18.8 per cent) and Denmark (18.0 per cent). In the period 1977-85, nine of the twenty countries experienced a reduction in the ratio of public pay to GNP but the growth in Ireland was the highest. O'Riordan's finding was that:

> while the number employed in the public sector expressed as a proportion of the total at work are not abnormal by OECD standards, the fraction of the GDP which these employees obtain is unusually high. Furthermore, there is no evidence that this proportion is tending to return to levels which are normal by OECD standards.

Public sector wage determination in Ireland is based on relativity claims rather than labour market factors. Rent-seeking is facilitated by the absence of market discipline on the employer side. For example, despite recommending a 35 per cent increase in the pay of a departmental secretary, Report No. 30 of the Review Body on Higher Remuneration in the Public Sector stated that "our investigations found, however, that there have been very few departures of chief executives to take up employment outside the public sector" (Review Body on Higher Remuneration in the Public Sector, Report no. 30, p. 29).

It also stated that:

> the hard evidence available does not show conclusively to what extent the remuneration of top public sector posts has had an effect on the decisions to leave, either among those in top posts or among public servants at lower management levels (Ibid., p. 22).

Since the wages paid were sufficient to attract and hold suitably qualified individuals the increase in pay proposed by the Review Body is a transfer of rent to those currently in post.

There is also a lack of linkage in the public mind between the tax burden and the public pay bill. The Irish tax system includes many examples of fiscal illusion such as a high burden of indirect tax and a categorisation of social insurance as insurance rather than taxation. In addition, the real cost of public pay and services is disguised by heavy government borrowing and large EU transfers. A further incentive to rent-seeking in Ireland is a belief that there is a large stock of uncollected taxes available to fund the expenditure proposed. Thus we have public spending programmes proposed by trade unions with the stated object that self-employed persons such as farmers should pay for them and proposals by other groups in the safe knowledge that the burden will fall on the average PAYE worker.

Ireland is thus an economy with large rent-seeking in labour and product markets. Resource allocation is distorted throughout the economy. There have been substantial outflows of both labour and capital from the economy. The 1995 GNP is predicted by the Central Bank to be 88 per cent of GDP, a sign of foreign indebtedness and capital outflows.

RENT DISTRIBUTION AGENCIES

The decision by government to intervene in a sector of the economy creates two layers of patronage for politicians, the distribution of the tax breaks and subsidies themselves, and the establishment of agencies for the purpose. The patronage of appointing supporters to boards of state bodies is a long established aspect of Irish politics. In the industrial development programme there are three industrial development bodies — IDA Ireland, Forbairt and Forfas — and regional bodies such as SFADCO and Udaras na Gaeltachta. There are functional bodies such as ABT and sectoral bodies such as An Bord Bia. In addition there are 89 recently established agencies comprising 35 county enterprise boards, 26 PESP area partnerships, and 28 Leader groups. These bureaucracies themselves become rent-seekers with tactics such as public relations campaigns to boost the budget of the agencies and opposition to any independent evaluation of their value. A typical tactic of the rent-seeking agency is to attribute all activity in the sector to the agency rather than the producers and to boost the incomes of those in the agencies far above those working in the sectors they were established to serve.

RENT-SEEKING AND ENTREPRENEURSHIP

The large scale emigration from Ireland over the last two hundred years, high unemployment, and poor economic performance compared to other countries over the last century or so has led to queries on whether Ireland and its people face inherent obstacles to economic growth or whether it is inappropriate policies and incentives that constitute the barriers to development. O'Connell (1992) supports the latter view:

> It is sometimes suggested that a "missing variable" in this relatively benign picture is entrepreneurship, i.e. Ireland's effort to converge to EC living standards will be frustrated by a dearth of entrepreneurs. This is difficult to sustain against the evidence that Irish people are highly aware of, and quick to respond to, opportunities for financial gain. Amongst this evidence is: the emergence of domestic entrepreneurs behind tariff barriers from the 1930s to the late 1950s, the exploitation of all manner of tax avoidance and evasion, the balancing of the return from entering the workforce against the return from not working (the poverty trap), the competition for entry to the traditional professions, etc. There is every evidence that Irish people are highly responsive to financial incentives. The incentive structure itself, however, it is now widely accepted, has been heavily biased against productive economic activity. Much of the country's best talent has been drawn into areas of economic activity where private returns frequently far out-weigh

social returns, an adverse development which economists have also drawn attention to in the UK and US. The promotion of an entrepreneurial environment requires, as is now accepted generally, a radical restructuring of incentives, the fresh air of competition to reduce economic rents and to deter the most talented young people from opting for unproductive activities which, although offering high private returns, have a low social return, and some reorientation of the education system in order to accommodate students with a more vocational than academic inclination.

Furthermore, Burke (1995) found that 26 per cent of Irish composers of music admitted to collecting some form of social welfare payment. In practice this is likely to be a low estimate as it must be presumed that a proportion of those surveyed would not have wished to reveal this action.

Baumol (1990) offers three propositions concerning entrepreneurship and rent-seeking. These are (a) the rules of the game that determine the relative payoffs to different entrepreneurial activities do change dramatically from one time to another; (b) entrepreneurial behaviour changes direction from one economy to another in a manner that corresponds to the variations in the rules of the game and (c) the allocation of entrepreneurship between productive and unproductive activities, though by no means the only pertinent influence, can have a profound effect on the innovativeness of the economy and the degree of dissemination of its technological discoveries.

Whether entrepreneurial activity is allocated to productive or unproductive activities is determined by the prevailing laws and legal procedures of an economy. Baumol's conclusion is that:

> We do not have to wait patiently for slow cultural change in order to find measures to redirect the flow of entrepreneurial activity towards more productive goals. . . it may be possible to change the rules in ways that help to offset undesired institutional influences or that supplement other influences that are taken to work in beneficial directions.

Tullock (1990) sees migration as a way of avoiding a rent-seeking economy:

> The émigré Chinese of southeast Asia and the United States perform extremely well, as do the émigré Indians of Africa. Only in

their own homelands do they fail to perform well (Tullock, 1990, p. 29).

The Irish export of both labour and private capital, plus the rent-seeking noted by O'Connell, point to the need for rule changes to reduce rent in the economy.

The diversion of entrepreneurial effort from serving the market and increasing productivity to rent-seeking behaviour prompts a warning by Porter (1990):

> Government's proper role in enhancing national advantage is the reverse of what is often supposed. Many see government as a helper or supporter of industry. Yet many of the ways in which government tries to "help" industry can actually hurt a nation's firms in the long run (for example, subsidies, domestic mergers, supporting levels of co-operation, providing guaranteed government demand, and artificial devaluation of the currency). These sets of policies mean that firms will fail to take the steps necessary to create sustainable competitive advantage and will slow the upgrading of the economy. Too much government support also makes it difficult to persuade industry to invest and take risk without it. At the same time helping creates the demand for more helping.

CONCLUSION: A POLICY PRESCRIPTION

Rent-seeking imposes large costs on the Irish economy. Ireland should therefore seek to reduce the volume of rent-seeking and to divert the resources employed in rent-seeking to directly productive activities The stimulation of the Irish economy towards productive entrepreneurship and away from rent-seeking, requires a wide range of policy reforms. The goal is to redeploy to the competitive market economy resources now diverted to rent-seeking. These include the resources transferred to the rent-seeking sector, the transaction costs of lobbyists, and the administrative costs of the rent-distributing agencies.

In taxation the goal of reform should be a simple system with a low standard rate without deductions, allowances, tax shelters and fiscal privilege. The low standard rate of tax would reduce the tax wedge between the cost of employment and take-home pay. It would also reduce replacement ratios of social welfare to after tax income from work. Furthermore, there would be a decrease in the return on lobbying governments for tax breaks for particular sectors. This contrasts with the present case where the high general rates of taxation increase the rewards for successful sectoral lobbying and where successful sectoral lobbying leads to even higher general tax rates. In the field of corporate taxation services should attract the same rate of taxation as manufacturing. The taxation of savings would be simplified to remove areas of fiscal privilege.

Thus the market would determine the allocation of resources through a reduced overall tax burden and the abolition of fiscal privilege for favoured sectors such as downtown apartments, movie making, and tree growing. The amount and location of retailing, banking and holiday making would be determined by an overall low tax regime rather than by fiscal privilege for some "designated" areas. The movement to lower and simpler taxes would also reduce the resources absorbed in tax compliance. The return on tax avoidance activities would also fall.

Fewer subsidies would reduce the burden of these payments on the productive sector. It would also reduce the size of the lobbying sector for subsidies and the cost to government of their administration.

In addition to tax reform and subsidy reduction, the elimination of rent-seeking in the market requires a programme of deregulation. In the unsheltered sector of the economy this has been sought by the abolition of economic frontiers within the EU for industrial products and by the GATT agreements. In agriculture and services, however, protectionist regimes still apply. CAP reform and the opening up of markets for transport, financial and professional services, telecommunications, media and energy, to competitive forces are the policies indicated.

Deregulation should also apply to labour markets. This requires removal of restrictions on entry traditionally enforced in some trades and professions. Income determination should be based on the incomes required to attract new entrants to an occupation rather than on the ability to exclude competition from new entrants.

The ability of rent-seekers to impose costs on taxpayers and consumers has frequently been assisted by lack of information about the costs and benefits to society as a whole. Institutional reforms are required to remedy the information deficit. The current Taoiseach, Mr John Bruton, when Minister for Finance proposed parliamentary reforms to secure simultaneous presentation of the costs and benefits of spending programmes and the appointment of a Public Expenditure Commissioner (A Better Way to Plan the Nation's Finances, 1982). A constitutional amendment to prohibit government borrowing was also proposed as a means to control intergenerational rent-seeking. For example, the introduction of a pay-as-you-go pensions is a windfall gain to older workers from the younger working population and future generations. Tullock (1990) proposes single issue referenda as a means of reducing rent: "Switzerland, which permits referenda on an immense number of things, has the smallest government of any European nation" (p. 81).

A major new external source of rent-seeking in Ireland has been the transfer of some £10 billion of EU structural funds over the years 1989-99. The funds were routed through the public sector and were apparently available only for public expenditure projects rather than for tax reform or debt reduction. The latter allocations would have applied generally throughout the economy through a reduction in tax rates. The allocation of the funds through the public sector invited rent-seeking in both the public and private sectors. The period of expansionary fiscal contraction from 1987 to 1989 changed the incentive structure of the economy away from public expenditure and towards exports but the allocation of structural funds by the EU to Ireland diverted the economy back from market-led activity to rent-seeking. Because additional finance from the national exchequer was required as part of EU funding the transfers brought an increase in taxation in the Irish economy, in addition to the resource misallocations caused by the change in the incentive structures. Given the problems of the Irish economy of rent-seeking, distortion of incentives, and resource misallocation, it is desirable that any future EU transfers be distributed as widely as possible so as to reduce rent-seeking, and be concentrated on the labour market. A programme of debt reduction leading to lower income taxation of low and average incomes is recommended as an alternative to the public spending programme of 1989-99.

In summary, the reduction of rent-seeking in the Irish economy has five major components. These are tax reform, subsidy reduction, deregulation of product and factor markets, institutional reform in the public sector and reform of EU transfer payments.

REFERENCES

Barrett, S.D. (1987): *Flying High, Airline Price and European Regulation*, London: Avebury.

Barrett, S.D. (1991): *Transport Policy in Ireland in the 1990s*, Dublin: Gill and Macmillan, Chapter 1.

Barrett, S.D. (1990): "Deregulating European Aviation — A Case Study", *Transportation*, 16: 311-327.

Baumol, W.J. (1990): "Entrepreneurship: Productive, Unproductive and Destructive", *Journal of Political Economy*, 98(5): 893-921.

Burke, A.E. (1995): "Employment Prospects in the Irish Music Industry", forthcoming in the *Journal of the Statistical and Social Inquiry Society of Ireland* (presented to the SISSI in January 1995).

Bhagwati, J.N. (1980): "Lobbying and Welfare", *Journal of Public Economics*, 14: 355-363.

Buchannan, J. (1980): "Rent-seeking and Profit seeking", in *Toward a Theory of the Rent-seeking Society*, Texas: Texas A&M University Press.

Callan, T. (1992): "Who Benefits from Public Expenditure on Education?", *ESRI Working Paper No. 32*.

Culliton, J. (Chairman) (1992): "A Time for Change: Industrial Policy in the 1990s", Report of the Industrial Policy Review Group, Dublin: The Stationery Office.

Commission on Health Funding (1989): "Commission on Health Funding", Dublin: Government Publications.

Government of Ireland (1985): "A Better Way to Plan the Nation's Finances", Dublin: The Stationary Office.

Government of Ireland (1989): "Programme for Economic and Social Progress", Dublin: The Stationary Office.

Government of Ireland (1994): "Irish Aviation Policy, a Green Paper", Dublin: The Stationary Office.

Johns, C. (1993): "Ireland's Record-Last in the Class?", *Studies*, 82(325): 9-23.

Kreuger, A. (1974): "The Political Economy of the Rent-seeking Society", *American Economic Review*, 66: 292-303.

Lee, G. (1994): *The Insider-Outsider Economy, Ireland 1987-1994*, Dublin: Irish Small and Medium Enterprises Association.

Cummins, P. and Keane, M. (1994): "New Approaches to Rural Development", Report No. 97, Dublin: National Economic and Social Council.

O'Connell, T. (1992): "Do Regions Naturally Converge or Diverge in an Economic and Monetary Union?", *Quarterly Bulletin Spring 1992*, Dublin: Central Bank of Ireland: 51-66.

Office of Population Censuses and Surveys (1986): "Occupational Mortality, The Registrar General's Decennial Supplement for Great Britain, 1979-80, 1982-83", London: HMSO.

O'Riordan, W. (1989): "Is Irish Public Sector Employment a Burden?", *Journal of the Statistical and Social Inquiry Society of Ireland*, 26(11): 1-22.

Porter, M. (1990): *"The Competitive Advantage of Nations"*, London: Macmillan: 681.

The Advisory Group on Third-Level Student Support (1993): "Report of the Advisory Group on Third-Level Student Support (The de Buitlear Report)", Dublin: Government Publications.

Review Body on Higher Remuneration in the Public Sector (1987): "Report No. 30", Dublin

Review Body of Higher Remuneration in the Public Sector (1992): "Report No. 35", Dublin.

Ryan, W.J. (1949): "Measurement of Tariff Levels for Ireland 1931, 1936 and 1938", *Journal of the Statistical and Social Inquiry Society of Ireland*, XVIII, 109-32.

Schultz, T.W. (1961): "Investment in Human Capital", *American Economic Review*, 51: 1-17.

Tullock, G. (1993): *Rent-seeking*, Aldershot: Edward Elgar.

Search, renew or reserve
www.buckinghamshire.gov.uk/libraries

24 hour renewal line
0303 123 0035

Library enquiries
01296 382415

Buckinghamshire Libraries
#loveyourlibrary

Buckinghamshire
libraryservice
CULTURE AND LEARNING

www.buckscc.gov.uk/libraries